First World War
and Army of Occupation
War Diary
France, Belgium and Germany

50 DIVISION
149 Infantry Brigade
Northumberland Fusiliers
1/4th Battalion (Territorials)
1 August 1915 - 31 July 1918

WO95/2828/1

The Naval & Military Press Ltd
www.nmarchive.com
Published in association with The National Archives

Published by

The Naval & Military Press Ltd

Unit 10 Ridgewood Industrial Park,

Uckfield, East Sussex,

TN22 5QE England

Tel: +44 (0) 1825 749494

www.naval-military-press.com

www.nmarchive.com

This diary has been reprinted in facsimile from the original. Any imperfections are inevitably reproduced and the quality may fall short of modern type and cartographic standards.

© **Crown Copyright**
Images reproduced by permission of The National Archives, London, England, 2015.

Contents

Document type	Place/Title	Date From	Date To
Heading	WO95/2828-1		
Heading	50th Division 149th Infy Bde 4th Bn Northumberland Fusrs May 1915-Jly 1918 To 39 Div 118 Bde		
Heading	149th Inf. Bde. 50th Div. 4th Battn. The Northumberland Fusiliers.August 1914 To May 1915 (4.8.14 To 31.5.15)		
Miscellaneous	4th Battn. The Northumberland Fusiliers August 1914 To May 1915 (4.8.14 To 31.5.15)		
Heading	149th Inf. Bde. 50th Div. 4th Battn. The Northumberland Fusiliers.June 1915		
Miscellaneous	4th Battn. The Northumberland Fusiliers June 1915		
Heading	149th Inf. Bde 50th Div. 4th Battn. The Northumberland Fusiliers July 1915		
Miscellaneous	4th Battn. The Northumberland Fusiliers July 1915		
Heading	149th Bde 50th Div. 1/4th Northumberland Fusiliers August 1915		
War Diary		01/08/1915	31/08/1915
Heading	149th Bde. 50th Div. 1/4th Northumberland Fusiliers September 1915		
Heading	War Diary Of 4th Batt Northld Fusiliers From August 31st To Sept 30th Volume III		
War Diary		31/08/1915	30/09/1915
Heading	149th Bde. 50th Div.1/4th Northumberland Fusiliers October 1915		
Heading	War Diary Of 4th Batt Northd Fusiliers From Oct 1st 1915 To Oct 31st 1915 (Volume I)		
War Diary		01/10/1915	31/10/1915
Heading	149th Bde. 50th Div. 1/4th Northumberland Fusiliers November 1915		
Heading	War Diary Of 4th Northd Fusiliers From Nov 1st To Nov 30th Volume (I)		
War Diary	Strazeele	01/11/1915	30/11/1915
Heading	149th Bde. 50th Div. 1/4th Northumberland Fusiliers December 1915 To 7 Jan 1916		
Heading	War Diary Of 1/4th Batt Northd Fusiliers From Dec 1st 1915 To Jan 31st 1916 Volume VI		
War Diary	Strazeele	01/12/1915	20/12/1915
War Diary	Canada Huts H.32.a.5.5 Sheet 28	21/12/1915	22/12/1915
War Diary	Trenches	23/12/1915	31/12/1915
War Diary	Hill 60	29/12/1915	07/01/1916
War Diary	Trenches	08/01/1916	31/01/1916
War Diary	Maple Copse	17/02/1916	20/02/1916
War Diary	In Trenches Sanctuary Wood	21/02/1916	24/02/1916
War Diary	Scottish Lines	25/02/1916	29/02/1916
War Diary	Trenches	01/02/1916	06/02/1916
War Diary	Scottish Lines	07/02/1916	12/02/1916
War Diary	Trenches Sanctuary Wood	13/02/1916	16/02/1916
Heading	War Diary Of 1/4th Batt Northd Fusiliers From Feb 1st 1916 To Feb 29th 1916 Vol VII		

Heading	War Diary Of 4th Batt Northd Fusiliers From March 1st 1916 To March 31st 1916 Vol VIII			
War Diary	Bedford House	01/03/1916	06/03/1916
War Diary	Trenches	07/03/1916	21/03/1916
War Diary	Dickebusch Huts	22/03/1916	24/03/1916
War Diary	Trenches	25/03/1916	27/03/1916
War Diary	Sq. Wood	28/03/1916	29/03/1916
War Diary	Canada Huts	30/03/1916	01/04/1916
Heading	War Diary Of 4th Batt Northd Fusiliers From 1st April 1916 To 30th April 1916 Vol IX			
War Diary	Locre	01/04/1916	02/04/1916
War Diary	Trenches	03/04/1916	08/04/1916
War Diary	Divl Res Locre	09/04/1916	13/04/1916
War Diary	Trenches	14/04/1916	25/04/1916
War Diary	Trenches Bde Reserve	26/04/1916	26/04/1916
War Diary	Rest Area X. 17 &16.	27/04/1916	30/04/1916
Heading	War Diary Of 4th Batt Northd Fus From May 1st To May 31st 1916			
War Diary	Meteren	01/05/1916	17/05/1916
War Diary	York Huts	18/05/1916	25/05/1916
War Diary	Brigade Reserve R.C Farm Etc	26/05/1916	28/05/1916
War Diary	Trenches KS & L.S.	29/05/1916	31/05/1916
Heading	War Diary Of 4th Batt Northd Fus From May 31st To June 30th			
War Diary	Trenches Ls & Ks	01/06/1916	01/06/1916
War Diary	Locre	02/06/1916	05/06/1916
War Diary	Trenches Ls & Ks	06/06/1916	09/06/1916
War Diary	R.C. Farm	10/06/1916	12/06/1916
War Diary	Trenches Ks & Ls	13/06/1916	17/06/1916
War Diary	Locre	18/06/1916	21/06/1916
War Diary	Trenches Ks & Ls	22/06/1916	25/06/1916
War Diary	Brigade Reserve R. C. Farm	26/06/1916	29/06/1916
Heading	War Diary Of 4th Batt. Northd Fus. From July 1st To July 31st 1916 (Vol 12)			
War Diary	Trenches Ks & Ls	01/07/1916	03/07/1916
War Diary	Camp Brulooze	04/07/1916	14/07/1916
War Diary	Durham Huts La Clytte	15/07/1916	19/07/1916
War Diary	Durham Huts	20/07/1916	21/07/1916
War Diary	Bulford Camp	22/07/1916	22/07/1916
War Diary	Trenches CS & DS	23/07/1916	26/07/1916
War Diary	Trenches D 3 4 5 + 6	27/07/1916	29/07/1916
War Diary	Bde. Reserve	30/07/1916	31/07/1916
Heading	War Diary Of 1/4th Batt Northd Fus From Aug 1st 1916 To Aug 31st 1916 Vol 13			
War Diary	Brigade Reserve Near Daylight Corner N.33.d.0.6	01/08/1916	03/08/1916
War Diary	Trenches D.3-D.6	04/08/1916	06/08/1916
War Diary	Locre	07/08/1916	07/08/1916
War Diary	Meteren	08/08/1916	11/08/1916
War Diary	Fienvillers	12/08/1916	17/08/1916
War Diary	Henencourt Wood	18/08/1916	31/08/1916
Heading	149th. Infantry Brigade 50th. Division 4th. Northumberland Fusiliers 149th. Infantry Brigade September 1916			
Heading	War Diary Of 4th Batt. Northd Fus From Sept 1st 1916 To Sept 30th 1916 (Vol 14)			
War Diary	Henencourt Wood	01/09/1916	09/09/1916

War Diary	Map. Ref Sheet 57 D. SE. 57 C. S.W Becourt Wood	10/09/1916	12/09/1916
War Diary	Mametz Wood	13/09/1916	14/09/1916
War Diary	Battle Form Action With Batt H.Q in Clark's Trenches	14/09/1916	30/09/1916
Heading	War Diary Of 4th Battalion Northumberland Fusiliers Volume 19		
War Diary	Prue and Starfish. Tr	01/10/1916	04/10/1916
War Diary	Millencourt	05/10/1916	17/10/1916
War Diary	Mametz Wood	18/10/1916	23/10/1916
War Diary	Trenches Flers Line	24/10/1916	27/10/1916
War Diary	Front Line Trenches Near Butte De Warlencourt	28/10/1916	31/10/1916
War Diary	Bazentin Le Grand	01/11/1916	04/11/1916
War Diary	Trenches Flers Lines And Hexham Road	06/11/1916	06/11/1916
Heading	4th Bn. Northld Fusrs. Confidential War Diary Volume 16 1st Nov-30th Nov 1916		
War Diary	Trenches Flers Line & Hexham Road	05/11/1916	05/11/1916
War Diary	Flers Line	06/11/1916	06/11/1916
War Diary	Bazentin Le Grand	07/11/1916	11/11/1916
War Diary	Trenches Snag Trench	12/11/1916	13/11/1916
War Diary	Hexham Road and Flers Line	14/11/1916	14/11/1916
War Diary	Snag Trench	15/11/1916	15/11/1916
War Diary	Flers Line	16/11/1916	16/11/1916
War Diary	Bazentin Le Grand	17/11/1916	17/11/1916
War Diary	Albert	18/11/1916	26/11/1916
War Diary	Trenches Hexham Road and Snag Trench	14/11/1916	15/11/1916
War Diary	Albert	27/11/1916	30/11/1916
Miscellaneous	4th Bn. Northld Fus. Appendice to November War Diary Casualties		
Heading	War Diary Of 4th Batt. Northumberland Fusiliers Volume 17 December 1916		
War Diary	Albert	01/12/1916	01/12/1916
War Diary	Bresle	01/12/1916	28/12/1916
War Diary	Becourt	29/12/1916	29/12/1916
War Diary	Balentin-Le-Petit	30/12/1916	30/12/1916
War Diary	Yarra Reserve	31/12/1916	31/12/1916
Heading	4th Bn. Northld Fusiliers Confidential War Diary Vol 18 Jan- 1st Jan 31st 1917		
War Diary	Yarra Reserve	01/01/1917	07/01/1917
War Diary	Bazentin Le Petit No 5 Camp (Lisser Hut)	08/01/1917	15/01/1917
War Diary	Support Trenches	16/01/1917	23/01/1917
War Diary	Nemetz Wood Camp	24/01/1917	25/01/1917
War Diary	Albert	26/01/1917	28/01/1917
War Diary	Dernancourt	29/01/1917	31/01/1917
Heading	War Diary Of 4th Battalion Northumberland Fusiliers February 1st To February 28th 1917 Volume 3		
War Diary	Dernancourt	01/02/1917	08/02/1917
War Diary	Mericourt Sur Somme	08/02/1917	10/02/1917
War Diary	Belloy	11/02/1917	18/02/1917
War Diary	N 34 A To T 4 A	21/02/1917	27/02/1917
War Diary	Foucacourt	28/02/1917	28/02/1917
Heading	War Diary Of 4th Battalion Northumberland Fusiliers From 1st March 1917 To 31st March 1917 Volume 3		
War Diary	Foucaucourt	01/03/1917	05/03/1917
War Diary	Bayon Villers	06/03/1917	09/03/1917
War Diary	Warfusee	10/03/1917	30/03/1917
War Diary	Boutillerie	31/03/1917	31/03/1917

Heading	War Diary Of 4th Battalion Northumberland Fusiliers From April 1st To April 30th 1917 Volume 3		
War Diary	Coisy	01/04/1917	02/04/1917
War Diary	Beauval	03/04/1917	03/04/1917
War Diary	Bouquemaison	04/04/1917	04/04/1917
War Diary	Sibiville	05/04/1917	07/04/1917
War Diary	Maizieres	08/04/1917	08/04/1917
War Diary	Beaufort	09/04/1917	10/04/1917
War Diary	Wanquetin	11/04/1917	11/04/1917
War Diary	Ronville Caves	11/04/1917	14/04/1917
War Diary	The. Harp South	14/04/1917	16/04/1917
War Diary	In Vicinity Of 149 & M.G.C. HQ.	17/04/1917	17/04/1917
War Diary	Wancourt	17/04/1917	20/04/1917
War Diary	The. Harp. North	21/04/1917	21/04/1917
War Diary	Ronville	22/04/1917	23/04/1917
War Diary	Wancourt	24/04/1917	25/04/1917
War Diary	The. Harp (North)	26/04/1917	26/04/1917
War Diary	Arras	27/04/1917	27/04/1917
War Diary	Mondi Court	28/04/1917	30/04/1917
Miscellaneous			
Miscellaneous	Fluctuation Of Strength		
Miscellaneous	50th Division. G.X. 3856	27/04/1917	27/04/1917
Diagram etc	Diagram		
Miscellaneous	50th. Divn. G.X. 3859	26/04/1917	26/04/1917
Miscellaneous	50th. Divn. G.X. 3867	29/04/1917	29/04/1917
Map	Detail And Trenches Revised To 21-4-17		
Map	Eterpigny		
Map	Map		
Heading	War Diary Of 4th Battalion Northumberland Fusiliers From May 1st 1917 (inclusive) To May 31st 1917 (inclusive) Volume III		
War Diary	Mondicourt	01/05/1917	01/05/1917
War Diary	Souastre	02/05/1917	02/05/1917
War Diary	Mercatel	03/05/1917	04/05/1917
War Diary	Mondicourt	05/05/1917	18/05/1917
War Diary	Boiry St Martin	19/05/1917	19/05/1917
War Diary	St Leger	20/05/1917	22/05/1917
War Diary	Croisilles	22/05/1917	24/05/1917
War Diary	St. Leger	25/05/1917	26/05/1917
War Diary	Moyenville	27/05/1917	27/05/1917
War Diary	Monchy-Au-Bois	28/05/1917	31/05/1917
Heading	War Diary Of 4th Battalion Northumberland Fusiliers From June 1st 1917 To June 30th 1917 Volume 3		
War Diary	Monchy-Au-Bois	01/06/1917	19/06/1917
War Diary	Boisleux-St-Marc S. 17c Ref Sheet 51 B S.W	18/06/1917	25/06/1917
War Diary	C Coy's in Egret Tr 'A' Coy Egret Tr 'B' Coy Egret Loop 'C' Coy 1/2 In Buzzard Trench 'D' Coy 1/2 In Egret Trench D Coy 1/2 At The Nest Battn H.Q The Nest	28/06/1917	30/06/1917
Heading	War Diary Of 4th Battalion Northumberland Fusiliers From July 1st 1917 (inclusive) To July 31st (inclusive) Volume III		
War Diary	Front Line Opposite Cherisy	01/07/1917	05/07/1917
War Diary	Front Line Near Cherisy	01/07/1917	05/07/1917
Map	Map 2		
Map	Map		

War Diary	Front Line Near Cherisy	01/07/1917	05/07/1917
War Diary	Henin	05/07/1917	10/07/1917
War Diary	Neuville Vitasse	10/07/1917	15/07/1917
War Diary	Front Line Vis-En-Artois Sector	19/07/1917	23/07/1917
War Diary	Front Line	23/07/1917	24/07/1917
War Diary	Support Area	24/07/1917	29/07/1917
War Diary	Front Line	28/07/1917	01/08/1917
Miscellaneous	Working Parties Supplied By 4th Bn. Northld Fusiliers		
Map	Map I		
Heading	War Diary Of 4th Battalion Northumberland Fusiliers From August 1st 1917 To August 31st Volume IV		
War Diary	Neuville Vitasse N 19b 7 1/2 9 1/2 Batt H.Q	01/08/1917	01/08/1917
War Diary	Neuville Vitasse Camp N 24d 2 1/2.8 Ref. Sheet 57b S. W. 1:10000	04/08/1917	11/08/1917
War Diary	Neuville Vitasse Camp M 24d 2 1/2.8	11/08/1917	12/08/1917
War Diary	Front Line	12/08/1917	16/08/1917
War Diary	Front Line-Croiselles Sector	12/08/1917	16/08/1917
War Diary	Support Area	16/08/1917	20/08/1917
War Diary	Fontaine Croiselles	16/08/1917	20/08/1917
War Diary	Cherisy Sector	16/08/1917	20/08/1917
War Diary	Support Area The Near	16/08/1917	20/08/1917
War Diary	Front Line Horse Shoe Sap to Puo Lane	20/08/1917	24/08/1917
War Diary	Bde Reserve Camp N 25a5.4	24/08/1917	28/08/1917
War Diary	Hindenburg Support Line Shaftty	28/08/1917	28/08/1917
Miscellaneous	Daily Working Parties		
Map	Map		
Miscellaneous	5 N.F Frontline 1/10,000 British & Boch Trenches Guemappe-Fontaine		
Heading	War Diary Of 4th Battalion Northumberland Fusiliers From September 1st 1917 To September 30th Volume V		
War Diary	Hindenburg Support Line	01/09/1917	01/09/1917
War Diary	Durham Lines Camp S 11 A Ref 51 B S W	02/09/1917	05/09/1917
War Diary	Left Section Right-Sub-Section Front Line	05/09/1917	06/09/1917
Map	Map		
Miscellaneous	4th NF		
War Diary	Right Sub-Section	06/09/1917	06/09/1917
War Diary	Left Sector Of Div. Sector	07/09/1917	09/09/1917
War Diary	Support Area Left Sector	09/09/1917	13/09/1917
War Diary	Left Section	13/09/1917	13/09/1917
War Diary	Right-Sub-Section Of Div. Sector	13/09/1917	17/09/1917
War Diary	Bde Reserve Camp N 21a-N15 Cad	18/09/1917	21/09/1917
War Diary	Nissan Hut Camp Camp A	21/09/1917	21/09/1917
War Diary	Durham Lines S 11 A	21/09/1917	25/09/1917
War Diary	Camp A	25/09/1917	25/09/1917
War Diary	Durham Lines Boisleux An Mont S 11a	26/09/1917	29/09/1917
War Diary	Durham Lines S 11a 57b S.W	29/09/1917	29/09/1917
War Diary	Rt Section Rt Sub Sect U 1a 23.5 to O 31b 75.15.	30/09/1917	30/09/1917
War Diary	Rt Section Rt Sub-Section U1a2 1/2 5b O31b75.15.	30/09/1917	30/09/1917
Map	Map		
Heading	War Diary Of 4th Battalion Northumberland Fusiliers 1st Oct 1917-31st Oct 1917 Volume 3		
War Diary	Front Line W. Of Cherisy	01/10/1917	05/10/1917
War Diary	Courcelles Le Comte	05/10/1917	18/10/1917
War Diary	Arneke	18/10/1917	20/10/1917
War Diary	Proven	21/10/1917	23/10/1917

War Diary	Hulls Farm	24/10/1917	24/10/1917
War Diary	Line H.Q U.12.b.4.4	25/10/1917	25/10/1917
War Diary	H.Q Taube Farm	25/10/1917	26/10/1917
War Diary	Caribou Camp	27/10/1917	31/10/1917
Operation(al) Order(s)	Operation Order No. 1 A Appendix A		
Map	Barrage Map		
Heading	War Diary Of 4th Battalion Northumberland Fusiliers From November 1st To November 30th 1917 Volume III		
War Diary	Caribou Camp	01/11/1917	08/11/1917
War Diary	Yser Canal Bank Near Boesinghe	08/11/1917	10/11/1917
War Diary	White Mill Camp Elverdinghe	10/11/1917	13/11/1917
War Diary	Zudrove	13/11/1917	30/11/1917
Heading	War Diary Of 4th Northumberland Fusiliers December 1917 Volume III		
War Diary	La Ronville	01/12/1917	11/12/1917
War Diary	Toronto Camp Brandhoek	12/12/1917	12/12/1917
War Diary	Line (Support)	16/12/1917	20/12/1917
War Diary	Brandhoek	20/12/1917	25/12/1917
War Diary	Potije (Whitby Camp)	25/12/1917	26/12/1917
War Diary	Seine	26/12/1917	31/12/1917
Map	Sketch Map		
Map	Map		
Miscellaneous			
Map	Message Map		
Miscellaneous	Message Form		
War Diary	War Diary Of 1/4th Battalion Northumberland Fusiliers 1st January-31st January 1918 Volume 4		
War Diary	Passchendael Sector	01/01/1918	01/01/1918
War Diary	Whitby Camp Ypres	02/01/1918	02/01/1918
War Diary	Brandhoek	03/01/1918	03/01/1918
War Diary	Watou Area Belgium	03/01/1918	18/01/1918
War Diary	Watou Area to Tilques Area	18/01/1918	18/01/1918
War Diary	St Martin-Au-Laert	18/01/1918	27/01/1918
War Diary	St Martin-Au-Laert St Lean	27/01/1918	27/01/1918
War Diary	Alnwick Camp	28/01/1918	31/01/1918
War Diary	St Jean	28/01/1918	31/01/1918
Heading	War Diary Of 4th Northumberland Fusiliers Vol IV February 1918		
War Diary	Alnwick Camp Potije	01/02/1918	01/02/1918
War Diary	Ypres	02/02/1918	02/02/1918
War Diary	Brandhoek	02/02/1918	06/02/1918
War Diary	Support at Seine	06/02/1918	09/02/1918
War Diary	Front Line	09/02/1918	12/02/1918
War Diary	Whitby Camp Potije	12/02/1918	16/02/1918
War Diary	Support Seine	16/02/1918	19/02/1918
War Diary	Front Line	19/02/1918	22/02/1918
War Diary	Ypres	23/02/1918	23/02/1918
War Diary	Zudausques	23/02/1918	28/02/1918
Map	Map A		
Heading	149th Brigade 50th Division. 4th Battalion Northumberland Fusiliers March 1918		
Heading	War Diary Of 4th Battalion Northumberland Fusiliers From 1st March 1918-31st March 1918 Volume III		
War Diary	Zudausques	01/03/1918	08/03/1918
War Diary	Moreuil	08/03/1918	08/03/1918

War Diary	Le Quesnel	11/03/1918	21/03/1918
War Diary	Brie	21/03/1918	21/03/1918
War Diary	Caulincourt	22/03/1918	22/03/1918
War Diary	St Christ	23/03/1918	23/03/1918
War Diary	Misery	24/03/1918	24/03/1918
War Diary	Foucaucourt	24/03/1918	24/03/1918
War Diary	Ashevillers	25/03/1918	26/03/1918
War Diary	Vauvillers	26/03/1918	27/03/1918
War Diary	Guillaucourt	28/03/1918	28/03/1918
War Diary	Guillaucourt & Ignaucourt	28/03/1918	31/03/1918
Heading	149th Brigade 50th Division 1/4th Battalion Northumberland Fusiliers April 1918		
Heading	War Diary Of 4th Battalion Northumberland Fusiliers From April 1st 1918 To April 30th 1918 Volume 3		
War Diary	Vironchaux	01/04/1918	03/04/1918
War Diary	L' Ecleme	04/04/1918	06/04/1918
War Diary	Cense La Vallee	07/04/1918	08/04/1918
War Diary	Arrewage	09/04/1918	09/04/1918
War Diary	Merville	09/04/1918	12/04/1918
War Diary	K12b To L7a	12/04/1918	13/04/1918
War Diary	J4a	14/04/1918	17/04/1918
War Diary	Mametz	18/04/1918	28/04/1918
War Diary	Colougnes Aisne	29/04/1918	30/04/1918
Heading	War Diary Of 4th Battalion Northumberland Fusiliers 1st May 1918 31st May 1918 Volume 4		
War Diary	Colougnes Aisne	01/05/1918	03/05/1918
War Diary	Colougnes	04/05/1918	05/05/1918
War Diary	Concevreux	06/05/1918	07/05/1918
War Diary	Front Line	08/05/1918	27/05/1918
War Diary	Concevreux	27/05/1918	31/05/1918
Heading	War Diary Of 4th Battalion Northumberland Fusiliers From 1st June 1918 30th June 1918 Volume IV		
War Diary	Congy	01/06/1918	02/06/1918
War Diary	Aulincaux	03/06/1918	09/06/1918
War Diary	Broyes	10/06/1918	23/06/1918
War Diary	Les Essarts	23/06/1918	29/06/1918
War Diary	Broyes	30/06/1918	30/06/1918
Heading	War Diary Of 4th Battalion Northumberland Fusiliers From 1st July 1918-31st July 1918 Volume IV		
War Diary	Broyes	01/07/1918	01/07/1918
War Diary	St Sophie Farm	02/07/1918	03/07/1918
War Diary	Fere Champenoise	03/07/1918	03/07/1918
War Diary	Pont Remy	04/07/1918	04/07/1918
War Diary	Hocquincourt	04/07/1918	12/07/1918
War Diary	Huppy	14/07/1918	18/07/1918
War Diary	Rouxmesnil	19/07/1918	31/07/1918

Woolf 282y

Wolf 2224j

50TH DIVISION
149TH INFY BDE

4TH BN NORTHUMBERLAND FUSRS
MAY 1915 - JLY 1918

149th Inf.Bde.
50th Div.

Battn. disembarked
Boulogne from
England 20.4.15.

4th BATTN. THE NORTHUMBERLAND FUSILIERS.

AUGUST 1914 TO MAY 1915

(4.8.14 to 31.5.15)

4th Battn. The Northumberland Fusiliers.

August 1914 to May 1915

(4.8.14 - 31.5.15)

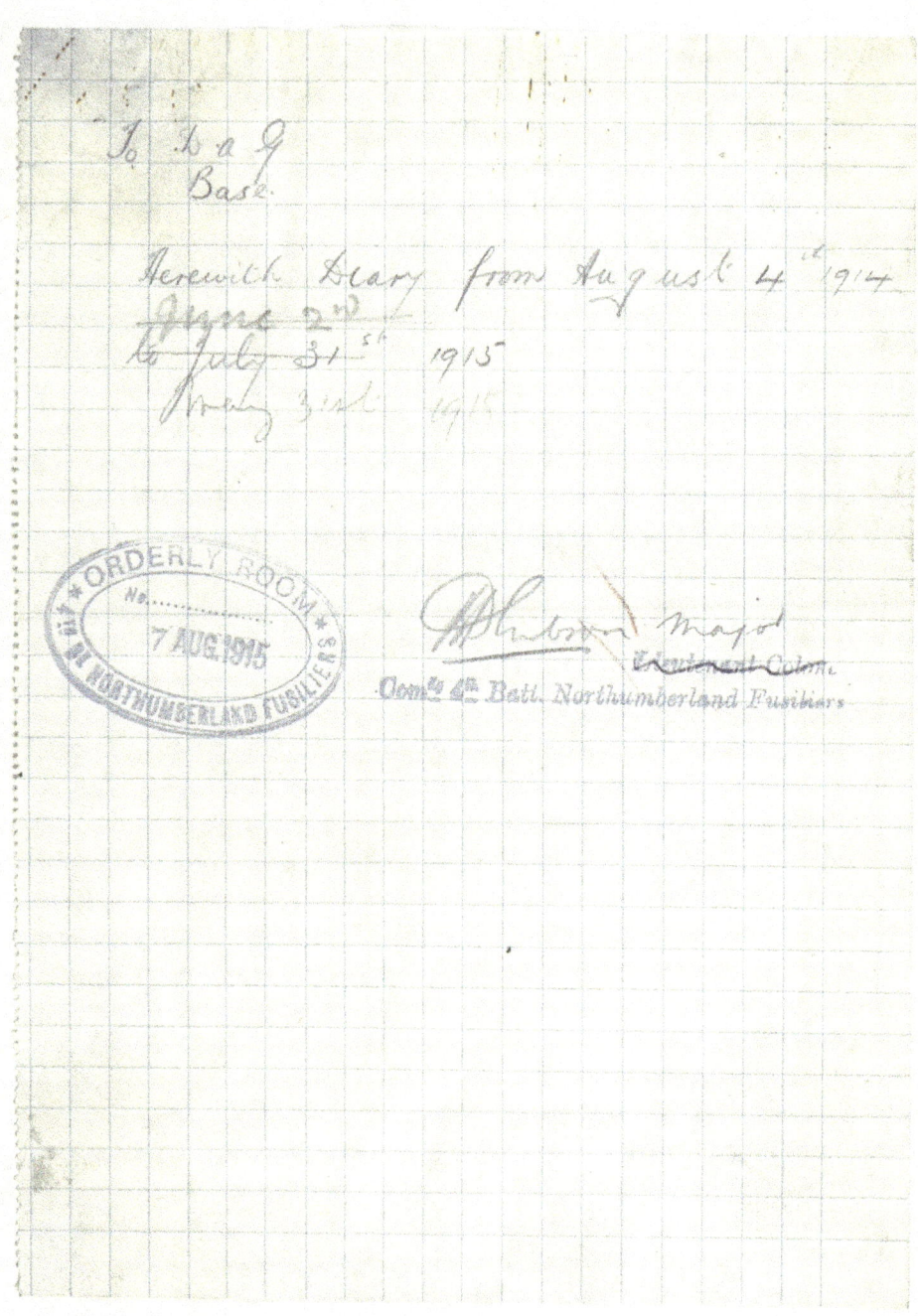

To D a G
Base.

Herewith Diary from August 4th 1914
to July 31st 1915
May 31st 1915

Comd 4th Batt. Northumberland Fusiliers

August 4th ordered to mobilise 6 p.m.

" 5th left HEXHAM 1.20 p.m. 40 minutes behind schedule time.
All officers & 657 O.R. i.e. 4 men less than laid down for N. SHIELDS.

" 6 dug trenches at EARSDON.
" 7. March to HEATON.
Transport arrived from HEXHAM by road. The train originally ordered for 4th day had been changed to 3rd day but the railway had not altered the day.

" 8 Marched to EARSDON. dug trenches for a week.
" 15. Marched to HEATON
" 18 — .— GOSFORTH PARK.
Nov 1 H.Q. to CLARENCE STREET N/c-on-Tyne. Billets.
Nov 16th marched to BLYTH.
April 14th Zeppelin over BLYTH.
April 18" Transport & M.G. leave for SOOTHAMPTON & HAVRE at 5 p.m.
" 20th ? Rn left 7.45; half 8.15. FOLKESTONE 7.30. BOULOGNE 8.50. B in Camp 11 p.m.
" 21st 11.20 parade. marched to PONT DE BRIQUES. entrained 1.30 p.m. in game

been as our Transport & M.G.
CASSEL 6.15, detrained in 30 min.
billets in farms near Station.
April 22 parade 10.0 a.m. OUDEZEELE about
3 p.m. Scattered billets. ordered to
leave at 3 p.m. next day. Heavy firing
heard.
- - 23. ordered at 7.30 a.m. to move at once.
marched at 9.40 to Bgde. H.Q. at
WINNIEZEELE. arrived 10.20
moved 1.0 p.m. via DOGLAND T. WATOU,
POPERINGHE to BRANDHOEK
about 14½ miles very dusty. no men
fell out. Took up position in the
dark.
- - 24th 5.30 p.m. order to move.
marched 6.0 thro' VLAMERTINGHE
& YPRES where we were halted one
hour under shell fire in the market
square. Some one in front had lost
direction in the town. 3 horses & 2 men
wounded.
- - 25th to POTIJZE where Bn lay in a field
in artillery formation, in 4 lines.
about 30 shells fell into the field.
One man wounded, Lt Scaife lost
speech thro' concussion.
Thence to WIELTJE. supported an
attack by 10th Brigade. L & N. F. went
in

further forward than intended & returned after dark to WIELTJE. Killed 1 O.R. wounded Capt. D.H. WEIR, Lt C.M. Pricy 2nd Lt W. Robinson, O.R. 33 missing O.R. 20 most of whom reported next day.

April 26. Attack by LAHORE Div. & a Canadian Bdge. Northd Brigade at 1.40 p.m. ordered to attack St JULIEN at 2.5 p.m. Very heavy shell & M.G. fire. reached our first line & a bit beyond in places. retired after dark as the line was too crowded. Our Bn was drawn by fire to the our LEFT.
Capt. Clifford when lying wounded in a ditch on St JULIEN road saw two men in service dress firing a M.G. from the dressing station out buildings at our troops. When being carried back he was fired at by the same men.
Lt Bunting also states that he was fired on from the same place, when he advanced to it with his platoon he was waved on by some hospital orderlies who were also seen by Major Gibson. Captain G.L. Huntly also states that he was fired on from the same place.

April 26th Killed 1 O.R. 19 Wounded Capts
C.Clipper L.D. Plummer, G.L. Hunting
Lt J.W. Barbey, H.B Spike, H.M.Carrick,
O.R. 188. Missing O.R. 98.
Mentioned. 2'Lt D.T. Turner.
    No 32 Sgt J.W. Smith.
    No 1592 L/Cpl E. Woodrow Killed
    No 1640 Pte A. Brown.
    No 1517 Pte G. Chadderton. D.C.M.

— — 27th in 2'd line trenches, burying parties.
— — 28th   do. Taube brought down in th
    evening. burying parties.
— — 29th 8pm – 3am all battalion digging
    trenches at BELLEWARDE Farm.
— — 30th Remainder of Brigade to HELL FIRE
    CORNER. Carrying party to Hill 60.
May 1st Shelled from 3 sides. shelt R.E in
    WIELTJE. all Bn digging 2'd line
    trenches in front of WIELTJE.
May 2 wet misty. balloons, no Taubes.
    Heavy shelled & gas at 4 p.m. some
    of 1st thing this hrs. deployed along dug
    outs on G.H.Q line, in case c-attack
    necessary. wet handkerchieves &
    caps comforter used. relieved 11pm.

Casualties April 24th to May 2nd

	K. Officers	O.R.	Wounded Officers	O.R.	Missing O.R.
24th April	—	—	—	5	—
25th	—	1	—	37	17
26th	—	19	6	188	98
28th	—	—	—	1	—
29th	—	—	—	2	—
2 May	—	—	—	5	—

May 3rd POPERINGHE at 6 a.m. billeted [in girls school. aeroplane bombed the town.] marched 8pm. to near WINNIEZEELE billets in farms Hard to find in the dark

4th billets adjusted. address by Sir J. French.

5th refitting & training.
to 9th — do —

10th marched to BRANDHOEK. bivouac in wood.

11th & 12th — do —

13th moved to 1000 yds N. of YPRES very wet. dug in in a field. moved to huts about 5.30 pm.

14th Huts. work party 200 men.

15th to VLAMERTINGHE CHATEAU. work party 200 men.

16th bivouac ½ mile N.W. in dugouts. working party 200 men. 2 wounded.

May 17th -do- 200 working party one O.R. wounded.
-- 18th -do- 400 -- --
-- 19th -do- 200
-- 20th -do- 250   two -- --
                German aeroplane brought down
                by French antiaircraft, fell in
                German lines.
-- 21st 300 working party two O.R. wounded.
-- 22nd 250 -- --   two -- --
-- 23rd 100 -- --   two -- --
Total wounded between 14th & 23rd while working 11.

May 24th. 2 a.m. German gas attack, very heavy bombardment. CO & Adj'n advance to No 2 pontoon followed by battalion. gas in canal still bad at 6 a.m. reported to 10th Brigade. Moved to 2nd Div. line W of St JEAN – WIELTJE road about 10 a.m. This line full of troops so advanced to support line at VIEW FARM. C & D coys then to trench in HILLTOP Farm. Heavy shelling gas shells. Ordered to send a company to SHELL TRAP Farm. O.C. Warwicks stopped C coy as he said we had no one there. ordered to support counter attack which did not come off. One gas shell burst in the trench, killed one & wounded one man, painful to the eyes, otherwise no harm done. Moved ½ B & ½ C to WEST along the road to avoid shelling.

24th May.

At dusk B coy ordered to trench E of St JEAN-WIELTJE road & S of WIELTJE, A & ½ C W of road. D in support W of road. ½ D sent to E. Lancs who asked for a company to fill a gap at TURCO FARM. Remaining ½ C reached A coy at 2 am 25th. Night counter attack by Somersets & Monmouths ordered. The message to Dublin Fusiliers re attack captured by enemy. Attack countermanded. Touch lost in the evening this officer with message to the remainder of the battalion being wounded.

4 N.F. in afternoon

```
                    ┌─┐HILL TOP Farm      HAMPSHIRE
       D coy           A coy              ═ Farm
                    ┌─┐VIEW             | | CROSS ROADS
                    └─┘Farm             | | Farm
        B coy          C coy
```

4 N.F. during evening

```
                    ┌─┐VIEW
                    └─┘Farm
       ½ B coy

                                        A & ½ C
       ½ B D & ½ C in 2nd Div line &    with WARWICK
              LA BRIQUE dugouts
```

4 N.F. One Hour after dusk.

WIELTJE

Warwicks A & ½ C coy   B coy
          D coy

½ C in dugouts near
LA BRIQUE

Wounded 2/Lt. W. J. Bunbury.
         Lt. R. W. Crantyes.
gassed & sprained ankle Capt. F. Robinson.

O.R. Killed 4. Wounded 24.
     gassed 9. Missing 4.

May 25th — ½ D shelled at 2 a.m. about 6 shells, ½ of them gas. One lot of gas rolled down the trench but did no harm. 6 a.m. this ½ D were in support trench E of road, other ½ D at Turco Farm. No touch. They went down at night on relief of E. Lancs. Barricade of support trench on road & house in rear crumped. B & C coy in all night & all day. Shrapnel hit some men of B.
Germans hit SHELL TRAP Farm in one shot; after that about 6 9.2 or 6 in on same place. We shelled BELLEWARDE Farm. In the early morning one of our aircraft drove away an enemy aeroplane. O.R. Killed 6. Wounded 27. Missing 1.

May 26th — Same position. at night ½ D. ⅔ round.
11th Brigade — A & D to Somerset Lt Infy in front line. C & B to 2nd Div line E of St JEAN. Working party to R.B. A. E of road. O.R. Killed 1. W. 2.

— 27th — ~~Same. C coy lost 1 killed rate of wound & 3 others hit from common shell bursting in the trench~~ Wounded O.R. 1. Working party to R.B.
RC

May 28th — same. Working party to R.B.
Wounded Capt J.R. Robb O.R. 1.

— 29th same working party to R.B.
O.R. wounded 5.

— 30th Worked on our trench by night.
in the evening Bombardment & attack by
the French.
C coy lost 1 killed 4 wounded (1 died)
from common shell bursting in the
trench.

— 31st same worked on our trench. Bombarded
by us. O.R. wounded 2.

June 1st G.O.C. 4th Div & Staff came down our
trench, 1 min later 2 common shell
byrst where they had been. 3 shells
also on crossroads.

149th Inf.Bde.
50th Div.

4th BATTN. THE NORTHUMBERLAND FUSILIERS.

J U N E

1 9 1 5

4th Battn. The Northumberland Fusiliers.

June 1915

June 1st. R.F.A. observation station in front of us shelled. C coy shelled. O.R.W. 1. worked on our own trench.

June 2nd. R.F.A. observation station, a cottage in front of us shelled & set on fire. 4 or 5 of our aircraft drove away an enemy aeroplane who came down in his own lines. Some R.F.A. observers drew salvoes on to C coy. One rifle & 1 pack smashed.

June 2nd
Heavy barrage of shell fire by enemy between POTIJZE & the MENIN road. relieved 10 pm & moved to S.W of VLAMERTI-NGHE by cops. to main road.
Men very stiff & tired & could hardly crawl along.

Casualties 24 May - 2 June

Officers wounded 3. gassed 1.

O.R Killed 12. wounded 67. missing 5
gassed 9.

June 3rd arrived at 2 am in wood about 1½ miles N of BRANDHOEK. Men very tired but in good heart.

" 4th inspected by brigadier. baths in VLAMERTINGHE. lecture by experts on respirators.

" 5th marched to other divisional area near OODERDOM. Men bivouac with crowded shelter available in case of wet.

" 6th training.

" 7 - do - officers reconnoitred road to new line.

" 8 to 10th - do -

" 11th marched 6 pm guides at KRUSSTAAT at 8.45 pm crossed canal at 9.15. delayed by battalion in front & jam of transport 2 waggons overturned in the road
PM

June 11th very muddy. hard marching. SANCTUARY WOOD at mid-night. one of relieving guides lost his way & one company & the M.G. did not get out that night. Company officers took over stores etc the night before. O.R. 3 wounded.

June 12th round trenches at 5 a.m. 3 of our own shells just over parapet & 1 short. one bless in our parapet. round again in the evening. a lot of work to do. a sniper seen on top of wall near HOOGE CHATEAU gates. fired at & disappeared. Killed O.R. 1 bullet thro head.

" 13th tried to find snipers positions for ourselves. trees make it difficult. Wounded O.R. 2

" 14th enemy sapping behind shield then after waiting half an hour got the man to expose himself. fired a volley of 3 rifles. Sgt Flannagan & 3 men of D Coy crawled out thro' bush about 5 p.m. Sgt shot an officer reading a newspaper against a tree & a man working on the trench. The others saw no one but were able to fire into dugouts at unexpected angles.

July 14th B coy spotted a M.G & a mortar near HOOGE CHÂU gates & directed guns on to them. direct hit on MG & mortar slewed round at dusk someone came & looked at them & was shot by Capt Dixon

July 15 Much wiring has been done & parapet now bullet proof. traverses, parados, & communication trenches made. Men enjoying themselves & in good fettle. Orders for next day.

June 16th ordered to be aggressive at 4:15 when bombardment stopped. not to leave the trenches. one M.G in 1st re-entrenchment in the salient. on coming back to old position a rifle grenade fell into bottom of trench killing 3 & wounding 4 men. more traverses, also small ones, to localise grenades. BS shelled by our guns.
Killed O.R 4 (one by bullet in head)
Wounded O.R 4

— — 17th worked in trenches. tried to snipe.
— — 18th sited rifle battery. O.R. Wounded 1.
— — 19th arranged relief. salient shelled by our own guns. relief arrived 10:30 completed 12:15. a lot of firing near BELLEWARDE. O.R. Wounded 6

July 11–19th O.R. Killed 5 Wounded 16

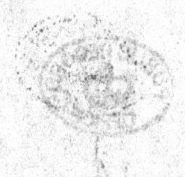

June 20th Reached bivouac 4 a.m.
— — 21st marched to ALDERSHOT huts
near NEUVE EGLISE. Very hot &
dusty. men very beat & heat but
soon recovered.
— — 22. Went round new trench. spotted
& shelled by enemy on way home. made
a small detour & avoided it.
A Coy took over SOUVENIR FARM,
B Coy — — SP4, N. MIDLAND & X dugouts
½ D Coy in SP5 & SP7. M.G. in SP4

— — 23 Companies resting training
— — 24 — do —
     25–27 — do — Wounded Lt. H. H. Bell.
— — 28. took over — D2 C coy 1 Platoon A coy.
S.P.4 1 Platoon D coy: S.P.5 1 Platoon D coy:
N. Midland dugouts 2 Platoon D coy.
SOUVENIR Farm 3 Platoon A coy.
X dugouts reserve M.G.
M.G. in D2 & SP5.
relief for S.P.7 not told off by incoming
& was late.
— — 29 2 15 lb shrapnel cases fell into D2.
— — 30 D2 & supports shelled

149th Inf.Bde.
50th Div.

4th BATTN. THE NORTHUMBERLAND FUSILIERS.

J U L Y

1 9 1 5

4th Battn. The Northumberland Fusiliers.

July 1915

July 1st "Lecture" on Smoke Helmets at
           Divisional H.Q.
  " - 2   H.E. & wooly bears in salvoes (two
           of 4 each) over front line. Bn

July 2:   Some rds of 5 & 6 N.F. hit rear our
           trench. no one hit.
  " - 3rd Spotted a wiring party in front of
      D2 from our listening post. opened fire.
           Several whistles blown by enemy.
           two bursts of rapid fire & M.G. in
           return.
           Wounded 2/Lt Gregory (bullet in face
              when on working party).
  " - 4th quiet.
  " - 5th 2 rifle grenades in front of D2.
           O.C. C coy returned 3. one short over, one blew
           up a post, one burst on parapet.
           a patrol found more wire up
           and the grass cut in front of enemy
           trench to a depth of 5 yards. also
           straw in communication trench
           near German wire.
  " - 6 Enemy sent 20 rifle grenades over,
           none in trench. We returned 12 some in
           trench. General Seely's farm shelled
           in the afternoon, common shell, 3 rounds
           in the evening. farm must be
           observable. Brigadier & C.O.
           narrowly missed near SOUVENIR
           Farm. 5/Lts Newton & McClafferty of C coy
           went out to try & capture enemy listening
           post which did not turn up. They
           threw 3 bombs into enemy trench causing
           some commotion. Coy relieved by A coy
              at

July 7th   Quiet
 "   8th   Much more shelling than usual.
           12 rifle grenades at D2 & quite
           40 others at our line.
 "   9th   at 4.30 a.m. our mining officer
           exploded a counter mine & blew up
           as G. mine. They had been heard
           under D4 & had just stopped.
           It seems likely that they would
           have exploded the mine soon, their
           trench being full of men who
           opened a heavy rifle, M.G. &
           light artillery fire. Our
           howitzers shelled during the night
 "   10th an allied aeroplane forced
           a German to descend in the
           morning. In the evening one of ours
           came down behind our lines
           the pilot wounded in the shoulder.
           One of our men in D2 shot a
           German who stood up to watch.
           Relief by 6 N.F. completed
           12.30 a.m. on 11th.
Wounded   During this tour in trenches, casualties
          were: 2nd Lt Gregory bullet while on
          working party, 1 O.R. bullet in leg when
          on listening patrol, 1 O.R. shrapnel in
          the head while carrying rations.

July 11th working party 5 off 150 O.R. Wounded 3 O.R.
Work delayed by explosion of one of our
mines which drew fire.
- - 12. resting & having working party of 3 off 150 O.R.
- - 13-15 - do -
- - 16th Marched 8 p.m. to ARMENTIERES.
guides at PONT DE NIPPE. one led
us round the town. a battalion cut
thro' us twice so that 2 coys were
lost for nearly an hour. relief
complete about 1.45 a.m.
- - 17th round trench 4 a.m. to 6 a.m.
- - 6 N.F. 3 p.m. Brigadier 3.30
Two of B coy visited German wire.
- - 18th round 3 a.m. C.O. to hospital.
- - 19th G.O.C. Div 10 a.m. Registered on trench
opposite trench 80 with catapult. trench
80 held by 6 N.F. under us.
usual routine go round in early &
see what work has been done.
go round in the evening & detail
work to be done.
Casualties 17th 1 O.R. wounded rifle.
18 1 O.R. killed rifle while shooting
19th 1 O.R. - - - over parapet
- - 20th Brigadier 11 a.m. our Howitzers
shelled opposite 80. 4 withers in
reply.

PM

July 21st T.80 Catapulted enemy. Sniper very busy on T.79 from Farm C in the evening.

" " 22 Our Howitzers shelled opposite 80. C.O.P.g. on patrol found a dead British soldier.

" " 23 Our Howitzers registered & shelled opposite EPINETTE. 6 N F patrol shot a G patrol.

" " 24 In the evening our trench howitzers shelled the sniper positions in Farm C with success. They also bombarded opposite T 80 earlier. 6 N.F Catapulted most of the day. Relief complete 11'50 p.m.
" Wounded 2 O.R.

" " 25 In billets in PONT DE NIEPPE. Voluntary Church Parade. Resting
" and ordinary company parades.

" " 26 Capt Suddas & 2nd Lieut Gibson proceeded on leave to England. Ba.ti wiring instruction at Brigade Headquarters. Training & bombing

" " 27th Wet. Billet inspection by Brig Gen Clifford. No complaints. Training bombing & wiring. Church on the PONT DE NIEPPE outskirts of ARMENTIÈRES shelled in the afternoon.
AL

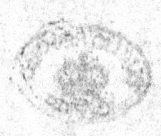

July 28th Battalion marching. Usual
company parades. Bombing instruction
Spraying of helmets. Digging party
at night one officer, 100 men.
Carried materials for making &
completing trench running just E
of HOUPLINES — to HOUPLINES —
EPINETTE road.

— 29th Working party 1 officer 50 men
8.30 a.m. working on same
trench as last night. Marching,
bombing instruction, Machine
Gun instruction, usual Coy
parades.

— 30th Marching bombing, Machine
Gun instruction, usual
Company parades. Working
party 2 Officers 100 men 7.30 p.m.
employed on same trench as two
previous parties.

— 31st Marching, bombing, machine
Gun instruction. Usual
Company parades. Instruction
& practice in detecting mounts
of guards etc. O.C. & Coy officers
went up to trenches before taking
over.

149th Bde.
50th Div.

1/4th NORTHUMBERLAND FUSILIERS

A U G U S T

1 9 1 5

Aug 1st Church Parade during the morning. The Battalion moved up to the trenches 7.30 p.m. occupying trenches 72, 72S, 73 & 73S. Relief carried out & no comment or casualties. Cy Andrewright.

Aug 2nd Quiet. Enemy shelled building a little in the evening. 1 O.R. wounded by rifle bullet whilst firing over the parapet. BL

— 3rd In the evening enemy shelled us with whiz bangs & then "bolos" on the parapet in two places with 2 shots. Killed 1 OR. firing over parapet. Bullet wounded 2 OR. Shell fire. BL

— 4th Enemy shelled PORT EGAL Farm with crumps. Also 72 & 73 with whiz bangs. Our mountain gun blew in their parapet in places. BL

— 5th Some shelling. Relieved about 11 pm. BL

— 6. 7. 8. Resting in Billets training. BL
— 9th Into Trench 67. BL
— 10th Fired two trench mortars & got two in reply in the morning. Howitzers shelled the barricade on the LILLE Road in the evening. Wounded O.R. 2. BL 1 on working party. One of our aircraft with engine stopped vol planed from G. lines & descended by our transport. BL

Aug 11th. Quiet. Work on repairs to front line & addition to support line. Communication trench converted to fire trench. BL

Aug 12th. Bombardment of T 69 or 70. BL

Aug 13th. Quiet. Relieved, marched to PONT DE NIEPPE. BL

Aug 14th. Resting. BL

Aug 15th Resting. Church parades in the morning. CJA.

" 16th Physical training. Marching. Bombing & M.G. instruction. Company parades. Capt Buddas left the Batt CJA.

" 17th P. Training. Batt used swimming baths. Wiring, Bombing & MG instruction CJA.

" 18th Ph. Training. Marching. Wiring practice, Bombing, M.G. practice. O.C. and adjutant went up to visit trenches. CJA.

" 19th Usual routine, O.C. Companies went up 5 p.m. to take over trenches 75, 76, 77 and 77 support. Batt moved into the trenches. Relief complete 10.35 p.m. CJA.

" 20th Situation normal along our front; Artillery exchanges in afternoon & evening. CJA.

" 21st Situation unchanged, wet, thick, very

little artillery fire. One man killed. (See Burial Book) CJA.

Aug. 22. Our Artillery more active during the whole day. Black redoubt in German lines successfully bombarded with large trench mortars. Retaliation with "whiz-bangs"; two men wounded. Otherwise our front was normal. CJA.

" 23. Nothing particular occurred the last 24 hours. Our own artillery situations have been normal. 2nd Lieut Thompson joined the battalion from 15th battalion. Col Innes Hopkins & Col Dunbar Stuart arrived, being attached for two or three days. CJA.

" 24. Morning normally quiet. At 5 p.m our trench howitzers fired on black redoubt in front of trench 75. Not very successful. Large variety of stuff sent back at us. No casualties but parts of trench damaged. Colonels Hopkins & Dunbar Stuart visited trenches. Lieut Gibson rejoined the Battalion from Machine Gun course at Wisques. CJA.

" 25. During the morning, artillery fired for some time on both sides. Germans set fire to farm just in rear of Batt. H.Q. Afternoon and evening quiet. One sausage of one football found in our trenches, which came over the previous day & failed to explode. Lt Cols

- Innes Hopkins of Dumbar Stuart left the Batt. after being attached for two days. 2 Lieuts. Allen, Stamberg & Morant joined the Battalion from England. (15th Bn.) 1 Officer & 4 men attached from 10th Hussars for instruction. C.Y.A.

Aug 26 Capt. Arkwright adjutant went home on leave. Lieut. C.O.P. Gibson acting adjutant. Capt. W. Robb reported sick & sent to hospital. Quiet during day. Four whizzbangs over trench 77 at night apparently to draw our batteries. No damage. C.O.P.G. Brig. Gen. Clifford inspected trenches.

" 27 And he was pleased with condition & work done. Quiet day. Very bright & hot. Aeroplane from enemy's lines flew over our lines about 5.30 p.m. Officer & men attached from 10th Hussars for instruction returned to unit and relieved by 4 men from 10th Hussars. Battn. relieved at night by 7th Battn. N.F. & moved to billets in ASYLUM ARMENTIERES.
2nd Lieut. C.A. Collingwood joined the Battn. from England.
C.P.G.

" 28. Resting till Breakfast. Baths for some of Coys. Inspection of arms, accoutrements, boots, clothing, &c. Armourer Sergt. inspected rifles. Working parties 1 N.C.O. + 20 men 2 p.m., 1 N.C.O. + 20 men 7 p.m. 3 N.C.O's + 60 men 8 p.m. 2 Officers + 75 men 8 p.m. under R.E. B.do. H.Q. Also ordered 2 Officers + 75 men 8.30 p.m. at 6th R? H.Q.

not seem to appeal to ....
party. C of P. G.

Aug 29. Church parade. Recit's Cook[?]'s parties
10½ 50 men at 8 p.m. M. G. 20 men
7 p.m. 2 M. G. 11. 40 men 8 p.m. 1 W. C. A.
10 men 8 p.m. 9th C. F. 15[?] 75 men
for 6th Div N. 3. Approved by C of ½ o.2.
their party consists of one ?? one Cpe.
as P. E. parts. Made a ??pt. particulars
to draw or P.T, 6 sections, bombers & officer
servants. Made out lists showing duties of
?? men in Batt. ?? C of P.G.

30. Physical training, musketry Instruction
& field ?????g on M. Pounding of R.E.
?? ?? of ?? Daily practice. Bombs,
instruction. M. G. action firing on ?
& general instruction. M. G. got a new Vickers
machine gun. N° 2139. Pt. H. F. Hacker A Co
detailed for permanent post under A.P.M.
ARMENTIERES to control persons passing
to & out of division's area. C of P.G.

31. Physical training. musketry Instruction
& field ???. Platoon Drill —
bayonet fighting. Bombing Pt. ?? ?? ??
?????? lecture in afternoon ??

149th Bde.
50th Div.

1/4th NORTHUMBERLAND FUSILIERS

SEPTEMBER

1 9 1 5

CONFIDENTIAL

WAR DIARY

of.

4th Batt Northd Fusiliers.

FROM August 31st TO Sept 30th.

(Volume III)

Aug. 31 Sent list of duties of Bn. to Bde. H.Q.
About 5 p.m. Asylum shelled but
portion in which 4 Bn. was billeted not
hit. 6th Durham L.I. had one man
wounded.
Battn. moved to factory PONT DE
NIEPPE at 8 p.m.
Brigade H.Q. moved to 3 RUE BAYARD
                                                    C.R.G.

Sept 1st Usual Battalion routine, marching
bombing etc. Day quiet. Heavy firing
heard further north towards HOOGE in
the evening & throughout the night.
                                                    C.A.

" 2nd Capt Good left for England on 6
days leave. Capt & Adjt C.G. Arkwright
returned from leave & resumed the
duties of adjutant. Lieut C.O.P.
Gibson took over the duties of M.G.
officer in Capt Good's absence.
Day very quiet. Nothing to record.
                                                    C.A.

" 3rd Very wet all day. Usual parades carried
out in the morning as far as possible.
Some officers went & inspected the 12th
Divisional line.   C.A.

" 4th O.C. Battalion, adjutant, and officers
commanding companies, took part in a
staff ride, for the purpose of testing

communications. 4th, 5th, & 6th N.F moved their H.Q. to positions to a point in rear of subsidiary line. 7th N.F. & 5th Borders moved up to subsidiary line. Enemy's supposed attack failed. Usual parades for the battalion in the morning. In the afternoon sports were held in the field joining the billets. CJA.

Feb 5th Church parades for all religions during the morning. CJA.

" 6th Battalion used swimming Baths in Armentières. CO inspected all companies, machine gun section and bombers. Promulgation of Court Martial in the case of Private Willis. The Battalion marched off 7.30 p.m. to take over trenches from 9th D.L.I. Relief completed at 10.35 p.m. CJA.

" 7th Front quiet except for usual artillery exchanges. C.O. of Regt inspected trenches. Supplied working party 8 men on M.G. emplacement; 15 men to R.E. for carrying, 20 men to R.E. for working.
Lieut Turner proceeded to England on leave.
CJA.

" 8th Our artillery lively in the morning with howitzers. Besides work done on the front trenches and support trenches we supplied two working parties to &

night for the R.E. Also two parties during the day for the same R.E. company. Very hot during the daytime. Capt Good returned from leave from England. CJA.

9th. Brigadier General H. Clifford inspected our trenches, and was quite satisfied with progress of work. Another hot day, but enemy quiet, except as usual about 10 a.m. when he fired some whizz-bangs & shrapnel. CJA.

10th. Our maxims fired on German trenches & at cross roads last night, resulting in a rather more violent artillery reply this morning, during which they shelled Brigade H.Q. at CHAPELLE D'ARMENTIERES. Our howitzer Batteries put fourteen rounds on to their trenches in the afternoon with good effect. Usual work in trenches, and working parties & carrying parties as well. CJA.

11th. Situation normal. Work proceeded with in trenches. A party on PORTE EGAL & another on a new communication trench dug during the night. During the day the 7th H.Q. were bombarded by whizz-bangs. We bombarded the germans' trenches with trench mortars and they replied with 'sausages'. CJA.

Sept 12th. Pretty heavy artillery fire by the Divn
on our right, trying to cut German
wire, situation otherwise normal.
The HAYSTACK FARM by the 7th N.F. Hq
again hit by whiz bangs. CJA.

13th Shelling on our right continued to-day,
not very much response by the Germans
until the evening, when they sent over
some "sausages" over, they also put about
½ doz heavies into & close to our 72 S.
trench, but only damaged trench in one
place; no one was hit. 2nd Lieut
Henderson proceeded to England on leave.
Three officers from 13th & 14th Batts were
attached to us for instruction. CJA.

14th Situation pretty normal. The three
officers who were attached left again.
Working party from 4th E Yorks came
to finish off communication trench
behind 71.S. CJA.

15th Divisional General came round trenches
but never got as far as ours. Fairly
quiet. Some whiz bangs into the
HAYSTACK FARM. Lt Gibson went out
at night and threw 2 bombs into
the German trenches. Lt Turner
returned from leave. CJA.

16. The Brigadier came round our trenches,
& was pleased with the work we had done

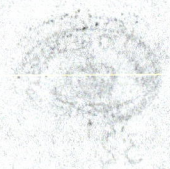

— 16th Enemy's artillery active in the morning putting some 50 shells over the trenches on our right, and some near our H.Q. An attack with the arrangements for reinforcing carried out in practice quite satisfactorily. C.G.A.

— 17th A quiet day on the whole. O C 5th DLI & officers commanding their companies came round the trenches, before their battalion comes in. O.C. went to meet the General at 6th Batt HQ. C.G.A.

— 18th Very quiet day, except for a few 'sausages' put over the trench on our right. Adjutant went down to ARMENTIERES to see the billets with Q.M. Not very good ones. Very hot. Relief complete at 9.18 p.m. & the Batt moved into billets without casualties. C.G.A.

— 19th In billets at ARMENTIERES. Battalion attended church parades; clothing issued, and sandbagging of gratings etc of cellars used in case of shelling. C.G.A.

— 20th All parades cancelled for inspection by General Plumer. Batt waited for one hour & half for him. When he appeared he seemed quite satisfied. C.G.A.

— 21st Battalion had use of baths. Parades carried out during the morning C.G.A.

— 22nd Batt marched to PONT DE NIEPPE for

instruction under Reg'd Serg't Major; usual parades under Coy officers, M.G & Bombing officer. CJA.

— 23rd Received orders to move up into trenches a day earlier into trenches 78, & 79. Colonel Gibson, Adjutant & Lieut Bell went up to the trenches in the morning & came in for pretty heavy shelling. One signaller killed while they were reconnoitering their wires. The C.O attended his funeral in evening. The Batt moved off 7.15 p.m & relief was complete 9.20 p.m. CJA. (See burial book for weather.)

— 24. Very heavy bombardment on the right of the 2nd Army, lasted all day being of extraordinary intensity. Our brigade occupies the right of 2nd Army. In conjunction with the proposed general advance of 1st & 3rd Armies & French, this Army is operating. In view of this our Batt to-day carried straw from behind support trenches to front line; when mist lifted enemy spotted the parties, 22 men were wounded, 7 out of our Batt. Cpl. Spark, L/c McGuire, Ptes G. Easter, Powell, Dodds, Teasdale, Thompson, parties brought off until dark. Pte Redpath wounded also, no WK, to rear of right. The night up till midnight was occupied in putting out the dry & wet straw
CJA.

Sept 25th. Very heavy bombardment on our right. Owing to misunderstanding the Batt on our immediate right set alight too early the straw, phosphorus bombs etc, gathered & put out last night. All the straw down the Divisional front became lighted & made strong cloud of smoke, added to which there were phosphorus bombs. The arranged Bombardment did not take place, too heavy a mist arose for observation. Situation here remained quiet through the day. We kept receiving information during the day of the advance of 1st Army in the south also of Divisions towards BELLWARDE in the south, these latter were forced back to their own trenches by German counter attacks late in the day. CJA

26th In spite of expected retaliation by the enemy the day passed without any particular activity on his part, except for machine gun fire at night. We had a patrol out by day up the Ruisseau which did good work & 11 bombs were thrown at night by a party into the German trenches. 2nd Lieut Bagnall proceeded to England on leave for six days. CJA

27th Day passed quietly with the exception of some whiz bangs. Capt Chesmond

returned from leave to England. The Batt.
was relieved from front line trenches by the
7th N.F. Two companies & half M.G Section
proceeded to the subsidiary line, the
remainder and H.Q to billets in ARMENTIERES
Relief reported complete at 6.20 pm. CJA

28th Companies in billets rested and carried
out company inspections. Two working
parties for R.E cancelled owing to wet
Remainder of Battalion came down from
the subsidiary line reaching the billets
at 8.25 pm. CJA.

29th The C.O. inspected all companies, the machine
gun section and bombers; during the day
nothing else carried out. Three working
parties at night for R.E. Raining hard at
time of starting and they were not
stopped until they arrived at their destination
and were then sent back very wet & having
done no work. CJA.

30th Battalion bathed at PONT DE NIEPPE
baths during the morning, and usual
company parades. Same working parties
as before but these were stopped by
rain before they started. CJA

149th Bde.

50th Div.

1/4th NORTHUMBERLAND FUSILIERS

OCTOBER

1 9 1 5

CONFIDENTIAL

War Diary

of

4th Batt Northd Fusiliers

From Oct 1st 1915   To Oct 31st 1915

(Volume I)

C Arkwright Capt
O/C 4 N.F.
31.10.15

Oct 1st. C.O and adjutant went up to see trenches before the battalion goes up in the evening. We had not been in these particular trenches before & found they were not very good. Battalion moved up at 6.15 p.m. taking two platoons of 8th Loyal North Lancs up with us for instruction. Relief complete without casualty at 8.45 p.m. CJA.

2nd Day quiet. Enemy appear to have been relieved and better troops come in, from air report, a good many more troops in LILLE, & activity on the railways. The two platoons of 8th Loyal North Lancs relieved by the other two platoons of the coy that we have attached to us. Relief carried out successfully. CJA.

3rd Certain amount of artillery fire during the day. For half an hour in the evening we used our machine guns on enemy's dumps and communication trenches. They answered with "whizz bangs" but did no damage. We had one man killed by a shell in the morning. (see burial book) CJA.

4th Another man killed this morning & was buried beside the other one (see burial book). Some enemy were sent early this morning from our trenches, who appear different from those a few days ago. After having had platoons of 8th L N Lancs up with us, the whole company came up to-night & took over one of the trenches held by our batt. Relief complete early without casualty. CJA

5. Adjutant went down to ARMENTIÈRES for the Court Martial of Pte Leathard D Coy. He was found not guilty. Very beastly wet day & trenches in a poor state not much shelling. The Coy of 8th L N LANCS went out of the trenches and our own men from the subsidiary line came up. Enemy's snipers very active, but artillery less so on the whole. CJA.

6. Quiet during the day, we supplied parties for R.E. & ourselves as we have done the last four days, & wiring parties at night. Fifty nine men of the draught came up to the trenches & joined their companies; they were guided up & got in without casualty. Lieut Bagnall came up having been on leave & on returning been of taken charge of the draught CJA.

7. For half an hour in the morning the enemy bombarded our trenches with rather heavy shells, which fell just

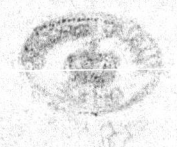

between our front & support lines and did no material damage. One man badly wounded was the only casualty belonging to MG section. Our retaliation blew in part of their parapet which we successfully prevented them from mending, with rifle & machine gun fire. CJA.

8th. Very thick all day, artillery on both sides quiet. Very heavy bombardment presumably about 8 miles south of us; started at 3 a.m. & lasted all day. Working parties during the whole day. Lieut Matheson proceeded on leave to England. A fresh draft of one officer and thirty men came from the base, & stayed down at H.Q. in the town. CJA.

9th. Cold and thick day, with the result that both the enemy & our own artillery were inactive being unable to observe well. Last night the digging of a broad trench in front of the parapet was started. The work was continued. Lieuts Allen and Lund returned from leave to England. Received information that the man wounded on 7th inst had died next day (See burial book. Pte McIntyre). Batt were relieved from present trenches by 6th N.F. and moved along into the two next trenches occupied by the 5th Borders who went down for rest to ARMENTIERES. Reliefs were carried out by 9 p.m; without casualty. CJA.

10th. The Brigadier General went round our trenches. Work carried on in the trenches and the trench in front of parapet continued. Usual artillery activity on our sector. A new 18 pounder battery put shells into the trenches on our right killing two men. Two platoons of 14th DLI came up for instruction remaining for 24 hours, got into trenches without casualty. CJA.

11th. The heavy bombardment heard in the south for the last two days, continued as hard or even to-day, presumably German counter attack, except for heavy maxim fire at night, our front was quiet; The Brigadier saw all O.C Battalions in the morning with reference to artillery demonstration tomorrow, during an attack further south by our 1st Army. CJA.

12th. Weather proved too thick and the artillery demonstration was off, no attack further south. The two remaining platoons of 14th DLI joined the two already in our trenches and they took over part of our 76 front line and part of 76 S

The Adjutant 14th DLI came up last night & stayed until 3 p.m. to day, the O.C 14th DLI came up in the evening. C.G.A.

13th The OC 14th DLI with us since last night. To day has been a "joy day"; at 2 p.m the artillery fired for an hour and half, 4000 rounds, & 800 rounds of H.E at a selected sector of the enemy's wire and trenches, at the same time, hundreds of phosphorous bombs were thrown over our parapet, & made a tremendous cloud. All this was done to try & keep as many of the enemy here as possible, while the 1st army attacked in the south. A good deal of material damage was done to one of our trenches. One man was killed and three slightly wounded of our battalion. C.G.A.

14th Very misty all day; during the afternoon our artillery continued firing with high explosive, but there was not much answer from the enemy. We were relieved by the 5th NF and proceeded to billets in ARMENTIERES. Relief carried out with one casualty, accidentally wounded. C.G.A.

15. The Battalion rested and had use of the baths. The latest

draught of 30 men joined their companies. We supplied two working parties of 50 men each to R.E. Lieut Mathison the Batt M.O. returned from England from leave. Lieut Walton proceeded on leave to England. C.J.A.

— 16th. The C.O. inspected the last two drafts to the battalion, and afterwards the battalion. Otherwise usual routine for companies. CJA

— 17th Church parades during the morning & for Transport in afternoon. CJA

— 18th. The Div General presented the DCM to 2/c Chadwester before the battalion. Usual parades. The Batt moved up to the trenches, & relieved the 6th Batt. Relief carried out by 7.30 p.m. without casualty. C.J.A.

— 19th Found working parties for the R.E, and did hard work ourselves, very cold, enemy's guns quiet on the whole. First introduction of steel helmets, found rather heavy for long use. News from further south that the enemy made another counter attack which failed. CJ.A.

— 20th Lieut Lees proceeded on leave to England. The enemy was exceptionally quiet with his artillery. One company of the 12th N.F came up and took over part of our front line and supports under our instruction. One company of ours retired to the subsidiary line, to make way for them. Relief was completed without loss. CJA.

21st The adjutant witnesses & prisoners proceeded to a COURT MARTIAL in ARMENTIERES, for the trial of Ptes Frazer & Allen. Enemy's guns just as quiet as yesterday. Two men of the 12th N.F. slightly wounded by rifle bullets. This company of 12th N.F. went out of the trenches to night, our company came up again from the subsidiary line. The first orders for the relief of the Division at some near date came out. CJA.

22nd Morning quiet. The artillery of one of the New Armies started registering in the afternoon, and succeeded in wounding two of our men in our own trenches. The retaliation of the Germans wounded two more. Very thick mist in the evening & through the night causing a good deal of rifle & M.G. fire. Lieut Walton returned from leave from England. CJA.

23rd Nothing very much to report. Mist very thick in the morning, two more men wounded. Orders received that we move out of the trenches to-morrow night right back for a rest. That is to say the whole division CJA.

- 24th In the early morning the adjutant left the trenches & proceeded to La Bieche about five miles behind the firing line, to detail the farms for the battalion to be billeted. The Battalion moved out of the trenches to billets in ARMENTIERES. CyA.
- 25th The Battalion stayed in ARMENTIERES. Capt Chipper proceeded to STRAZEELE to arrange the billets for the final resting place. CyA.
- 26th The C.O proceeded to England on leave, in the early morning. The Batt. moved off by companies at intervals to billets near the village of La Bieche & arrived about 4 p.m, and stayed at various farms for the night. CyA.
- 27th Pouring rain the battalion moved off from billets at 9 a.m for final billets at or near STRAZEELE, about twelve miles behind the firing line & arrived at 12.30 & got into billets very wet. CyA.
- 28th Did nothing very much, & started settling down. CyA.
- 29th Parades & smartening up the battalion started in earnest, & the formation of a grenadier coy commenced. CyA.
- 30th Day cleared up & the battalion got to work. Physical training, marching, coy drill. CyA.
- 31st Church parades in morning. Very wet. Lieut Bagnall returned from bombing course at TERDEGHEM. CyA.

149th Bde.
50th Div.

1/4th NORTHUMBERLAND FUSILIERS

NOVEMBER

1 9 1 5

WAR DIARY
~~INTELLIGENCE SUMMARY~~
(Erase heading not required.)

Army Form C. 2118

CONFIDENTIAL

War Diary
of
4th North'd Fusiliers
from
Nov 1st to Nov 30th
Volume (I)

WAR DIARY or INTELLIGENCE SUMMARY

Army Form C. 2118

Instructions regarding War Diaries and Intelligence Summaries are contained in F. S. Regs., Part II. and the Staff Manual respectively. Title Pages will be prepared in manuscript.

(Erase heading not required.)

Place	Date	Hour	Summary of Events and Information	Remarks and references to Appendices
STRAZEELE	Nov 1st		About Coy parcels, machine gun, and grenadier instruction and parades carried out as far as possible, but growth interfered owing to rain. A league football competition was started for representative teams throughout the Battalion. C/A.	
"	2nd		Leave has been doubled for the Batt. Parades today interfered with by the wet. C/A.	
"	3rd		Col Gibson returned from leave from England. Lieut Bell proceeded on leave to England. Wet all day. C/A.	
"	4th		Still very wet. C.O. was round the billeting area. Parades carried out in the morning. Of the football league proceeded with in the afternoon. C/A.	
"	5th		The Batt moved to its hope billets into an area N.W. of STRAZEELE about a mile outside the village. Reference Map Sheet 27. W 10 and 16. Billets much better for the men, but officers quarters not so good. C/A.	
"	6th		Day devoted to usual parades and settling into new billets. The football league fixtures were continued during the afternoon. C/A.	
"	7th		Church Parade for all denominations. C/A.	
"	8th		A further reshuffling in the billetings. C Coy which had been left in the old area joined up with the Batt to-day. L/Cpl M Wynnford went on leave to England. C/A.	
"	9th		The C.O. went to a meeting at Brigade H.Q. Four cases were tried by F.G.C.M. Ptes Parkinson, Forester, Skate and Renwick. The latter was acquitted. C/A.	
"	10th		Lt Bell returned from leave to England. The Corps Commander, Sir Charles Ferguson, inspected the Brigade by Battalions of stated he was very pleased with the work we had done in the trenches and our appearance. C/A.	

Army Form C. 2118

WAR DIARY
or
INTELLIGENCE SUMMARY
(Erase heading not required.)

Instructions regarding War Diaries and Intelligence Summaries are contained in F.S. Regs., Part II. and the Staff Manual respectively. Title Pages will be prepared in manuscript.

Place	Date	Hour	Summary of Events and Information	Remarks and references to Appendices
STRAZEELE	Nov 11	—	Programme of work has been largely interfered with by the wet. The Batt work at present consists of "attack on enemy's trenches" on the lines of recent attacks at HOOGE & LOOS. C.g.A.	
"	12	—	Nothing to record. C.g.A.	
"	13	—	Usual routine, raining wet C.g.A.	
"	14	—	Church parade. C.g.A.	
"	15	—	In view of the practice to be carried out tomorrow of attacking enemy's front of second line of trenches from our own trenches, companies carried this out on a field, bombers and machine gunners co-operating. Trenches have been prepared outside STRAZEELE the same as German trenches in front of our trench 80, in front of ARMENTIERES, taken by aeroplane photos. C.g.A.	
"	16	—	Attack on trenches carried out by two Coys the same as yesterday; a complimentary letter was received from the Brigadier on Capt. J.R. ROBB's or our C.g.A.	
"	17	—	Wretched day. The CO inspected platoons for the inter-platoon competition for turn out, handling of arms & squad drill. First three as follows A COY, C COY & B COY. C.g.A.	
"	18	—	Nothing to record. C.g.A.	
"	19	—	Batt took part in a brigade route march; the whole brigade being inspected by Gen PLUMER on route. Capt Robinson proceeded on leave to England C.g.A.	
"	20	—	Company Training. C.g.A.	

WAR DIARY

Army Form C. 2118

Place	Date	Hour	Summary of Events and Information	Remarks and references to Appendices
STRAZEELE	Nov 21st		Church parade. C.g.A.	
"	22		Remaining coys did practice attack on the Skeleton trenches. Received the order that the Brigade would go back to CALAIS, but the order was cancelled the next morning. 2/Lieut N.R. Allen went on leave to England. C.g.A.	
"	23		Coy parades carried out. The Brigadier Major lectured to all officers of the Brigade. C.g.A.	
"	24		J/S Bradley returned from leave to England. Two hundred men of the Batt went as a fnd through demostration filled with gas from cylinders; very successful. C.g.A.	
"	25		Coy training C.g.A.	
"	26		Batt concentration went in a heavy mow storm. C.g.A.	
"	27		Company in attack practice by all coys. C.O. inspected boys for the rifle coy competition in Physical Training, Won by C Coy. C.g.A.	
"	28th		Church Parades. Capt Robinson returned from leave to England. Capt Ainscough went on leave. a brigade bombing competition was held in which the first prize was obtained by B coy Grenadiers of N.F. C.g.A.	
"	29th		Nothing to record C.g.A.	
"	30th		Company in attack practice for all coys. 2/Lieut W.R. Allen returned from leave to England C.g.A.	

149 th Bde.
50th Div.

1/4th NORTHUMBERLAND FUSILIERS

D E C E M B E R

1 9 1 5

to 7. Jan 1916

Army Form C. 2118

WAR DIARY
or
~~INTELLIGENCE SUMMARY~~
(Erase heading not required.)

CONFIDENTIAL

War Diary
of
1/4th Batt. Northd. Fusiliers
From Dec 1st 1915 To Jan 31st 1916

Volume (~~IV~~ VI)

Army Form C., 2118

WAR DIARY
or
INTELLIGENCE SUMMARY
(Erase heading not required.)

Instructions regarding War Diaries and Intelligence Summaries are contained in F. S. Regs., Part II. and the Staff Manual respectively. Title Pages will be prepared in manuscript.

Place	Date	Hour	Summary of Events and Information	Remarks and references to Appendices
STRAZEELE	Dec 1		Batt route march. C.y.A.	
"	2nd		Batt drill and attack formation carried out. C.y.A.	
"	3rd		Wet. Brigade concentration route march cancelled. C.y.A.	
"	4th		Wet. Medical inspection and lecture held. C.y.A.	
"	5th		Church parade. C.y.A.	
"	6th		Batt route march, stand postponed owing to wet. C.y.A.	
"	7th		Batt carried out an attack practice in a position on ROUGE CROIX road. C.y.A.	
"	8th		Batt took part in a brigade concentration route march. Capt Arkwright came back from leave 9 th day. C.y.A.	
"	9th		Batt attacked Wilton Hamlets at STRAZEELE. Lieut Collingwood and Howard proceeded on leave to England. C.y.A.	
"	10th		Wet. C.y.A.	
"	11th		Inspection by the Brigadier just off owing to the wet. C.y.A.	
"	12th		Church parade. C.y.A.	
"	13th		Company parades. Captains Robinson and Arkwright went to 2nd Army H.Q. for Staff instruction for the day. C.y.A.	
"	14th		Capt Turvey & Lieut D. Turner went to England on leave. C.y.A. Lieut Steenberg returned from leave. C.y.A.	
"	15th		Advanced parties started off for the new area, to the west billets to hand at the time at Hill 60. C.y.A.	
"	16th 17th 18th		Companies left to themselves for final arrangements, for equipment and move; 2 Lieut Collingwood returned from leave. C.y.A.	

WAR DIARY
or
INTELLIGENCE SUMMARY

(Erase heading not required.)

Army Form C. 2118

Instructions regarding War Diaries and Intelligence Summaries are contained in F.S. Regs., Part II. and the Staff Manual respectively. Title Pages will be prepared in manuscript.

Place	Date	Hour	Summary of Events and Information	Remarks and references to Appendices
STRAZEELE	19th		Church parade. EYA	
"	20th		The Batt moved to new area; marched to STRAZEELE station and proceeded to POPERINGHE by train and marched from there to CANADA HUTS near DICKEBUSCH; the mud and dirt was appalling even in the camp.	
CANADA HUTS H.32.a.5.5 Sheet 28.	21st 22nd		The Batt was at CANADA HUTS. The C.O, second in command and O.C. Coys went up & reconnoitred the trenches and reserve points which the Batt are going to take up. EYA	
TRENCHES	23rd		The Batt moved up into brigade reserve at H.30.a Sheet 28. and to BEDFORD HO+ BLAUE POORT farm for one day. EYA	
"	24th		The Batt took over trenches at Hill 60, the line running approximately from I.34.1.9.6 to I.29.d.7.8. This is the Bulgars area, the brigade occupying the right sector of the Divisional area. Xmas day in the trenches EYA. And really fairly unnoticed, though there was a good deal of artillery fire. The trenches are frightfully appalling and the mud unbearable. We were worried and at night while returning by a Boche french mortar EYA Smash the same artillery banned out in all strafes. The French murder too inmostly misshaven itself and damage our dansters & quite hard to stop. EYA	
"	26th 27th		The Batt was relieved by 1st N.F. and went into brigade reserve at BEDFORD HOUSE, got shelled a bit the second day but nothing direct EYA	
"	28th			
"	29th 30th 31st		For the next 3 days we were lying pretty quiet, as we were made observation from a	

WAR DIARY

or

INTELLIGENCE SUMMARY

(Erase heading not required.)

Army Form C. 2118

Instructions regarding War Diaries and Intelligence Summaries are contained in F.S. Regs., Part II. and the Staff Manual respectively. Title Pages will be prepared in manuscript.

Place	Date	Hour	Summary of Events and Information	Remarks and references to Appendices
Hill 60	29th 30th 31st		Abt hours but snow enough for the Bosch to know all about us. On the night of 31st we go up to relieve the 6 N.F. again, which brings us into the trenches for New Year, as well as having had Xmas in C.T.	
"	Jan 1st 1916.		As the same old trenches and nearly quite cheery. 2Lt Richardson on attd on leave to England. Lieut Hindmarsh Thompson returned. Shone very cosy night from the French mortars, but we silenced them eventually. Belgian batteries loosed off a lot of rapid fire and the Bosch at 5 minutes to 12 ushers in a New Year greeting, this being the time the Germans kept it. C.T.A.	
"	2nd		Nothing very particular. As usual on a Sunday, our artillery fired heavily, and to the day of trench ammunition supply. More shouts from Fritz & mortars at night. C.T.A.	
"	3rd		Quite a quiet day. Cap. Chopper dep. trenches, to proceed on leave to England. Cap. Stammers returned from leave. C.T.A.	
"	4th		Battn relieved by 6 N.F. & proceeded to CANADA HUTS. C.T.A.	
"	5th		Resting.	
"	6th		Ditto and Batt bathed at POPERINGHE C.T.A.	
"	7th		Owing to the whole Div at this time got to be to the same night, we had to go up again a night earlier, I relieve 6 N.F. Lieut Bagnall returned at CANADA HUTS to proceed on leave to England tomorrow. C.T.A.	

Army Form C. 2118

WAR DIARY
or
INTELLIGENCE SUMMARY
(Erase heading not required.)

14th B.2. January 1916

Instructions regarding War Diaries and Intelligence Summaries are contained in F.S. Regs., Part II. and the Staff Manual respectively. Title Pages will be prepared in manuscript.

Place	Date	Hour	Summary of Events and Information	Remarks and references to Appendices
Trenches	Jan 8		Relief carried out last night quite quietly. Nothing much to report to-day. our guns did a little barrage practice behind their front line in front of our trenches. EyR.	
"	9		A very good strafe against the enemy's lines on and around Hill 60, doing apparently some damage, they retaliated on our trenches with a little. Got connection lost of 14 pr of gun trench. EyA.	
"	10		Quiet day. EyA.	
"	11		We were relieved by 6 N.F. yester dawn to BEDFORD HOUSE. 2 other Richardson returned from leave EyA.	
"	12, 13		Left Bn working parties EyA.	
"	14, 15		Ditto, Batt went up to the trenches, this time to the right sector + relieved 5 N.F. The Batt's in future changing over sectors. EyA.	
"	16, 17		This sector is much better in every way to the left, and away. I fn our machine gun when the enemy got too close to HQ, was quite a quiet dinner. EyA.	
"	18		Relieved by 6. N.F. and proceeded to CANADA HUTS EyA.	
"	19, 20, 21		Resting	
"	22		Batt proceeded to POPERINGHE to ms of DIV Baths EyA	

WAR DIARY

or

~~INTELLIGENCE SUMMARY~~

(Erase heading not required.)

Army Form C. 2118

Instructions regarding War Diaries and Intelligence Summaries are contained in F.S. Regs., Part II. and the Staff Manual respectively. Title Pages will be prepared in manuscript.

Place	Date	Hour	Summary of Events and Information	Remarks and references to Appendices
Trenches	Jan 23		Came back to trenches and relieved 8NF. CyA	
"	" 24		An unfavourable day. In the morning three men and one Sergt were wounded, the latter badly by one of our own shells. At night two officers were wounded whilst patrolling 2 Lieut Allen and Collingwood CyA	
"	" 25		Went down came back from leave last night. Cpl. YEOMANS was killed this morning by (see turn of book). A quiet day, the thickness of the water interfered with artillery fire. CyA	
"	" 26		A quiet day. Work on proceeded with well and some good evening work out during the night in front of the parapet. CyA	
"	" 27		A quiet day again; the relief to-night was rather different - in view of a new dispn. by relieving the trenches, to be taken up on the first day of next month. The DIV on our right took over our own three night trenches, I incidentally am then that over, the remainder of the relief was carried out by 8MNF & we proceeded to Bedford House. CyA	
"	" 28 } " 29 } " 30 }		On different, and a quiet phase. There were early wounds during these few days, of which we had warning from G.H.Q. McLeod, but my corner of the Armee strong etc was stopped by the bullet on mask. CyA	
"	" 31st		In the evening we relieved 8th NF in the trenches, we left passed off well in we relieved 5th NF as well and on thepilod over time, taking over trenches of the left sector we use. CyA	

WAR DIARY

Army Form C. 2118

Place	Date	Hour	Summary of Events and Information	Remarks and references to Appendices
MAPLE COPSE	Feb 17th		relieved from front line somewhere by 6th N.F. and went into close support redoubts. H.Q. went to MAPLE COPSE. Capt J.R. ROBB and 2Lt Scaife returned from leave and no officers being due, all leave was stopped for the men. G.A.	
"	18th 19th 20th		Nothing much to record for these four days. The Batt. supplied two working parties each night and lay in support during the daytime. On the night of the 20th we carried up to trenches again & took over from the 6th N.F. owing to our strength being so weak just at present. The 7th N.F. took over this town each night too. C.G.A.	
On attached SANCTUARY WOOD	21st		A good deal of snow on the ground, but artillery on either side kept fairly quiet. C.G.A.	
"	22nd 23rd 24th		All these three days passed quietly, and there being no communication [trench]	
SCOTTISH LINES	25th 26th 27th		Nothing. The Batt. went to Reforeighe for baths on the 25th. On the 27th we had to pitch a camp for two battalions who were coming up to SCOTTISH LINES previous to the push for taking back the "Bluff", and the Batt. moved up to CANADA and had to entrench huts that night. Colonel Gibson such C.G.A.	
	28th		Received orders to move up to night but these were cancelled, & we got further orders to go up at 10 tomorrow night to Bedford House to be ready in case we were wanted for the show. Colonel Gibson went back to hospital. Lent in a Taxicab again. The Batt to form the Reserve. C.G.A.	
	29th		Major Hunt of the 7th & 21 took over command after Batt. The Batt. proceeded to Bedford House. C.G.A.	

WAR DIARY
or
INTELLIGENCE SUMMARY
(Erase heading not required.)

Army Form C. 2118

Place	Date	Hour	Summary of Events and Information	Remarks and references to Appendices
Trenches	Feb 1st		The enemy much more active with rifle grenades. We had an unfortunate accident during the a trench bombing promiscuity. Pte ROBERTS was killed, and four men badly wounded, one died the next day. C/A	
"	2		During last night Pte HEDLEY of B coy was killed. The enemy were this very active with grenades. PTE ROBSON D coy was wounded and in the evening our machine gunner PTE RIGBY and PTE WATT of A coy were killed. We replied vigorously all day with rifle grenades and bombs. The artillery strapped on the Huns trenches C/A Hill 60.	
"	3		2 Lieut STEPHENSON A coy was wounded by a rifle grenade. PTE URE was killed in the morning. This has really been an unfortunate tour this time. Owing to the new obstacles in the brigadiers "Kid the Bosch coming in, we were only in the line three days. We were relieved by 8th N.F. and proceeded to Bedford Ho. C/A.	
"	4		The C.O. went to look at the new sectors on the left. We had an awful time at Bedford House; we were shelled do 13·0, 5·9" shells in an hour and a half, so stuck was no one was even wounded. The ninth company was not so lucky, we had four or five men wounded and Lieut SHARP was wounded and died soon after.	
"	5			
"	6		We were relieved by 4th YORKS and marched back to SCOTTISH LINES for 6 days rest, which is going to be very acceptable.	
SCOTTISH LINES	7th 8th 9th 10th 11th 12th		On the whole quite a good rest. The batt had to carry out a programme of work laid down by the brigade. The weather was very wet. On the night of the 12th we went up and relieved the 9th Btl in trenches in SANCTUARY WOOD. Relief quite quiet C/A.	

WAR DIARY or INTELLIGENCE SUMMARY

(Erase heading not required.)

Army Form C. 2118

Place	Date	Hour	Summary of Events and Information	Remarks and references to Appendices
Trenches SANCTUARY WOOD	Feb 13		A very active day. At 8 a.m. and long after the whole day the enemy shelled the HOOGE RIDGE just on our left. SANCTUARY WOOD came in for a bit of shelling and we had a few men wounded. The enemy at 10 wounded put our about two shells during the day. The night passed off fairly quietly. CYR	
"	" 14		During the morning there was only shell of HOOGE RIDGE and attacked and we were beaten back. A good amount of stuff was thrown over our trenches and we had four men killed and about thirteen wounded (see burial book). Also on the night of this Division the 7th Div this morning in the afternoon bombarded very heavily and attacked them fray when returning through KRUISSTRAAT were shelled and had one Corporal killed, two men wounded. The night was disturbed and quiet at 4.30 am a counter attack was made on the lost trenches but failed. The whole of the day was rather disturbed, the enemy started HOOGE RIDGE and around about, but nothing further happened. During the attack on our left on the 14 night, some of the enemy came and opposite our trenches, but they were spotted and dispersed. During the night two rifles, two grenades and two belongings of one of them who was shot were safely brought into our trenches. The information gained turned out to be of great value to G.H.Q. At 8 p.m. another counter-attack was made on the lost trenches and succeeded, suffering frantically. CYR	
"	" 15			
"	" 16		The whole of the day was quiet on both sides. In the evening the Batt was	

CONFIDENTIAL.

WAR DIARY
of
1/4th Batt North'd Fusiliers

Feb 1st 1916 To Feb 29th 1916

Vol VII

Army Form C. 2118

WAR DIARY
or
INTELLIGENCE SUMMARY
(Erase heading not required.)

Confidential

WAR DIARY
of
4th Batt Northd Fusiliers
from
March 1st 1916
To
March 31st 1916

Vol VIII

WAR DIARY or INTELLIGENCE SUMMARY

Army Form C. 2118

(Erase heading not required.)

Instructions regarding War Diaries and Intelligence Summaries are contained in F. S. Regs., Part II. and the Staff Manual respectively. Title Pages will be prepared in manuscript.

Place	Date	Hour	Summary of Events and Information	Remarks and references to Appendices
BEDFORD HOUSE.	March 1st		In view of possible strenuous times, the Batt came up to this place last night and found shelter in any available squashed up. At 5 p.m. in three guns of ours the whole of our guns opened up on enemies bombardment on the "Bluff" and the adjoining trenches. This stopped as abruptly as it started. The night was pretty quiet considering conditions, but at 4.30 a.m. on the morning of the 2nd, the	
"	2		enemy started another bombardment, which in various degrees lasted all day; the attack soon succeeded in all trenches being recovered. Prisoners were taken - a lot of which about ¾ of the wounded men were taken into the dressing station at Bedford House. Right & Left the Germans worked from us to go and help us at 2 a.m. at Hill 60, where the Germans had put up an enormous artillery fire; one of them was killed and three were wounded. CyA.	
"	{3 4 5 6		Except for being shelled a bit each day, there have always been more or less quiet; we had one more man killed. On the night of 6/7 ins we went up to the Hill 60 trenches. CyA.	
Trenches	7		The trenches are in an awful state; after quite heavy snow and a partial thaw, a great deal of them had fallen in. B Co had one or two men wounded today, but on the whole things were fairly quiet. CyA.	
"	{8 9		These two days seemed but trying for us, we had three sergeants killed and a good many wounded, and very heavy shelling. The little aid it necessitated a lot of heavy work, especially owing to our very low strength, CyA.	

WAR DIARY
or
INTELLIGENCE SUMMARY
(Erase heading not required.)

Army Form C. 2118

Instructions regarding War Diaries and Intelligence Summaries are contained in F. S. Regs., Part II. and the Staff Manual respectively. Title Pages will be prepared in manuscript.

Place	Date	Hour	Summary of Events and Information	Remarks and references to Appendices
Trenches	March 10		The day started quietly but grew more noisy as time wore on. We had a few men wounded though only 1, although we were subjected to severity of artillery during the day. The 5th M.F. came up and relieved us & we proceeded to where they had come from namely S.G.W.REWOOD CYP.	
Trenches	11th 12th 13th 14th		We had two more surgeon wounded the first day, and one man killed, when they shelled heavily in relation to turn. These other three days passed very quietly, and we were relieved on the night of 14/15 by 3rd Borders. We marched back to just outside Ypres where they had a barn for us down to Poperinghe Resting and very pleased to get it too. We expected to be only two days.	
	15th 16th 17th 18th		Battalion buried several severe cases (measles). Received orders to move up again, which we did, and were very annoyed about it too, we have only had four days rest approx. all. We moved up to H.30.a and came under the 150th Brigade and our underwent over the 1419th CYP	
	19th 20th 21st		In support at H.30.a. BLAVE POURTROM and ARMAGH WOOD. Except one N.C.O. wounded and Sergt. Major SHARP killed (see Summ of work) there were three quiet days. On night of 21/22 most the Battalion relieved by the 4th Yorks Regt and came back to Dickebush Huts; rather a tired rest on there was a congestion of traffic. CYP.	

WAR DIARY
or
INTELLIGENCE SUMMARY
(Erase heading not required.)

Army Form C. 2118

Instructions regarding War Diaries and Intelligence Summaries are contained in F. S. Regs., Part II. and the Staff Manual respectively. Title Pages will be prepared in manuscript.

Place	Date	Hour	Summary of Events and Information	Remarks and references to Appendices
DICKEBUSCH HUTS	March 22, 23, 24		Usual nightthing, rect clothing, company parades. On the 23rd Gen. Sir Douglas Haig came and inspected the Battn; it was a wet day and he only saw the men in their huts. A concert was held the same night in the Y.M.C.A. that went off successfully. On the night of 24th the Battn went	
Trenches	25th, 26th		up to the trenches at Mount Sorrel between Hill 60 and Sanctuary Wood. Guide a quiet two days; on the 26th officers of the Canadians who are coming up to relieve us came round & saw the trenches; they seemed quite a good lot. C.J.A.	E9/A
	27th		The Battn was relieved by 3rd N.F.A. & proceeded to close support, with Battn HQ at Square Wood. C.J.A.	
Sq. WOOD	28th, 29th		Again quite a quiet time, only two men wounded. On the night of the 29th the Battn was relieved by 16th Battn Canadians & proceeded to CANADA HUTS. C.J.A.	
CANADA HUTS	30th, 31st, April 1st		The Battn prepared three days for the march to the new area.	E9/A
			The Battn marched early the 30th down to LOCRE in the new area.	E9/A

WAR DIARY

Army Form C. 2118

CONFIDENTIAL

War Diary
of
4th Batt North'd Fusiliers

From 1st April 1916 To 30th April 1916

Vol IX

Army Form C. 2118

WAR DIARY
or
~~INTELLIGENCE SUMMARY~~

(Erase heading not required.)

Instructions regarding War Diaries and Intelligence Summaries are contained in F. S. Regs., Part II. and the Staff Manual respectively. Title Pages will be prepared in manuscript.

Place	Date	Hour	Summary of Events and Information	Remarks and references to Appendices
Trenches LOCRE	April 1st	—	Batt moved off from CANADA HUTS. Orders were changed and instead of going back to the Connection Road area, for two days before taking over the new trenches, we marched down to LOCRE and billeted in various places in the village. C̲y̲A̲	
"	2nd	—	To-night the Batt moved into the trenches. Coy Commanders and others had reconnoitred them before and they were found to be very poor, nothing more than a breastwork; what work that had been done appears to have been done might behind the firing line & be very no fighting value C̲y̲A̲	
Trenches	3rd 4th 5th 6th 7th 8th	—	This was a two days tour in the trenches, and even nearly and very heavy. We lost about eight men wounded, but they were all slight, from splinters to which cases have been avoided, had the trench been a proper one. On the eighth we had a piece of bad luck, as a heavy shell got a direct hit on a dug out in R.7 L. Killing two men and wounding four (see trench book). The Batt was relieved & this night by 5th N.F. and proceeded to Div Road in LOCRE, as far as we know for 6 days C̲y̲A̲	
Div Res LOCRE	9th 10 11 12 13	—	Period in Div. reserve interrupted however, by artillery activity on the part of the enemy which caused several casualties and to bad weather on the last two days. the 5th N.F. was relieved by this batt, on night of 13th &c. Intermittent shelling. &c.	

WAR DIARY
or
INTELLIGENCE SUMMARY
(Erase heading not required.)

Army Form C. 2118

Place	Date	Hour	Summary of Events and Information	Remarks and references to Appendices
Trenches	April 16th		Two quiet quiet days CJA	
	17th			
	18th		Enemy artillery put over during the day three heavy but short artillery barrages, our divisional artillery responded very well with retaliation, we were very lucky to have no casualties. The Batt: was relieved by the 5th NF and proceeded to Brigade reserve. Three companies being back in dugouts and one Coy. in support trenches. All leave had previously been stopped, and are men on leave recalled. Those to attend courses back to-day. CJA.	
"	19th		Being fine day out of the trenches. Coys bathed and had use of the baths at LA CLYTTE. CJA	
"	20th		To-day I made a year ago the Batt: started for France and disembarked at 10 pm at BOULOGNE. To-day the C.O. went and inspected the KEMMEL Defences, previous to our sending our companies there, in accordance with instructions to be taken up as 1000 week. CJA	
"	21st		Nothing for division to record. Services were held on 21st, Good Friday, and on	
"	22nd		night of 22nd Batt: relieved 5th NF in front line trenches. CJA	
"	23rd		St Georges day. Batt: are now near CJA	
"	24th		Except for the one days barrage of the North, this was a quiet tour, during	
"	25th		the three days, when we were relieved by the 13th Batt Kings Liverpool Regt. On night of 25th Batt. went back into the Brigade Reserve, for one day & night only CJA	

WAR DIARY or INTELLIGENCE SUMMARY

Place	Date	Hour	Summary of Events and Information	Remarks and references to Appendices
Trenches Pde Ronval.	April 26th		The 3rd Division is either relieving the 3rd Division; the Batt was relieved in the evening by 1st N.F. and proceeded to and area between BAILLEUL and METEREN, two Coys who proceeded to KEMMEL HILL, encamped near the defences of the Hill, for which the Brigade is responsible. The rest of the Batt though at rest is at one hour's notice to man the defences at KEMMEL eyA.	
REST AREA X.17 + 16.	27th		Resting.	
	28th		Resting, had to supply working parties of 200 men eyA.	
	29th		Batt had one of Battns. south of METEREN eyA.	
	30th		At 1 P.m the gunners tied off gas opposite the E. Crème Res. Batt warned to join Division man KEMMEL DEFENCES, and started off by companies independently but order was cancelled before arriving, the gas attack failed. eyA.	

Army Form C. 2118

WAR DIARY
or
INTELLIGENCE SUMMARY
(Erase heading not required.)

CONFIDENTIAL

War Diary
of
4th Batt. North'd Fus
From
May 1st to May 31st
1916

OC Arkwright Capt & Adjt
OC 4 H 31-5-16

Army Form C. 2118

WAR DIARY
or
INTELLIGENCE SUMMARY
(Erase heading not required.)

Instructions regarding War Diaries and Intelligence Summaries are contained in F.S. Regs., Part II. and the Staff Manual respectively. Title Pages will be prepared in manuscript.

Place	Date	Hour	Summary of Events and Information	Remarks and references to Appendices
METEREN	May 1st		To day is the first day for Batt commencing training after the four days complete rest after coming out of the trenches, then transhed by company and platoon slice for all, Lewis Gunners and Bom bers included CyA	
"	2nd 3rd 4th		This company and platoon Drill's started for four days and then the specialists carried on on their own CyA	
"	5th		Gas courses, bayonet fighting and other courses started and the Batt carried out the programme of work laid down by the Brigade CyA	
"	6th 7th 8th 9th		Brigadier General Clifford inspected the Brigadiers CyA. Training carried out CyA. S.H.Q. A football competition between Batts, in which the Brigadier is getting a cap, started to day, We played the 3rd NF and drew, on the 8th by we were beaten two goals to one. CyA. Training was inspected by Divisional General. Training carried out CyA.	
"	10th 11th 12th		Training, nothing else to record. CyA. Training. During the 12nd week, all ranks were inoculated again who had not been done within last 12 months. The final of the Brigadiers left was played off between 5 and 7 NFs, won by the latter CyA.	
"	13th 14th 15th		Battalion is still carrying and carrying out training. Many officers and other ranks are away on various courses, such as bombing, gas and bayonet fighting CyA	

WAR DIARY or INTELLIGENCE SUMMARY

Army Form C. 2118

(Erase heading not required.)

Instructions regarding War Diaries and Intelligence Summaries are contained in F.S. Regs., Part II. and the Staff Manual respectively. Title Pages will be prepared in manuscript.

Place	Date	Hour	Summary of Events and Information	Remarks and references to Appendices
METEREN	May 16th		The Batt held Sports during the afternoon. B Coy did not compete owing to being on guard duty. The Brigadier General was present and presented the prizes. CYA	
"	17th		Resting. CYA	
YORK HUTS	18th		The Battalion had to turn out of their camp near the Remoned Defences and proceeded to YORK HUTS 20cRE, the Japans continue to be carried out here. We believed the 7th NF here, and the 204 Lewis Gun section still remained at Kemmel. CYA	
"	19th		Resting. We supplied working parties at night for 5th Corps Signals on Kemmel Hill. CYA	
"	20th			
"	21st		The Lewis gun of B Coy came from Kemmel and joined the Batt. We played the final Batt outfit for Football beating them 2-0. CYA	
"	22nd		Resting. Coy Sergt Maj SMITH and 2/Cpl MOGERLY was Bandsman FOSTER and CAMERON received their D.C.M medals from the Army Commander at FLETRE. CYA	
"	23rd			
"	24th		Resting. CYA	
"	25th		About 6.30 p.m received heard of orders to proceed to Brigade reserve. The Batt moved off at 7.30 p.m and occupied SIEGE and RE Farms, this was owing to a scrap on the front of the Bosche, but no further development occurred. CYA	
Brigade Reserve RE FARM etc	26th 27th 28th		Remained in Brigade Reserve and found working parties at night and 7th through of the 28th when the Battalion relieved the 3rd NF in the K and L Trenches being	

Army Form C. 2118

WAR DIARY

~~INTELLIGENCE SUMMARY~~

(Erase heading not required.)

Instructions regarding War Diaries and Intelligence Summaries are contained in F.S. Regs., Part II. and the Staff Manual respectively. Title Pages will be prepared in manuscript.

Place	Date	Hour	Summary of Events and Information	Remarks and references to Appendices
	May 28		The storm seden on we were in before our month's rest. Relief was carried out without casualties.	
Trenches K5 & L5	29th		Except for a little trench mortaring WNM. one O.R. wounded. C.y.A. during the day was quiet. 2.O.R. wounded. 2 Lieuts Wilson and Rewe joined the Battalion from England. Also 8. O.R. A trench mortar strafe on an enemy crater was carried out at 12.30.a.m. C.y.A.	
"	30th		Rather more activity to-day on the part of the enemy. Our trench mortars succeeded in shutting him up in the morning. There was a certain amount of Artillery action in the morning and evening. We carried out another trench mortar strafe on enemy crater at 10.30 p.m. 1. O.R. Killed. C.y.A.	
"	31st		Enemy were active during the early morning with trench mortars, the rest of the day passed very quietly. one O.R. wounded. C.y.A.	

WAR DIARY

Army Form C. 2118

Vol XI

WAR DIARY
of
4th BATT NORTH'D FUS
From May 30th To June 30th

G. Arkwright Lt Col
ody A.H.N.F.
30-6-16

Confidential

Army Form C. 2118

WAR DIARY
or
INTELLIGENCE SUMMARY
(Erase heading not required.)

Instructions regarding War Diaries and Intelligence Summaries are contained in F. S. Regs., Part II. and the Staff Manual respectively. Title Pages will be prepared in manuscript.

Place	Date	Hour	Summary of Events and Information	Remarks and references to Appendices
Trenches L.S. & R.S.	June 1st		Enemy threw several bombs at us in the early morning during a fog, and caused casualties, 3 O.R. and 1 officer 2/L Scarfe wounded. The rest of the day was quiet. We were relieved in the evening and proceeded to Div Reserve at V.D.C.R.E.	eg/A
10 C.R.E.	2nd		Baths. Resting.	C.g.A
	3rd		Resting. Short courses on defensive gas measures and the Tower Respirator. Three officers have joined us the last few days. 2/Lts Wilson, Reeve, Bradshaw and Long.	C.g.A
	4th		In the evening we relieved the 3rd N.F. in the left sub-sector, during the night we had 4 O.R. wounded.	C.g.A
Trenches L.S. & R.S.	5th		Fairly a quiet day on our front. We registered on enemy crater at 2 p.m. with trench mortars and Stokes gun, in preparation for a "strafe". 2 O.R. and one officer, Copt. Y. Good wounded. Connections had a very bad day in the area from Hill 60 to Hooge.	C.g.A
	6th			
	7th		A quiet day. French mortars were again engaging in the afternoon on the craters. No casualties.	C.g.A
	8th		The demonstration on the crater took place at 3.30 a.m. with trench mortars, 2 Stokes guns, 28 fd'm and 2 howitzers. The shooting of all of them was excellent and the effect appeared good. The retaliation from the enemy did not last long and the only casualty we suffered was one O.R. slightly wounded. The rest of the day was particularly quiet.	C.g.A

WAR DIARY
or
INTELLIGENCE SUMMARY

(Erase heading not required.)

Army Form C. 2118

Instructions regarding War Diaries and Intelligence Summaries are contained in F. S. Regs., Part II. and the Staff Manual respectively. Title Pages will be prepared in manuscript.

Place	Date	Hour	Summary of Events and Information	Remarks and references to Appendices
Trenches Rs & LS	June 9th	—	The enemy put over a long burst of trench mortars during the afternoon and breached the parapet in a few places, but we were otherwise lucky, having only 2 O.R. wounded. In the evening we were relieved by 3rd N.F. & proceeded to Brigade Reserve at R.E. Farm. C9A	
R.E. Farm	10th	—	Baths C9A	
"	11th	—	Church Parade C9A.	
"	12th	—	Brigade Reserve still. Battalion supplied working parties of 200 men each night C9A	
Trenches Rs & LS	13th	—	The Battalion relieved the 3rd N.F. in trenches. Relief carried out without casualties C9A	
"	14th	—	Enemy shelled and trench mortared our trenches, in answer to our shelling of the PETIT BOIS. Two O.R. wounded C9A	
"	15th	—	Quiet day C9A	
"	16th	—	Another quiet day, but a very active night. A very intense bombardment took place to the north in the Ypres salient, about twelve midnight. A bombardment burst and to the south of us and grew nearer though gradually not actually as near to station from which front to the right. A smoke gas attack was made on the 24th division to our right but nothing further happened. We suffered no casualties then, but had two O.R. wounded earlier in the day. C9A	
"	17th	—	A Captain wounded by artillery accidentally by the enemy, and trench mortar. 2 Lieut LEES was killed by shrapnel. The Batt. was relieved by 3rd N.F. & proceeded to Bn Reserve LO-RE	

WAR DIARY
~~INTELLIGENCE SUMMARY~~
(Erase heading not required.)

Army Form C. 2118

Instructions regarding War Diaries and Intelligence Summaries are contained in F.S. Regs., Part II. and the Staff Manual respectively. Title Pages will be prepared in manuscript.

Place	Date	Hour	Summary of Events and Information	Remarks and references to Appendices
LOCRE	June 18, 19, 20, 21		Batt in Divisional Reserve at Locre. Baths used at Westoutre. Battn in usual amount of routine carried out the Battalion worked. On the night of the 18th the Battalion relieved the 5th N.F. in the trenches. Two O.R.s were wounded, and one O.R. belonging to the Batt, but attached to the Brigade working party was killed. C.y.A.	
Trenches K sq L5	22nd 23rd		An absolutely quiet day. C.y.A. On the whole a quiet day, but we had bad luck for when the enemy retaliated with the trench mortars, seven of our men got caught, two being killed and five wounded. The rest of the day was quiet. The road outside H.Q. was being damaged in the evening C.y.A.	
"	24th		An organized 'strafe' was carried out on the enemy's wire and C.T.s. by the artillery and trench mortars and kept up at intervals during the night. Mirrour the day was quiet. C.y.A.	
"	25th		There was practically no retaliation from the enemy for the artillery strafing last night. The Batt was relieved by 5th N.F. and proceeded to Brigade Reserve C.y.A.	
Brigade Reserve R C Farm	26th 27th 28th 29th		Batt supplied large working parties, but there were cut down to half each night owing to an discovery outbreak being a new etc. The court martials on Sergt Davies, Pte Burdon, Fiddes, and Routledge were held and sentences promulgated. For the night of 29th the Batt relieved the 5th N.F. in trenches K2 — L5. Relief carried out without casualty. C.y.A.	

1875 W: W 593/826 1,000,000 4/15 J.B.C. & A. A.D.S.S./Forms/C. 2118.

Army Form C. 2118

WAR DIARY
~~INTELLIGENCE SUMMARY~~
(Erase heading not required.)

Vol 12

SECRET.

WAR DIARY
of
4th BATT. NORTHD FUS.

FROM July 1st TO July 31st
1916.
(Vol ~~IX~~)

WAR DIARY or INTELLIGENCE SUMMARY

Army Form C. 2118

(Erase heading not required.)

Instructions regarding War Diaries and Intelligence Summaries are contained in F.S. Regs., Part II. and the Staff Manual respectively. Title Pages will be prepared in manuscript.

Place	Date	Hour	Summary of Events and Information	Remarks and references to Appendices
Trenches R5 & L5	July 1st		Quiet day, both them on the 2nd the Col. & the officers of 3rd Z.L. came to look round the trenches. C/A.	
	2nd		Another quiet day. The Battn was relieved by the 3rd Z.L. and proceeded to a camp close to BRULOOZE. C/A.	
Camp BRULOOZE	3rd			
	4th		The Battn during this time supplied working parties of 300 men each night, burying cable in rear of VIERSTRAAT. During the day those who had not been	
	to 9th		out the night before had off issued parades. C/A.	
	10th		The Battn exchanged camps with the 7th N.F. & moved close to LA CLYTTE. This	
	to 14th		moved an exchange of working parties at night. If there were employed on support line behind the M trenches, & on carrying parties from RIDGEWOOD to Support time. Comrades during this period one man wounded. C/A.	
Durham Huts LA CLYTTE	15th		During the last few days 2Lts Tutley, Hope Wallace, Rennison & Pearson joined the Battalion from the Reserve Batt. Only intermittent working parties were sent out at night and programme of work was carried out. The Battn was in the M and N trenches and the Battn was in Brigade Reserve for 8 days. C/A.	
	16th			
	17th			
	18th			
	19th		A draft of 171 men and 2 C.O.'s joined us from the Base. And a programme of training for the Battn was carried out & warmth specialists. Three officers from the 8th H.L.I. joined the Battalion with the draft.	

WAR DIARY
or
INTELLIGENCE SUMMARY

(Erase heading not required.)

Army Form C. 2118

Place	Date	Hour	Summary of Events and Information	Remarks and references to Appendices
DURHAM HUTS	20th		Officers proceeded to look over the new trenches previous to going in tomorrow night, but the order was cancelled the same evening and early the next morning, orders were received to be ready to move, which we did at 2.30 pm and proceeded to BULFORD CAMP near NEUVE EGLISE, scantily where we	CyA
"	21st		were a gun and a month ago. The same night we received fourteen officers from the base.	CyA
BULFORD CAMP	22nd		Officers proceeded up to have a look out the time in the morning and the Battn went into the trenches the same night.	CyA
[trenches] C & D's	23rd		Our trenches and our's standard regarding and the 'Borts' wasted a heavy retaliation which damaged our trenches in a few places. Casualties 1.O.R. killed and five wounded.	CyA
"	24th		Quiet day. Large amount of rifle & M.G. fire at night.	CyA
"	25th		A certain amount of trench mortaring on our left, which did not come down to our trenches. 1 O.R. & 1 Officer 2/s MUIR were wounded out serving at night.	CyA
"	26th		Quiet day. Our front was modified, the Battn going up two trenches on the right and taking over three on the left. the Battn HQ moved from ST QUENTIN CABARET to COOKERS FARM. 1 O.R. 1 Officer Capt. S. TURNER were wounded. Officer the actg Adjt. who commd while the Battn was holding trenches D3 – D6 inclusive.	CyA

WAR DIARY
or
INTELLIGENCE SUMMARY

(Erase heading not required.)

Army Form C. 2118

Instructions regarding War Diaries and Intelligence Summaries are contained in F. S. Regs., Part II. and the Staff Manual respectively. Title Pages will be prepared in manuscript.

Place	Date	Hour	Summary of Events and Information	Remarks and references to Appendices
Trenches D 3 4 5 + 6	27ᵗʰ	—	A quiet day. Enemy rifle and machine gun fire was active after dark. C.9.A.	
"	28ᵗʰ	—	We were relieved by the 5ᵗʰ N.F. & proceeded into Brigade Reserve, and	
Bde. Reserve	29ᵗʰ 30ᵗʰ 31ˢᵗ	—	found working parties each night. C.9.A.	

Vol 13

WAR DIARY
of
1/4th BATT NORTHD FUS.
From Aug 1st 1916 To Aug 31st 1916
(Vol. XI)

CONFIDENTIAL

G. Ankough (?) Capt
Adjt 1/4 NF
1-9-16

WAR DIARY

~~INTELLIGENCE SUMMARY~~

(Erase heading not required.)

Army Form C. 2118

Instructions regarding War Diaries and Intelligence Summaries are contained in F.S. Regs., Part II. and the Staff Manual respectively. Title Pages will be prepared in manuscript.

Place	Date Aug.	Hour	Summary of Events and Information	Remarks and references to Appendices
Brigade Reserve near DAYLIGHT CORNER N33.d06	1st		Nothing to report. Batt: is in Brigade Reserve and supplying working parties of 200 men each night. Lieut Gibson had a gate from his house and proceeded to hospital on the 2nd. Major Robinson took over command of the Battalion. CYA.	
	2nd			
	3rd		Batt: relieved 5th N.F. in trenches D3 – D6 inclusive. During the relief 2.O.R. were killed Sgt Charlton R.A.M.C. and Pte Grant of 2/y Leaden CYa	
Trenches D.3 – D6.	4th		Enemy opened a shrapnel and mortar & artillery shrapnel on our trenches, 5.O.R were wounded. One Pte Sandison subsequently died. Damage to trenches slight. CYA.	
	5th		A few 200 mm trench mortar have been put in & registered during the afternoon. The enemy replied heavily with trench mortars & artillery. 2.O.R. wounded. Damage to trenches slight. CYA.	
	6th		Nothing to report. No activity of any sort on either side.	
Longueval	7th		Quiet day. Batt: were relieved in trenches by 8th North Staffs and 10th Royal Warwicks and proceeded to Badajos Hut. Loire gun	
Meaulte	8th		Batt: proceeded to billets near Meaulte gun	

WAR DIARY or INTELLIGENCE SUMMARY

Army Form C. 2118

Place	Date	Hour	Summary of Events and Information	Remarks and references to Appendices
METEREN	9th	—	Nothing to record, the Batt. is in Corps Reserve JCR	
	10th	—	Nothing to record, the Batt. is extremely busy preparing to leave Second Army. JCR	
	11th	—	The Batt. moves out of Vth Corps Reserve at Meteren and entrains at Bailleul for Doullens, after detraining at Doullens we have three hours march to Fienvillers where we are billeted. The Division is now transferred from the 2nd Army to the Reserve Army; this being the first time that we have really left the neighbourhood of Ypres since first arriving in France nearly sixteen months ago. JCR	
FIENVILLERS	12th 13th 14th		after detraining at DOULLENS, the Batt had a 7 mile march to Fienvillers CPA. These three days were given up to route marching, the result of these being a marked improvement in the Batt which had become soft from continuously being in the trenches. CPA	
	15th		The Batt made an early start, at 4.40 a.m marched to NAOURS a distance of about 8 miles, there, bivouaced for one day CPA	

Army Form C. 2118

WAR DIARY
or
INTELLIGENCE SUMMARY
(Erase heading not required.)

Instructions regarding War Diaries and Intelligence Summaries are contained in F. S. Regs., Part II. and the Staff Manual respectively. Title Pages will be prepared in manuscript.

Place	Date Aug.	Hour	Summary of Events and Information	Remarks and references to Appendices
	16th		Battalion marched from NAOURS & remained there for the night	CJH
	17th		Battalion marched from PIEREGOTTE to HENENCOURT WOOD where we started training the same evening	CJH
HENENCOURT WOOD	18th 19th 20th 21st 22nd		These five days were spent in Batt. Training, chiefly Batt. in attack or Trenches	
"	23rd to 28th		Batt. Training consisting of attack on trenches, which subsequently developed into Brigade attack. Combined Patrols carried out by the Signallers in conjunction with aeroplanes were successfully carried out. One or two night attacks were also done. Several Military Medals were presented by the Corps Commander to men of the 50th Division, on account of the hard weather the 149th Infantry Brigade were the only Brigade who attended the presentation	
"	29th to 31st		During these three days the wet weather interfered considerably with the Batt. Training in one day it was impossible to do any work at all. The Batt. together with the 7th N.F. carried out night operations on the night of the 31st.	

149th. INFANTRY BRIGADE

50th. DIVISION

4th. NORTHUMBERLAND FUSILIERS

149th. INFANTRY BRIGADE

SEPTEMBER 1916.

Army Form C. 2118

WAR DIARY
or
INTELLIGENCE SUMMARY
(Erase heading not required.)

Vol 14

Confidential

WAR DIARY
of
4th BATT. NORTHD FUS.

From Sept 1st 1916 To Sept 30th 1916

(Vol X)

WAR DIARY

~~INTELLIGENCE SUMMARY~~
(Erase heading not required.)

Army Form C. 2118

Instructions regarding War Diaries and Intelligence Summaries are contained in F.S. Regs., Part II. and the Staff Manual respectively. Title Pages will be prepared in manuscript.

Place	Date SEPT	Hour	Summary of Events and Information	Remarks and references to Appendices
HENENCOURT WOOD	1st		Training of the Batt. carried on with. The men are now getting very fit & taking a keen interest. CyA.	
"	2nd		Weather appalling and consequently drawing was must curtailed. Routh marches when possible and worked into the drawing spaces, in view of Brigade Sports which are to come off shortly. The Div. General came and inspected the transports of the Brigade. Ours was a very good show and we were complimented on the turn out.	
"	3rd 4th 5th		Training CyA.	
"	6th		The Brigade Sports which should have taken place to-day were put off owing to movement and were a great success. This Batt. did extremely well & carried off a large proportion of first & second places in a lot of events. At the conclusion the Brigadier presented the prizes. CyA.	
"	7th			
"	8th			
"	9th		During the night of the 8th and early hours of the 9th the 3rd and 6th Battalions moved up to positions first in rear of the front line. On the evening of the 9th inst. the 8th & 9th Inf. Bde. took over part of the front line. The 5th Batt. took over in the front line and the 6th Batt. were in support. This Battalion moved off from HENENCOURT WOOD at 3p.m. on 9th inst. and proceeded via MILLENCOURT and ALBERT to BECOURT WOOD about 2 miles E. of ALBERT	[signature]

1875 Wt. W593/826 1,000,000 4/15 J.B.C. & A. A.D.S.S. Forms/C. 2118.

WAR DIARY

of
~~INTELLIGENCE~~ SUMMARY

(Erase heading not required.)

Army Form C. 2118.

Instructions regarding War Diaries and Intelligence Summaries are contained in F. S. Regs., Part II. and the Staff Manual respectively. Title pages will be prepared in manuscript.

Place	Date	Hour	Summary of Events and Information	Remarks and references to Appendices
Map Ref Sheets 57DSE 57c 5W BECOURT WOOD	Sept 10	7.	The Batt. marched to BECOURT WOOD. Both officers & NCO's accommodated front & support lines both in the morning & the afternoon. Brigadier General CLIFFORD was killed while inspecting 147 TRENCH which had been dug on a jumping off position. Lt Col TURNER CMG took over command of the Brigade A draft of N.R.I.C.&R.S. (50 men) arrived	
"	"	11	The 149th Inf Bde extended its front to the left to JUTLAND ALLEY inclusive. The boundary between it & the 150 Inf Bde now being Junction S.8.c.9.7 — O.E. Trench S.14.a.2.6 — N.W. corner MAMETZ WOOD. At 7 a.m. the positions of Batts. were Strand front — CLARKS TR & foot. in front Part of 6TH AVENUE. E — 5TH N.F. New intermediate TR, E of JUTLAND ALLEY Support Line — 16TH N.F. Quadrangle TR — 7TH N.F. BECOURT WOOD — 4 N.F. On the night of/9 left of the 149° Inf Bde reached am front of the front line on the night to	

Army Form C. 2118.

WAR DIARY
~~INTELLIGENCE~~ SUMMARY.
(Erase heading not required.)

Instructions regarding War Diaries and Intelligence Summaries are contained in F.S. Regs., Part II. and the Staff Manual respectively. Title pages will be prepared in manuscript.

Place	Date	Hour	Summary of Events and Information	Remarks and references to Appendices
	6/7	12"	The 142nd Inf Bde (47th DIV) The boundary between 47th & 30th Div's now running – Point S.3.d.2.6½ in CLARKE'S TR (front line) — WINDMILL at S.9.c.3.9½. — Road at point S.8.d.9.1½. — cross roads (inclusive to 149th Inf Bde) at S.14.b.1.5 — point on road at S.13.b.1.0. — road inclusive to 149th Inf Bde to X.24.a.8.8. — Menu de pent in quadrangle TR at X.23.c.4.6½.	
		13"	The positions of Batts were carried unchanged. Between the hours of 5 & 6 a.m. the Batt moved by platoons to MAMETZ WOOD (S.W).	
MAMETZ WOOD		14"	During the whole day & also the following day the Batt was engaged with all material to complete its full fighting order. At the C.O's meetings all Batt formations, Artillery arrangements etc were thoroughly gone into amongst officers, Brigadier Gen. OVENS. C.M.G. took over command of the Bde.	
Batt H.Qrs in Q.4.A.R.5.0.5			At 9.30 p.m the Batt moved from MAMETZ WOOD via the "Quarry" then overland to its Batt. positions in the aug 27 Aro ducker of the Bde sector, namely from a point S.3.f.6.6. to S.3.f.0.5½. The Batt formations were completed about 3 A.M, Coy running from right to left as follows B.coy, A.coy, B.coys, D.coy. The following officers went to be action	
Headquarters			M. Col. B.D. Gibson.	2/b. R.D. Browne (wounded)
			Capt. J.G. Jenkins. Adgt (Adjt)	2/h. R.W. Bromage (Sig.off)
			Capt J.C. & 2.Lt. Wilson (2nd off)	2/h.Lt. N.C. Longchin (Bde Liaison off)
				2/b J.A. Bagnall (B.D) Killed

WAR DIARY
or
INTELLIGENCE SUMMARY
(Erase heading not required.)

Army Form C. 2118.

Place	Date	Hour	Summary of Events and Information	Remarks and references to Appendices
	Sept. 14th		H. Coy — Capt. J.J. Henderson (killed) 2/Lt. G.P. Watton (wounded) 2/Lt. R. Pathick (killed) B. Coy — Capt. L.D. Plummer (killed) 2/Lt. E. McGuer (wounded) 2/Lt. H.A. Long (killed) C. Coy — Capt. H. Chessmond (wounded) 2/Lt. A.S. Wade (wounded) 2/Lt. J.J. Midwell (killed) D. Coy — Capt. H.H. Bell (killed) 2/Lt. H. Tully (wounded) 2/Lt. J. Fleming (killed) 2/Lt. G.J. Balfour (killed) Attached — Stokes Mortar Lt. Currie (wounded) M.G. Coy Lt. Taylor (killed) Carrying Party Lt. Robson (wounded)	
	Sept. 15th	At 3 a.m.	the dispositions of the Bde were as follows Bde H.Q. — The Quarry S.8.Z.8.1 Front line — 4th N.F. — On the right with H.Q. in Craters TR at S.3.c.4.9 — 7th N.F. — " Left " — S.3.a.1.0 Support — 6th N.F. with H.Q. at New Quarry S.8.d.9.9½ Reserve — 3rd N.F. — " Old Quarry S.8.Z.8.1	

WAR DIARY
or
INTELLIGENCE SUMMARY.
(Erase heading not required.)

Army Form C. 2118.

Place	Date	Hour	Summary of Events and Information	Remarks and references to Appendices
	Sept 15th		The 150th Bde occupied the left front & the 149th Bde the right front of the Div sector the 151st Bde was in Div Reserve. The 47th Div were on the right & the 13th Div on the left of the 50th Div. The 18th London Regt (London Irish) were on our immediate right & will the 19th Batt in support to them. At Zero time 6.20 a.m. this Battn aucling Barrage left then jumping off trenches for the first objective. First in front of this assault two of the new Tanks went forward to the Northern left of the 149th & the 149th Inf Bde. This caused the enemy to send up the S.O.S. signals at once, which after 4 minutes brought down the enemy barrage to front of his own front line, just before Zero time. About 7.6 A.M. a message was received from Capt Plummer from the left of the Battn front that the 1st objective had been gained with but small opposition, that he was to push on with D Coy and the 7th N.F. Shortly after this wounded men began to come back. End one further messages were received from Coys for some time. At 7.20 P.M. the advance to 2nd objective (STARFISH TR) began under a barrage advancing 50 yds per minute and 1st objective was occupied by a Coy of 6th N.F. under Capt TWEEDY. The Coy of 6 N.F. under Capt COOKE which should have	

WAR DIARY
or
INTELLIGENCE SUMMARY.

(Erase heading not required.)

Army Form C. 2118.

Place	Date	Hour	Summary of Events and Information	Remarks and references to Appendices
	Sept 15th		replaced the Latter toward HIGH WOOD & made some trouble the extreme end of C.O.H.N.F.	
		7.43 A.M.	A message was received from Bolts that the attack of 47th DIV on HIGH WOOD on our right was held up & that 2 enemy Batts were going forward. The moon & our right flank had to be carefully watched and was subjected to rifle fire and was in the rear.	
		8.20 A.M.	A further message was received from Bolts saying left brigade of 47th DIV was trying to work around HIGH WOOD, & obtaining the Batt to assist with stokes Mortars and lewis guns from BETHEL SAP, a chance to working at right angles to our jumping off trenches and up our volume sight. Col Gibson having no one in the CHARL'S TR. wired for another coy to form defensive flank in BETHEL SAP, & sent 2/Lt Wilson to obtain information as to the position in the night of our final objective. 2/Lt Wilson reported that top of BETHEL SAP & right of final objective was occupied by M.G. fire from HIGH WOOD. Shortly after Capt Bramford 2nd N.F. this coy were placed at the disposal of Col Gibson by O.C. 7 N.F. Half this coy was sent to BETHEL SAP & half to the tops of final objective to work along ½ right and form a defensive flank.	
		9.25 A.M.	A message was received from Bolts, saying Division directed that	

WAR DIARY
~~INTELLIGENCE SUMMARY~~
(Erase heading not required.)

Army Form C. 2118.

Instructions regarding War Diaries and Intelligence Summaries are contained in F. S. Regs., Part II. and the Staff Manual respectively. Title pages will be prepared in manuscript.

Place	Date	Hour	Summary of Events and Information	Remarks and references to Appendices
	Sept 15		HOOK TR. must be made good & strengthened on far right as Div Boundary. The strengthening of Mr y BETHEL SAP was completed as far as possible & the flank made secure. Bombing parties of gunners from HIGH WOOD were dispersed by our machine, Lewis gun and Stokes Mortar fire.	
		At 10.35 A.M.	a coy of 3rd N.F. under Lt Doyle's command & guns and CLARK's TR at 10 H.C.A.M. 2/Lt Wilson was again sent forward to obtain more information as to further 1st objective. Half of Lt Doyle's coy was then up to 1st objective & bombed round HOOK to right and got touch with BETHEL SAP.	
		At 11.30 A.M.	Heavy Artillery bombarded N W corner of HIGH WOOD and as the #7 Div gradually worked round HIGH WOOD the enemy commenced retiring & were again caught by our M.G. fire. About 100 gunners caught by this were endured. HIGH WOOD was then cleared step by step. 2 coys of our forward attack on our 2nd & 3rd objectives came on slowly only disconnected stations from wounded men for some time being received. At 11.40 A.M. 2/Lt Wilson returned confirming his previous report. 2/Lt Wittope R.F.A. reported that all officers of C coy were hit & that he had taken on this coy till he turned over his coy to watch a Corporal had led to lead it against the	

WAR DIARY
or
INTELLIGENCE SUMMARY

Army Form C. 2118.

(Erase heading not required.)

Place	Date	Hour	Summary of Events and Information	Remarks and references to Appendices
	Sept 15th 1916		2nd objective which it appeared to gain.	
		At 12 noon	the whole of 6 L.N.F. supporting Batty, being up in various parts of the attack, Col Spain, OC 6 L.N.F. moved his HQ up to CLPRKS TR.	
		At 3.30 p.m.	Col Gibson moved his HQ forward to HOOK TR. This was badly knocked about. Two of 4, 5, 6, & 8 Coys of 7 N.F. were found all crowded up into Col Gibson then organised the whole of these objectives, getting all the various Battalions together, establishing commander on the redoubt beyond unit. Battalion of 47th DIV. As this piece of them were 100 men of 7th NF. in SUNKEN RD in front of HOOK TR. 650 men of the Bde further forward had become considerable, together a handful who withdrew with 2/1 Bosone about 1.30 am (16th inst) on the arrival of part A of 47th DIV. This was the situation at dusk & the position of affairs that was reported to Bde.	
		About 7.30 p.m.	the 151st Bde came through the 1st objective; pursued by HOOK TR to attack & consolidate the 2nd & 3rd objectives, a task to which the situation had been in our town all day. This attack did not succeed.	
	Sep 3 16th	4.45 a.m.	A moving was received from Brigade, stating 151st Bde were making every effort to occupy and consolidate STARFISH LINE (2nd objective)	

WAR DIARY
or
INTELLIGENCE SUMMARY

(Erase heading not required.)

Army Form C. 2118

Place	Date	Hour	Summary of Events and Information	Remarks and references to Appendices
	Sept 16th	6.45 am	Further messages were received that 151st Bde were to occupy PRUE. TR.	
		9.25 am	At 9.25 am a 15 minute bombardment. This attack did not succeed. During this time the Battn with H.Q. maintained its position in HOOK TR. which was continuously shelled with 5.9's. From subsequent information it seems clear that the 4th N.F. took part of the 2nd objective and advanced to the 3rd objective (PRUE. TR) on the morning of 15th. Both these trenches were evacuated by the enemy on the attack, & only held afterwards at east end of our front by M.G.S. & bombers. In the afternoon 149th Inf. Bde went into Div. Reserve & the Battn left HOOK TR for MAMETZ WOOD. Total casualties, 17 officers & wounded above. O.Rs. Killed 110, Wounded 229, Missing 143. 3 Guns went into action, 22 officers and 895 O.Rs. The Battn was congratulated in very flattering terms by the G.O.C. Bde & Division for its conduct in the action of the 15th.	
	Sept 17th	12.12 am	At 12.12 am a message was received that a counter attack was to be expected in the neighbourhood of HIGH WOOD and the Batt "stood to", but nothing developed. A draft of 30 men joined the Battalion. Casualties were checked as far as possible and a present strength got out of 17 officers & O.R. 262. Incorporated in this were officers who had been kept back and the transport being kept back as	
	Sept 18th		The remainder of the day and also the next were spent in re-equipping the Battn	

WAR DIARY

Army Form C. 2118

Place	Date	Hour	Summary of Events and Information	Remarks and references to Appendices
	Sep 1	19th	A further draft of 39 arrived, of the re-equipment of the Batt was completed. The trench strength now was	
	Sep 1	20th	Another draft of 40 arrived. The Batt. arrived from MAMETZ WOOD at 3 pm. by coys and proceeded to CLARK'S TR. together with 7"N.F. On arrival at 8" B21. had not been relieved so the Batt dug themselves in in shell holes in rear of CLARK'S TR. At dusk 1 coy was to go to a strong point at 5.3. & 9.5, and 3 coys to HOOK TR. The latter was in such a bad state that Col Gibson got permission from Bde for these 3 coys to remain where they were. B coy under Lt Carrick went to the above strong point at dusk. The 5"N.F. also came to CLARK'S TR at dusk.	
	Sep 1	21st	These dispositions remained for the day of 21st. Orders were received from Bde for the Batt with working party of 5"N.F. & covering party of our own, to dig at 7.30 pm a jumping off trench, midway between the front line (the BOW), and the STARFISH LINE, with a view to an attack on the latter. Buy the orders also stated that 3 on completion of the jumping off trench, the covering party found by the STARFISH LINE was tagally or most held attack, then the covering party was to take it, if a garrison be just in. All preparations for this were being made and at 7 p.m. all these orders were cancelled & further orders received that STARFISH trench and PRUE TR. beyond, had to be assaulted and captured.	

Place	Date	Hour	Summary of Events and Information	Remarks and references to Appendices
	Sept 21st		The Brigadier arrived and established Bde HQ in CLARK'S TR. and consulted with Col Gibson & Lt Col Jackson 7th N.F. Colonel Gibson with the Batt Bombers and some selected men, 20 men of D coy, A coy, and 200 men detailed from 2 coys of the 5th N.F. in original working party at once proceeded to SUNKEN RD, where Col Gibson established his H.Q., and made his dispositions for the attack on the STARFISH LINE. One coy of the 5th N.F. was sent to HOOK TR. in rear of SUNKEN RD to be at his disposal & the 4th coy of 5th N.F. with their Batt HQ remained at CLARK'S TR. Remainder of 7th Bath was as follows. Remainder of C&D coys at CLARK'S TR. and B coy at strong point mentioned above. This coy did not move during the whole of these operations. The 7th N.F. were holding the front line (BoN TR) with coy in support at SUNKEN RD & HOOK TR. The 8th N.F. were in rear of CLARK'S TR.	
		10.15 pm	Attack was launched from the BoN against STARFISH. Three bodies of bombers and picked men in front under Lieuts Carrick, Hindleyson, & Long, and interval of about 100 yds and A coy and 20 men of D coy under Lieuts Stephenson, Micks & Benson in support. STARFISH was occupied without opposition & 100 men of 5th N.F. commenced to dig A.C.T. to it from the "BoN". The remaining 100 men of 5th N.F. were sent into STARFISH TR. on the left of 4th N.F. C coy of 4th N.F. joined 4th N.F. on right.	[signature] Copy 9/3 OH

		Army Form C. 2118

WAR DIARY
or
INTELLIGENCE SUMMARY
(Erase heading not required.)

Instructions regarding War Diaries and Intelligence Summaries are contained in F.S. Regs., Part II. and the Staff Manual respectively. Title Pages will be prepared in manuscript.

Place	Date	Hour	Summary of Events and Information	Remarks and references to Appendices
	Sept 21st		Another coy of 5th NF arrived & was placed on the extreme left of STARFISH. Col. Gibson handed over the H.Q. at SUNKEN RD to Col. Jackson and moved to STARFISH about 3. a.m. The attack on PRUE TR. was then organised. Two bombing parties from the 4th N.F. & 5th N.F. respectively were in front, with 4th N.F. on the right & 2 coy of 5th NF on the left in support. About 5 A.M. PRUE TR. was occupied without opposition, but the 4th N.F. had a number of casualties from our own artillery. The 8th N.F. occupied STARFISH with one coy of 5th N.F. on the left. Col. Gibson handed over H.Q. to Col. Stain and went forward to PRUE TR. about 5.45 A.M. A draft of 45 O.R. arrived as the transport today.	
	Sept 22nd		On the early morning the dispositions of the Battalions were, 4th N.F. with 2 coy of bombers & 5th N.F. in PRUE TR. 8th N.F. in STARFISH. 7th N.F. in their original front line and support trenches & 5th N.F. H.Q. and remaining coys in CLARK'S TR. Rather in the morning the 7th N.F. moved their H.Q. back to CLARK'S TR & Col. Gibson moved his H.Q. back to SUNKEN RD. Patrols were pushed forward & reported that the high ground in front was clear. Posts were established about 300 yds further forward the same evening. The E.D. was again congratulated in very flattering terms on the manner in	M. Cox Lt Col

WAR DIARY or INTELLIGENCE SUMMARY

Army Form C. 2118

Place	Date	Hour	Summary of Events and Information	Remarks and references to Appendices
	Sept 22nd		which the operations had been conducted. Casualties, Lt Carrick & 2 others wounded. 2/Lt Stephenson received slight shell shock but remained at duty. O.R. killed 4. Wounded 28. Missing 1.	
	Sept 23rd		For the remainder of the 22nd & the 23rd these positions remained unchanged. The Batt was in touch with the Gloucesters (1st DIV) on the right & with 23rd DIV on the left. On the night of the 23rd the Brigade was relieved by the 150th Bde and became Brigade in DIV Support. The Batt was relieved by 5th Yorks & proceeded to O.C. line BAZENTIN LE PETIT.	
	Sept 24th		The 151st Bde relieved the 149th Inf Bde which there by became DIV Reserve. The Batt moved to MAMETZ WOOD (SW) at 2 p.m. where a further draft of 80 O.R. joined the Battalion.	
	Sept	25th 26th 27th 28th	The Battalion remained in DIV Reserve and supplied working parties both by day & by night, varying from 100 men to the whole Battalion, working on roads and trench tramway. On 26th another draft, 139. O.R., joined the Battalion. Corpl W. Ross rejoined the Battalion and took over the command of D Coy. The Battalion relieved the 4th Coy Yorks and in the afternoon moved up again to the O.C. line BAZENTIN LE PETIT. The 149th Bde having again become Brigade in support.	
	Sept 29th			
	Sept 30th		Messages received that Batt would move tomorrow to take part in further advance. Orders were sent forward to reconnoitre by the Batt Commd & Officers	

Army Form C. 2118.

WAR DIARY
or
INTELLIGENCE SUMMARY

(Erase heading not required.)

14/30

Vol 15

CONFIDENTIAL

WAR DIARY VOLUME 19

4 Battalion

Army Form C. 2118.

WAR DIARY or INTELLIGENCE SUMMARY

(Erase heading not required.)

Place	Date	Hour	Summary of Events and Information	Remarks and references to Appendices
PRUE and STARFISH TR.	Oct 1st	—	The Battalion moved up from the O.G. Line at Bazentin to PRUE TR. and STARFISH with two guides in the tackle. The 7"N.F. were lying to our left in both these trenches. The 5th & 6th N.F. were to th And to the 161st Inf Brigade who were attacking. Zero time 3.20 p.m. An intense bombardment of our artillery took place on german front line & then lifted. The german barrage was late in coming down and we got through with little loss. We took all our objectives and pushed forward posts. The 117 Div on our right got into FAUCOURT L'ABBAYE and were held up & did not gain the objectives. On the night of 1/2 Oct we suffered severely from fire. In the 8th & 9th Bns in front line.	
	Oct 2nd	—	The two coys in STARFISH who went forward to occupied position left in PRUE TR. left by 7th N.F. who had gone further forward. Late in the day three coys were relieved on the 7th N.F. coys were redumming there. We hoped to be relieved of that night. At 3 p.m. orders were received that the 8th N.F. would relieve the Durhams in the front line. We relieved the 8th S21st & the 3rd Borders. The weather was appalling & the mud of that fire. A large number of bombs had to be carried up & the men were absolutely beaten out	

Army Form C. 2118.

WAR DIARY
or
INTELLIGENCE SUMMARY
(Erase heading not required.)

Instructions regarding War Diaries and Intelligence Summaries are contained in F.S. Regs., Part II. and the Staff Manual respectively. Title Pages will be prepared in manuscript.

Place	Date	Hour	Summary of Events and Information	Remarks and references to Appendices
	Oct. 3rd		And the relief was not completed until about 9 a.m. on the morning of 3rd. Day pretty quiet, but the mud was appalling, causing great difficulty in getting food & water up to the front line – the wounded retired at 12 mid-night by the 11th N.F. 23rd division & proceeded to MAMETZ WOOD. The men were so exhausted, it was breaking day before some coys got in.	
	4th	2 p.m.	The Batt moved by Coys to billets RUE de PERONNE ALBERT.	
MILLENCOURT	5th	12.15p	— The Batt moved to MILLENCOURT. The C.O. proceeded for 14 days leave to England. Major Robinson took over command of the Batt	
"	6th 7th		Training & reorganisation of the Batt & specialists."	
"	8th		Church Parades, five men on draft came from Base as reinforcements. The G.O.C. Both inspected all drafts to the Batt since 15-9-16 & was very pleased with their appearance	
"	9th 10th 11th 12th 13th		Training continued. On 10th inst 14 O.R. came on draft from the Base.	

C.Y. Arkwright Lt Capt
Adjt

WAR DIARY or INTELLIGENCE SUMMARY

Army Form C. 2118.

Place	Date	Hour	Summary of Events and Information	Remarks and references to Appendices
MILLENCOURT	Oct. 14th		Training continued. The Batt carried out an exercise on night operations on the same lines to be adopted tomorrow night when the whole Division is to carry out a similar exercise. 19 men arrived from Base as an draft. Church Parades. The Batt took part in divisional night operations. 59 O.R. arrived as draft from Base.	
"	15th			
"	16th		All specialists carried on training. The Batt. stood for a route march.	
"	17th		Orders had previously been received that the Batt. would proceed to ALBERT to relieve 7th N.F. working on the roads. This was cancelled, and orders were received to proceed to the vicinity of MAMETZ WOOD for working. Woods under the Div. C.R.E. The Batt arrived at 5.20 p.m. and pitched camp. The party of 2 officers and 100 men from VIVIERS joining the Batt. The camp was shelled during the night.	
MAMETZ WOOD	18th		Batt. provided party of 400 men at 6 a.m. on working party. The camp was moved more up to MAMETZ WOOD. One officer 2/Lt WARREN arrived from the Base last night.	

J Arkwright Capt
A/Lt/Col 1st N.F.

WAR DIARY
INTELLIGENCE SUMMARY

Place	Date	Hour	Summary of Events and Information	Remarks and references to Appendices
MAMETZ WOOD	19/9/16 20/9/16 21/9/16		Battalion provided working party of 500 men for R.E.'s to work on roads near BAZENTIN, BOTTOM WOOD and CATERPILLAR VALLEY. On 21/9/16 Lt Col B.S. Gibson returned from leave in England. (continued on next page).	

Army Form C. 2118.

WAR DIARY
or
INTELLIGENCE SUMMARY
(Erase heading not required.)

1st Bn Northumberland Fusiliers

Place	Date	Hour	Summary of Events and Information	Remarks and references to Appendices
MAMETZ WOOD	22/10/16		Battalion under canvas outside S.E. corner of WOOD. Working party of 500 men attached to R.E. mending roads near "BAZENTIN-LE PETIT", BOTTOM WOOD and CATTERPILLAR VALLEY.	
Trenches FLERS LINE.	23/10/16 24/10/16		Battalion moves up into forward area to FLERS LINE in support to 6th Batt. N.F. who are in to front line trenches S.E. of BUTTE de WARIENCOURT. Route taken MAMETZ WOOD – BAZENTIN LE GRAND – S.E. corner of HIGH WOOD – COUGH DROP. Battalion Headquarters at COUGH DROP and FLERS LINE.

During this move owing to soft condition of the ground, it was impossible to take up Lewis Guns on hand-carts. The Guns and ammunition drums had to be carried and special carrying parties attached from companies was by pack ponies. The only method of bringing rations up owing to soft condition of roads. Cavalry pack ponies were attached for this purpose. | |

Army Form C. 2118.

WAR DIARY
or
INTELLIGENCE SUMMARY
(Erase heading not required.)

Instructions regarding War Diaries and Intelligence Summaries are contained in F.S. Regs., Part II. and the Staff Manual respectively. Title Pages will be prepared in manuscript.

Place	Date	Hour	Summary of Events and Information	Remarks and references to Appendices
Trenches FLEERS LINE.	25/10/16		Conditions very wet and muddy. Company Officers reconnoitre front line. 2nd Lt. C.A. BARDEN sprained his ankle and goes to hospital. 26/10/16. Men engaged in cleaning out and improving trenches. All cooking done at COUGH DROP and dinners carried up.	939.
	27/10/16		Battalion relieves 6th N.F. in front line trenches (Opposite BUTTE de WARLENCOURT) as follows. A.Coy. in SNAG TRENCH. D.Coy in SNAG TRENCH and ABBAYE TRENCH. 2 Platoons B.Coy in ABBAYE TRENCH. 2 Platoons B.Coy in FLEERS LINE. C.Coy in FLEERS LINE. Battalion Headquarters in two Boche deep dug-outs near HEXHAM ROAD. Relief started at 6.30 pm and was not completed until 3.30 am. At 4 pm. an intense barrage was opened up by enemy chiefly in ABBAYE, ABBEY (which were hut and trenches fully in ABBAYE LANE, PIONEER ALLEY (which were hut and trenches behind) and HEXHAM ROAD. This barrage lasted for 1½ hours until 5.30 pm. The night was fairly quiet. Covering for front line was carried out by Coys. also in being two and three up at HEXHAM ROAD and carried up.	

WAR DIARY
or
INTELLIGENCE SUMMARY

(Erase heading not required.)

Army Form C. 2118.

Place	Date	Hour	Summary of Events and Information	Remarks and references to Appendices
Front line Trenches near BUTTE de WARLENCOURT	28/10/16		Cold day but fair. Enemy Artillery fairly quiet. Our artillery very active, 'practising' an SOS barrage at 10 p.m. At 8.30 a.m one of our aeroplanes was brought down. It nose dived and burst into flames. May enemy snapper. Our snipers were active and slain 2 Huns.	940-
	29/10/16		Fine day but wet night. Enemy Artillery active, especially on HEXHAM ROAD. The two coys. in FLERS LINE move up and relieve the two front coys "A" and "B" who must trek into FLERS LINE.	
	30/10/16		Cold day but very wet night causing the trenches to become full of water. The sides of PIONEER ALLEY fell in at several places, weaker, the older trenches three deep in mud. Enemy shelling again active on PIONEER ALLEY and HEXHAM ROAD.	
	31/10/16		Fine day. Trenches very wet muddy. PIONEER ALLEY being almost impassable. Relief commencing 5 p.m Battalion relieved by 7th N.F. 1st Battalion moves to BAZENTIN l.e and finishing 4 p.m and Kensho in huts, men in dug outs and trenches, GRAHDS, officers in huts.	

WAR DIARY
or
INTELLIGENCE SUMMARY

Army Form C. 2118.

Place	Date	Hour	Summary of Events and Information	Remarks and references to Appendices
BAZENTIN LE GRAND	1/11/16		Battalion in German old 2nd line system of trenches near BAZENTIN LE GRAND. Very busy acclimatization. Dug and revetans new dawn from R.E. dump and new dug out made. Very wet weather, ground very sodden. Men re-equipped with clothes, and boots as far as possible. Battalion resting. Very wet weather.	
	2/11/16 3/11/16			
	4/11/16	3pm 8pm	The Battalion served under the command of G.O.C. 151st Infantry Bde. Commencing from Battalion moved by Companies to FLERS LINE, between DROP ALLEY and PIONEER ALLEY, as right Reserve Battalion to 151 Inf. Bde. who attacked BUTTE TRENCH, HOOP SAP and GIRD LINE next morning. Batn. HdQrs in FLERS LINE. Very wet night.	Attached map
TRENCHES FLERS / HEXHAM ROAD	5/11/16	9.10am	Fine clear morning, strong wind. Zero hour. A front of 8th & 5th (from left to right) and 9th & 6th D.L.I. 8 D.L.I. (from left to right) could be seen advancing towards BUTTE de WARLENCOURT and HOOP SAP. Enemy barrage fired at 9.15 am but was not at first very intense. Enemy communicated with his artillery by means of an Ex Cellent panoramic display of coloured lights.	943–

WAR DIARY or INTELLIGENCE SUMMARY

Army Form C. 2118.

CONFIDENTIAL

4th Bn NORTHLD FUSRS.

CONFIDENTIAL WAR DIARY

VOLUME 20

1st NOV – 30th NOV 1916.

WAR DIARY or INTELLIGENCE SUMMARY

Army Form C. 2118.

Place	Date	Hour	Summary of Events and Information	Remarks and references to Appendices
Trenches FLERS LINE & HEXHAM ROAD	5/11/16		The Australians also could be seen advancing towards GIRD LINE on the night of the 8th S.L. The 9th S.L. and part of 6th S.L. were soon seen on the BUTTE itself and the attack here seemed to achieve its objective. The 8th S.L. were not successful.	94
		3 pm	Orders received that 8th S.L. would fall back to reorganise; 5th Border Regt. to relieve them. FLERS LINE to reorganise, 5th Border Regt. to attack at dawn with SNAG TRENCH and to prepare to attack in SNAG TRENCH and to prepare to attack with 4th N.F. in support.	
		7 pm	"A" Coy and "B" Coy 4th N.F. moved to HEXHAM ROAD, the Battalion now under orders of Lt. Col. HESLEY, 5th Border Regt. Readjusted H.Q.P. at HEXHAM ROAD.	
		11.30 pm	Word received that 9th S.L. and 6th S.L. had been heavily counter-attacked and driven back to their original position in MAMMET TRENCH. 4th N.F. ordered back to FLERS LINE immediately East of PIONEER ALLEY and to proceed to move with other units of Right Section on crest of ridge.	
FLERS LINE	6/11/16		Quiet day in FLERS LINE. After dark Battalion were relieved by 4 "YORKS" in FLERS LINE and proceeded to BARENTIN LE GRAND. Battalion was under command of 149th Inf. Bde.	

Wt. W14957/M90 750,000 1/16 J.B.C. & A. Forms/C.2118/12.

Army Form C. 2118.

WAR DIARY
or
INTELLIGENCE SUMMARY
(Erase heading not required.)

Place	Date	Hour	Summary of Events and Information	Remarks and references to Appendices
WARLENCOURT LE GRAND.	7/11/16		Very wet day. More accommodation than one each was here. 20 additional tents provided. Battalion provide working parties for Roads & advanced Divisional Headquarters at SABOT COPSE.	
"	8/11/16 9/11/16 10/11/16		Working parties provided for Roads and Advanced Divisional H.S. Weather showery and cold.	
Trenches SNAG TRENCH	11/11/16 12/11/16		Commencing 10pm Battalion moved up. Companies and relieved 4th YORKS in SNAG TRENCH. 'B' and 'C' Coys in SNAG TRENCH and SNAG SUPPORT. 'A' Coy in ABBAYE TRENCH. 'D' Coy in PEAS LINE. Battalion warned to be ready to attack HOOK SAP. Col. Gibson visited front line system of trenches and reported that Communication Trench was impassable in many places and the condition of SNAG front line and support was extremely bad. SNAG TRENCH was 6ft wide and almost impossible to move along it. In several instances men sat completely stuck in the mud and took over an hour to be dug out.	944-

Army Form C. 2118.

WAR DIARY
or
INTELLIGENCE SUMMARY
(Erase heading not required.)

Place	Date	Hour	Summary of Events and Information	Remarks and references to Appendices
Trenches SNAG TRENCH	19/11/16		Rifle fire was fairly heavy during early morning of the 12th and the 5th Grenadier Guards (German) who were opposite to us being more active than the SAXONS who were relieved during previous afternoon.	945-
		9.30am 10am	Intended hop over this report jumped on HOOK S.P. to postpone till 14th and will be carried out by 5th N.F. and 7th N.F.	
			Work continued on SNAG new Support during morning. Enemy systems heavily shelled during morning, he put over about 20 (or more) and several new trench mortars. C.O.G. ARKWRIGHT wounded (slightly) and so well. Capt. Adj. O.G. ARKWRIGHT wounded (but not temporarily dug as well. SNAG new Support was dug comp[le]te about 12/13. SNAG new Support was dug comp[le]te about PIONEER ALLEY was cleared as far as approach about 200 which made were carried up to SNAG being line and all Cross wires in the trench. A made to barricade.	
		5.15	A change there was carried out by our Artillery on HOOK S.P. and S.A.P. LINE. Enemy Retaliation was very severe especially on HEXHAM ROAD where an extreme barrage was put up for an hour. Battalion was not several casualties from shell fire.	

WAR DIARY or INTELLIGENCE SUMMARY

Army Form C. 2118.

946-

Place	Date	Hour	Summary of Events and Information	Remarks and references to Appendices
Trenches SNAG TRENCH	13/11/16		Battalion relieved by 5th N.F. Commencing 8pm, proceedings back to FLERS LINE. Except A Coy and B Coy who remain at HEXHAM ROAD. During night 5th N.F. and 7th N.F. moved into position to attack HOOK SAP and GIRD LINE at dawn.	
HEXHAM ROAD and FLERS LINE	14/11/16	6.45 a.m.	5th N.F. and 7th N.F. attacked HOOK SAP and GIRD LINE. Australians attacking at same time on our right. Weather poor but very misty. Attacking troops could not be seen on occasion from FLERS LINE. Enemy barrage on this occasion started at 6.47 (2 mins after zero). A & B Coy at HEXHAM ROAD were ordered to Report at FLERS LINE. Lieut B.W. CRANAGE was slightly wounded by Shrapnel in FLERS LINE. Under orders of 7 N.F. proceeded from HEXHAM ROAD to D. Coy under orders of 7 N.F. to continue this C.T. towards that held by PIONEER AYRES. A.P. Machine gun fire was so heavy that party returned to HEXHAM ROAD.	
		2.30 pm	A Coy placed at disposal of 5th N.F. by 2 Lieut T. POYNER and 50 ndy against GIRD LINE on right (held by 5th N.F.) used trench to right occupy left flank portion of Hook so as to entrust in heavy hand fighting all wet day.	

Army Form C. 2118.

WAR DIARY
or
INTELLIGENCE SUMMARY

(Erase heading not required.)

Instructions regarding War Diaries and Intelligence Summaries are contained in F. S. Regs., Part II. and the Staff Manual respectively. Title Pages will be prepared in manuscript.

948.

Place	Date	Hour	Summary of Events and Information	Remarks and references to Appendices
SKYS TRENCH	18/11/16		Enemy shelling fairly heavy all day.	
	16/11/16	2:45 am	Relieved by 4th YORKS. Party in GIRD LINE relieved by 4 "E."YORKS. Man. Bn. to FLERS LINE.	
FLERS LINE	17/11/16		In the afternoon relieved by 10th GLOUCESTER REGT (1st DIVISION) and marched back to BAZENTIN LE GRAND.	
BAZENTIN LE GRAND	18/11/16		Proceeded by Rail to ALBERT. Billets in FELIX FAURE.	
ALBERT.	18/11/16	12 noon	Battalion clothing & re-equipping. Bathing.	
	19/11/16		Re-organising as far as possible. Training specially.	
	20/11/16		Each day after 21st party of 20 men working on men transport (lines).	
	21/11/16		Party of 20 men unloading coal.	
	22/11/16		20 men sent to DIVISIONAL SCHOOL NORTHEY to meet landing Skeer.	
	23/11/16		Party of 3 officers and 160 men widening ALBERT Street.	
			Re-equipping.	
	26/11/16		Party of 3 officers and 180 men working on ALBERT - BAPAUME ROAD.	

WAR DIARY or INTELLIGENCE SUMMARY

Army Form C. 2118.

Place	Date	Hour	Summary of Events and Information	Remarks and references to Appendices
SUCKEN, HEXHAM ROAD, and SNAG TRENCH.	14/11/16	3.30 a.m.	C.O. moved to HEXHAM ROAD. "B" and "C" coys. move to HEXHAM ROAD. "B" coy moves up to SNAG front line.	947
	Sep		"B" coy moves up to SNAG trench C.T. between HOOK y PIONEER.	
		1.30	"B" coy moves to SNAG trench. C coy moves to SNAG trench by ALLEY and HOOK SAP. Captain R.T.W. ROBINSON O.C. "B" Coy. PIONEER ALLEY. Captain R.T.W. ROBINSON's HOOK SAP was who got out a patrol to reconnoitre to forward & killed.	
		N-OM	Lt-Col B.B. GIBSON and Major WRIGHT (6th Y.R.) re-organise the front line for an attack.	
	14/11/16	12.30 a.m.	An attack was launched at 12.30 am. but owing to intense enemy barrage and heavy rifle and M.G. fire did not succeed. The following were the Casualties: Killed Capt. T.W. ROBINSON, 2nd Lt. F.T. LANNEN wounded Lt. Col. B.B. GIBSON (injd. at duty) missing 2nd Lt. F. BONNER	
		N.o.m	Reorganised and defend SNAG TRENCH.	

Army Form C. 2118.

WAR DIARY
or
INTELLIGENCE SUMMARY
(*Erase heading not required.*)

Place	Date	Hour	Summary of Events and Information	Remarks and references to Appendices
ALBERT	27/11/16		Party of 3 officers and 100 men cleaning ALBERT STREETS.	
	28/11/16		Party of 4 officers and 200 men working in ALBERT BAPAUME Rd. Lt Col B.S. GIBSON assumes temporary Command of Bn. Maj. Bule Wee A. Col. SCOTT-THOMSON granted leave of absence.	
	29/11/16		Party of 3 officers and 100 men in ALBERT Street.	
	30/11/16		Cleaning up and preparing for move to BRESLE in See.M	

949

R Allen Capt

4th Bn. Northd Fus.

Appendix to November War Diary
Casualties

950-EB

Officers

Capt	ROBINSON	J.W	Killed in action 15/11
2 Lieut	LARKEN	F.T	(7th N.F.) Killed in action 15/11
2 Lieut	DERRICK	A.J	(7th N.F.) wounded & missing 15/11
2 Lieut	MOORHOUSE	A.E	Killed in action 15/11
	BALDEN	C.A	Wounded 14/11
	BONNER	T	do 14/11
Lt-Col	GIBSON	B.D	Wounded slightly at duty 15/11
Capt	CRANAGE	R.W	do do

Other Ranks:

1 O.R wounded 1/11			
2 O.R wounded 5/11			
1 O.R wounded 8/11			
11 O.R do 12/11			
9 O.R do 13/11	4 O.R Killed 13/11		
23 O.R do 14/11	8 O.R Killed 14/11		
37 O.R do 15/11	11 O.R Killed 15/11		
2 O.R wounded 16/11	2 O.R Killed 16/11		
1 O.R wounded 18/11	2 O.R Killed 18/11		
2 O.R missing 6/11	2 O.R missing 14/11		
2 O.R missing 15/11	1 O.R " 16/11		

Totals

	Killed	Wounded	Missing
Officers	3	4	1 (wounded & missing)
Other Ranks	27	91	3
Totals	30	95	4

CONFIDENTIAL

Army Form C. 2118.

WAR DIARY
or
INTELLIGENCE SUMMARY

(Erase heading not required.)

Vol 17

WAR DIARY
of
4th Batt. NORTHUMBERLAND FUSILIERS
—
VOLUME III
—
DECEMBER 1916.

14ª

Army Form C. 2118.

WAR DIARY
or
INTELLIGENCE SUMMARY

(Erase heading not required.)

Instructions regarding War Diaries and Intelligence Summaries are contained in F.S. Regs., Part II. and the Staff Manual respectively. Title Pages will be prepared in manuscript.

Place	Date	Hour	Summary of Events and Information	Remarks and references to Appendices
ALBERT. BRESLE	1/12/16	8 a.m.	The Battalion moved off by Companies to Camp at BRESLE a small village 4 miles S.W. of ALBERT. A working party of 4 officers and 200 men reported to 2nd LABOUR Battalion at 7.30 a.m. for work on the ALBERT- BAPAUME ROAD. This party marched to BRESLE and arriving there at 3 p.m. The Lewis Gun handcarts were drawn by pack ponies for the first time. This was not a success.	
BRESLE	2/12/16		Organisation completed. Lt-Col. GIBSON returned from leave. Infantry Brigade and Trench Command. He inspected the Battalion.	
"	3/12/16		Church Parade at no. 50 PRINCES STREET, BRESLE. Brigade and Regimental Canteens opened. Capt. C.E. ARKWRIGHT and Lieut. J.Q.M. W.H. WYNNEFORD returned from leave.	
" BRESLE	5/12/16		Training chiefly drill for all (specialists included).	

Army Form C. 2118.

WAR DIARY
or
INTELLIGENCE SUMMARY
(Erase heading not required.)

Instructions regarding War Diaries and Intelligence Summaries are contained in F. S. Regs., Part II. and the Staff Manual respectively. Title Pages will be prepared in manuscript.

Place	Date	Hour	Summary of Events and Information	Remarks and references to Appendices
PRESLE	6/2/16		The Brigade was inspected by Lieutenant General Sir W. P. PULTENEY near BREDE WOOD at 9 a.m. He thanked the Brigade for their work since Sept. 15th. Expressed himself as pleased with the turn out of the Brigade.	
	7/2/16		Battalion Training — Musketry on the Range	
	8/2/16		Rain practically prevented any training being done	
	9/2/16		Battalion went for a Route March	
	10/2/16		Church Parade in the Brigade Canteen at 10.15 a.m. Capt. J. R. ROBB took over Command of Battalion, Lt. Col. B. D. G. IBBSON having proceeded to Commanding Officers' conference at 4th Army Infantry School of Instruction, FLIXECOURT.	
	11/2/16 12/2/16		Training. Capt. R. ALLEN having returned from 149th Infantry Brigade resumes duties of Acting Adjutant. Major F. ROBINSON returned from leave.	
	13/2/16 14/2/16		Training. 2nd Lt. B. R. P. HAWKEN takes on duties of Transport Officer whilst Lt. W. H. FOSTER is on leave.	

Army Form C. 2118

WAR DIARY
or
INTELLIGENCE SUMMARY
(Erase heading not required.)

" Instructions regarding War Diaries and Intelligence Summaries are contained in F. S. Regs., Part II. and the Staff Manual respectively. Title Pages will be prepared in manuscript.

Place	Date	Hour	Summary of Events and Information	Remarks and references to Appendices
BRESLE	15/12/16		Training. Lt A.L. Thompson took over duties of Acting Adjutant. Church Parades in Brigade Canteen and BRESLE franc. Church.	
"	16/12/16		"	
"	17/12/16		Training.— Capt. J.R. ROBB inspected all companies. The NINETS (Brig. Inf. Brigade (french)) Gave their first performance at the Brigade Canteen.	
"	18/12/16		Lt Col SCOTT JACKSON 7th N.F. is acting Brigadier. Brigadier inspected the Brigade Lt Col B.D. Gibson, having returned from C.O.'s conference at the Army School, resumes command of the Battalion.	
"	19/12/16			
"	20/12/16		Training.	
"	21/12/16		"	
"	22/12/16		Training. Inspection of Coot by Lt-Col SCOTT JACKSON, 7th N.F., acting Brigadier.	
"	23/12/16		Brig. Gen. R.M. OVENS inspected Hqrs Brigade near BRESLE wood	
"	24/12/16		Church Parades a.o on 17/12/16.	

Place	Date	Hour	Summary of Events and Information	Remarks and references to Appendices
BRESLE	25/12/16		The men had their Xmas Dinner at 1 p.m. — The Brigadier and Officer Commanding went round the lines during Dinner. In addition to the ordinary rations, pork, plum pudding and beer were provided. The Divisional Band (50th Div.) played at BRESLE in the afternoon. The NIVETS performed in the Gloucester.	
	26/12/16		The Battalion went for a Route March. — Lt.-Col. BD GIBSON, CAPT. HERRIOT, Lt. D.T. TURNER, and 2/Lt. COATSWORTH went forward to the part of the line we are taking over to reconnoitre. The Brigadier inspected A & B Coys in full marching order. Preventions for to-morrow's move.	
	27/12/16 9.30 a.m.			
	28/12/16 9.20 a.m.		The Battalion left BRESLE at and marched to 'A' Camp, BECOURT, when they relieved the 5th GLOUCESTER REGIMENT. The camp consists of NISSEN huts, which are (cont)	

WAR DIARY or INTELLIGENCE SUMMARY

Army Form C. 2118.

Place	Date	Hour	Summary of Events and Information	Remarks and references to Appendices
BÉCOURT	29/1/44	13:00	The Battalion left A Camp and marched to BAZENTIN-LE-PETIT into NISSEN huts. Some Shells were falling close to the huts and some hit Quartermaster Stores but returned unshell the Castles.	
BAZENTIN-LE-PETIT	30/4/44	14:30	The morning was spent in getting shuffling man for the Trenches. The Battalion left camp & proceeded to the Trenches via a duck-board track. N.E. of HIGH WOOD. "C" Company & a few Sect men were left behind at MAMETZ WOOD CAMP. The 4th N.F. relieved Us (1st Battalion SOUTH WALES BORDERERS) Support Trenches. A Coy took position in YARRA AVENUE, "B" Coy in YORK LANE, D Coy NORTH ROAD. Battalion HQ is in YARRA RESERVE. 5th N.F. is on the left & 7th on the right. 4th & 6th NF Supporting 4, 5, 7th NF are the front line with ...	
YARRA RESERVE	31/4/44		Lt. Col. B. D. GIBSON marched on position in the morning. Together with Lt-Col WRIGHT 5.N.F. he reconnoitred the position. Lt-Col WRIGHT 5.N.F. between Btn "aid posts" YARRA & left portion of our front line. AVENUE was shelled in the afternoon. Casualties 2 O.Rs Ranks (A Coy)	

4th Bn Northld Fusiliers

Confidential War Diary

Vol 3

Jan 1 - Jan 31 1917

WAR DIARY
or
INTELLIGENCE SUMMARY

(Erase heading not required.)

Army Form C. 2118.

Place	Date	Hour	Summary of Events and Information	Remarks and references to Appendices
YARRA RESERVE	1/11/17		The following officers of H.J. Battalion were the recipients of awards in London Gazette.	237
			Lt.Col. B.D. GIBSON. — D.S.O.	
			Capt. H. CHEESMOND — M.C.	
			Capt. C.G. ARKWRIGHT. — M.C.	
			—	
			Major. F. ROBINSON, — Mentioned in Dispatches.	
			Lt. Adjt. W.H. WAWAUSFORD — "	
			2/Lt. W.M.E. WILSON — "	

Army Form C., 2118.

WAR DIARY
or
INTELLIGENCE SUMMARY
(Erase heading not required.)

Place	Date	Hour	Summary of Events and Information	Remarks and references to Appendices
YARRA RESERVE	1/1/17		A great deal of work was done in improving the condition of the trenches, in TURK AVENUE and YARRA AVENUE. TURK AVENUE, YARRA AVENUE and NORTH ROAD were shelled intermittently with 5.9's. The guns appear to be along BARRY ?? and fire from the direction of LE BARQUE. 1 officer and 50 men carried ?? stores up to YARRA BANK at night.	
	2/1/17		The whole area occupied by the Battalion was shelled intermittently. The junction of YARRA RESERVE and YARRA AVENUE was heavily shelled with 5.9's between 8am and 9am. Five direct hits were obtained on YARRA AVENUE. Work continued on reclaiming and improving trenches and shelters. 2 officers and 50 men carried duckboards up to the front line at night. A considerable quantity of material etc. was salved by the Battalion.	
	3/1/17		The Battalion relieved the 5th N.F. in the front line about 8pm. The Artillery did not effect relief but a Machine Gun was turned on the last platoon relieved. On the left sector, "B" Company took over the right sector [nos. 1, 2, 3, 4.] from YARRA BAND to M.24.b.66. "D" Company took over left — (Sheet 57c S.W.). Three platoons D'd Company	239

WAR DIARY or INTELLIGENCE SUMMARY

Army Form C. 2118.

Place	Date	Hour	Summary of Events and Information	Remarks and references to Appendices
YPRES RESERVE	3/1/17		Sector [Posts. 5,6,7,8.] From the left of B Company [after a Coy of about 70 s/g to M.24 a.2.9. From there there is a Coy of about 60 s/s. at call the end of which the 6th N.F. have their right post. The trenches were in a bad condition & a good deal of time was spent during the night in improving them. Enemy is almost very Quiet on our front. A few isolated bombs were landed behind and on the left flank front. A party of 3 N.C.O.'s and 32 D. Company during the night. Casualties. Killed 2 wounded men carried wire and revetting material to the front line. Other Ranks. The enemy within	240?
	4/1/17		A Quiet day in the front line. at times & waved to our about in the open During the day wire was put up in front of YPRES men. A 50 yds. of wire was put up in front of D Company hurriedly BANK. An enemy relief was effected. An offr of D Company hurriedly sent from B & D Coy'n. On of D Company seemed to be taking place — Men were reported thereabout Seconds. BARFOUR officers On a large party of the enemy moving down anything had attention & this relief.	

2449 Wt. W4957/M90 750,000 1/16 J.B.C. & A. Forms/C.2118/12.

Army Form C. 2118.

WAR DIARY
or
INTELLIGENCE SUMMARY
(Erase heading not required.)

Place	Date	Hour	Summary of Events and Information	Remarks and references to Appendices
YARRA REDOUBT	3/1/17	5.30pm	COBHAM TRENCH was shelled as usual. Message sent to Artillery that an enemy working party were working at a trench in rear of MAZE M.24.b.8.5. between L.3.9. Artillery replied about 4 pm with salvoes of HE's. Shrapnel which appeared to be effective. Work done on Right Border Bay on wiring and drains. 150 yds. wiring completed, 1 & 2 drains dug, one of which was revetted.	29/7
	5/1/17		3 Platoon "D" Company relieved by "A" Company on the Left Section. 3 platoon "D" Company went to COBHAM TRENCH. On the right Section 3 platoon "B" Company was relieved by 1 platoon "A" from COBHAM TRENCH, 4/B Company took relief from (platoon 1/B which one platoon of "D" from Headquarters, 2 platoon Hd [Quarters] who had been acting as Camp Guard. Rest as B/B Company came & Headquarters. The remainder of "B" Company remained at YARRA BANK as a camp platoon. CASUALTIES Other Ranks 2 wounded.	

WAR DIARY or INTELLIGENCE SUMMARY

Army Form C. 2118.

Place	Date	Hour	Summary of Events and Information	Remarks and references to Appendices
YARRA RESERVE	6/1/17		Work was continued at night on YARRA BANK. Sandbag while of the front of YARRA BANK was raised in front, and the proposed support trench was sited and taped out. The drains were completed and revetted. On the left sector the trench was cleaned out and dried after last night's rain and 10 duckboards put in. —	
		10:30	Information sent to Artillery that an enemy working party were working in front of our left sector. It was dispersed by artillery. Another working party was dispersed by artillery on same information.	
		10:45	Reinforcements from Lng. Rgt. F.? arrived behind no. 8 Post. Okrania enemy was seen in front in large no.6 junction of YARRA RESERVE COBHAM TRENCH and the junction of YARRA AVE and YARRA AVE NUE were also shelled heavy. CASUALTIES. R.O.R. 1 wounded	24

2449 Wt. W14957/M90 750,000 1/16 J.B.C. & A. Forms/C.2118/12.

Army Form C. 2118.

WAR DIARY
or
INTELLIGENCE SUMMARY
(Erase heading not required.)

Instructions regarding War Diaries and Intelligence Summaries are contained in F. S. Regs., Part II. and the Staff Manual respectively. Title Pages will be prepared in manuscript.

243.

Place	Date	Hour	Summary of Events and Information	Remarks and references to Appendices
	7/1/17.		A certain amount of work was done on drain through YPRES BANK during the day.	
		5.30	The Batt. Relief came up - 5th Yorks Rgt. relieved us & by 8 p.m. relief was reported to be complete.	
			The Batt. proceeded by Coys. to Dicoa Nutmeg Camp Bazentin-le-Petit.	
			No Casualties occurred either during day or after relief.	

2449 Wt. W14957/M90 750,000 1/16 J.B.C. & A. Forms/C.2118/12.

Army Form C. 2118.

WAR DIARY
or
INTELLIGENCE SUMMARY

(Erase heading not required.)

244*

Place	Date	Hour	Summary of Events and Information	Remarks and references to Appendices
Bagati-b (P&N) No 5 Camp (Chain Nat).	8/1/17		The Day was devoted to cleaning equipment rifles etc. Coy. inspections of general turn out took place & returns of requirements with regard to clothing & equipment were rendered to O.R.	

Army Form C. 2118.

WAR DIARY
or
INTELLIGENCE SUMMARY

(Erase heading not required.)

Instructions regarding War Diaries and Intelligence Summaries are contained in F. S. Regs., Part II. and the Staff Manual respectively. Title Pages will be prepared in manuscript.

2454

Place	Date	Hour	Summary of Events and Information	Remarks and references to Appendices
	9/1/17	4 p.m.	The following working parties were found by the Batt:—	
			1 N.C.O. & 30 men at Clarke's Dump S.3.a.4.7. reporting to 178 Manlukin Field Coy R.E. to put tank tks. to M.30.c.4.0.	
		7 p.m.	1 N.C.O. & 25 men at Clarke's Dump S.3.a.4.7. at 7 p.m. to reporting to 179th Tunnell. Coy R.E. to put trolly & Factory Corner & Flers Dump.	
		1 p.m.	1 N.C.O. & 25 men to report Clarke's Dump at 1 p.m.	
		4 p.m.	3 Officers & all remaining available men (120) to R.E. Brigade H.Q. 15 38 at Cent. Drop at 4 p.m. for dismd. cable layg.	

WAR DIARY or INTELLIGENCE SUMMARY

Army Form C. 2118.

Place	Date	Hour	Summary of Events and Information	Remarks and references to Appendices
Nos Camp	10/1/17	1 p.m.	Working parties found as under:— 1 N.C.O & 25 men to report to CLARKE'S DUMP at 2.30 p.m.	
Bazentin le petit		4 p.m.	1 N.C.O & 30 men to report at CLARKE'S DUMP at 4 p.m. Frank Trench to M.30.c.4.0	
		7 p.m.	1 N.C.O & 25 men to report to above mentioned place to put tracks to FACTORY CORNER	
		5 p.m.	All available men of Coys including Off. servants sent 2 / Coy & 2 Officers/2 Officers Rinaldi to report to R.E. Signals Brig. Ny. Conf. prep. for cable buried — hands shown at B.dump.	
	11/1/17	4 a.m.	26 N.C.Os & men reported at CLARKE'S DUMP. Another party arr. strength 40 CLARKE'S DUMP at 7 p.m. with Harvard Rations	
		7 p.m.	1 N.C.O & 8 men to report to 174 Tunnel. Coy R.E. Road Workers at BAZENTIN CIRCUS (S.20.d.8.9) with Harvard Rations.	
	12/1/17	1 p.m.	Working parties under following arrangements:— 1 N.C.O & 25 men at Nugt Unsort Stilery S.30d.4.7 at 1 p.m. & report to representative of 174 Tunnelly Coy R.E.	
		4 p.m.	1 N.C.O & 25 men at Clarks Dump S.20.d.4.7 at 4 p.m. & representative of 1st Nottingham Field Coy R.E.	
		6 p.m.	1 N.C.O & 8 men trip't to report to representative 174 Tunnell. Coy R.E. at 6 p.m. at BAZENTIN CIRCUS — Harvard rations.	
		12 noon	Brigadier General Owen inspected the huts of the Camp.	

246

Army Form C. 2118.

WAR DIARY
or
INTELLIGENCE SUMMARY

(Erase heading not required.)

Instructions regarding War Diaries and Intelligence Summaries are contained in F.S. Regs., Part II. and the Staff Manual respectively. Title Pages will be prepared in manuscript.

247x

Place	Date	Hour	Summary of Events and Information	Remarks and references to Appendices
LISSENHOEK CAMP N°5	13/1/17	4 p.m	1 N.C.O. + 16 O.R. Report at CLARK'S DUMP	
BAZENTIN G-PETIT.		5.30"	2 N.C.O's + 28 men inclinely H/Qr. to SEVEN DIALS DUMP at 7 p.m. with H. rations	
		6 p.m	1 " + 20 men Report at R.E. Dump (Nr Leafy Circus) at 6 p.m.	
		"	1 " + 8 " " " BAZENTIN CIRCUS at 6 p.m. with Harvard Rakes	
		7.40	1 " + 6 " " " HIGH WOOD Sta. (Nr CLARKES DUMP)	
"	14/1/17		Usual working Parties found.	
"	15/1/17	4 p.m.	Inst Cy left for trenches to relieve 5th Yorks Regt. in Support. Some trenches in trenches town of duty.	
		7 p.m.	Relief reported complete - Dispositions of 3 Coys & Hrs as under - "D" Coy into H/Qrs at CANVAS CAMP BAZENTIN in two occasions impressed during the night.	
			A Coy - TURK ALLEY which was improved during the night.	
			B " - NORTH ROAD dug-outs &c billets	
			C " - 2 Matoos with B Coy - 1 Matoo with A Coy & 1 Platoon - part of YARRA AVENUE which was v.dry & cleaned.	

WAR DIARY or INTELLIGENCE SUMMARY

Army Form C. 2118.

Place	Date	Hour	Summary of Events and Information	Remarks and references to Appendices
Suffolk Tabular	16/1/17		Whole day very quiet - workey parties were provided in enemy YA sent to YARRA BANK. Sky cleared up. Material from TURK'S DUMP worked on CT from YARRA BANK to Rt Sectn Coy Hq.	
	17/1/17		Dead heavy mouldes during night 16-17. Slight inclination of snow during morng. Turk HEY cleared forward latrines, dug out & sunk a shelter 11/2" x YARDS around shelter. Bags. Hand at myself - hand worky party rout for YARRA BANK. With men & letts organised & men sent to dramis though BANK. & reretty V.C.T. Command.	
	18/1/17		Hard weather still holding - slight increased frost. Slight increased frost of dry frost in TURK ALLEY next to CRIP2 commenced. Worky parties use dug out to YARRA BANK as usual & good progress maid with alterns thing to the CT tracks V.C.T.	
	19/1/17		15th on TURK ALLEY & new ladder AS dug out. AT J.M.C & B Coy & work up a relieved 5th NORFORD J Cot/schers Coys at CUBNAN Field dug out	2 E 1 +

2449 Wt. W14957/M90 750,000 1/16 J.B.C. & A. Forms/C.2118/12.

Army Form C. 2118.

WAR DIARY
or
INTELLIGENCE SUMMARY
(Erase heading not required.)

Instructions regarding War Diaries and Intelligence Summaries are contained in F. S. Regs., Part II. and the Staff Manual respectively. Title Pages will be prepared in manuscript.

Place	Date	Hour	Summary of Events and Information	Remarks and references to Appendices
	20/1/17		Day was quiet & fine, but there'd amount of intermittent shelling around Park area. C Coy did usual work on front & trench revetting & duckboards. Lewis gun & stokes work from B & D MG Lewis & C.T. Hugh Boose slung down aby wounded & large amount of material. Co continued to carry a supply up to sectors.	
	21/1/17		Ground still very heavy. Coys cont'd earlier on B area and much trench work with cont'n effected & deep dug outs.	2.49 x
		4pm 5pm	C Coy relieved C Coy & Lgt Feld & A-04 AM back in shelters at C. BHAM. Relief complete by 6 pm Coy took over on TAMBRACINE lines - A co on left front & B co on right. O.C. with 1 Stokes mortars by enemy.	
		1 pm	Enemy bombard heavily around Lgt Flat 1 Lby Coy & the to get some things out & frilly. Yeoman firing & were in on just below & half of Reav & Lt Lift	
		4 pm	the Coy 4 corp. 1 self. Stokes mortars? shed over very heavily all over.	
	22/26		Day very fine. Coys went out & cont'd day work & first stood worked every yard of the Batty. Nought. 3rd of 6th Regt. Convention of relief very fine.	
		6.30	Co complete by 6.15 pm	
		8.15		

Army Form C. 2118.

WAR DIARY
or
INTELLIGENCE SUMMARY
(Erase heading not required.)

Instructions regarding War Diaries and Intelligence Summaries are contained in F. S. Regs., Part II. and the Staff Manual respectively. Title Pages will be prepared in manuscript.

Place	Date	Hour	Summary of Events and Information	Remarks and references to Appendices
Mametz Wood Camp	24/1/17		Day spent in cleaning up & preparing for next day. Coys. working party	
	25/1/17	16.30/h 9.10/h	50 yards for camp. Guarding went CLARK'S DUMP. Marched to A1 B.2.3.8 Fair flight in Bns H.Q. R. BOULEAU. No huts available	
ALBERT	26/1/17		and a few latrine, H.Q. parade held. Inspection etc. And many thanks left	
	27/1/17		C.O. inspected lines in billets. Training continued	
	28/1/17		Draw of R.A.C. unfitted hut in billets. Training hawle held during morning.	
DERNANCOURT	29/1/17	18.30	Batt marched to billets in Canteleux Wood DERNANCOURT (about 2 miles). Aft. Coy inspection of roads paraded held at 3.10 /h	
			G.T.M.R. Canteleur was established opposite own right	
	30/1/17		Training as issued "B" weather was decreed into the weeks. Coys attended well did not permit of full programme of training being observed	
	31/1/17		Parade as per Coy toppers, Sa Training Continued - Lieut T B L Bly-OKF 2-LT's ... Delete ? Wt Batt & Lieut Draft.	25.Y + B

Army Form C. 2118.

WAR DIARY
or
INTELLIGENCE SUMMARY.
(Erase heading not required.)

WAR DIARY

of

4th BATTALION NORTHUMBERLAND
FUSILIERS.

1917.

FEBRUARY 1st to FEBRUARY 28th

VOLUME 3.

Vol 19

19ª

Army Form C. 2118.

WAR DIARY
or
INTELLIGENCE SUMMARY.
(Erase heading not required.)

Instructions regarding War Diaries and Intelligence Summaries are contained in F. S. Regs., Part II. and the Staff Manual respectively. Title pages will be prepared in manuscript.

Place	Date	Hour	Summary of Events and Information	Remarks and references to Appendices
DERNANCOURT	1/2/17.		Battalion continued to train as on previous days. A party was detailed to proceed to RUE des ILLIEUX, ALBERT to fix up bathing apparatus for the whole Brigade. In spite of pipes being frozen the majority of the men were bathed.	
	2.2.17		Training continued. Boys were practised in musketry on range allotted to us.	
	3.2.17			
	4.2.17			
	5.2.17		G.O.C. 149th Inf Brigade inspected the Battalion in full marching order.	
	6.2.17		Lieut T.A.L. THOMPSON returned from leave on 4.2.17. Capt. C. STEPHENSON also returned from leave. 2 Lieut. W. CLEMITSON & 17 Other Ranks reported from BASE.	
	7.2.17			
	8.2.17		The Battalion moved off at 9.0am for MERICOURT sur SOMME. Progress was very slow on account of having to halt whilst Divisional Train Transport, 2nd Field Ambulance 9 & 46 Field Coy R.E. closed up with remainder of column. Route lay via BUIRE CROSS ROADS - VILLE - MORLANCOURT - CHIPILLY - CERISSY - MORCOURT - MERICOURT sur SOMME. Battalion was billeted on houses & farms. Remainder of Brigade	

Army Form C. 2118.

WAR DIARY
or
INTELLIGENCE SUMMARY.
(Erase heading not required.)

Instructions regarding War Diaries and Intelligence Summaries are contained in F. S. Regs., Part II. and the Staff Manual respectively. Title pages will be prepared in manuscript.

Place	Date	Hour	Summary of Events and Information	Remarks and references to Appendices
MERICOURT Sur SOMME	8.2.17		were billeted in large huts in vicinity of village. Intense cold prevailed. An enemy aeroplane flew over about 10.30 p.m. & dropped bombs. No casualties to this Battalion.	
		9 a.m	Boys exercised in Company drill.	
		10.2.17	Battalion proceeded by march route to BOIS TOUFFU via CHUIGNOLLES — CHUIGNES approximately 7 miles. Bivy out accommodation was found for the whole Battalion.	

Army Form C. 2118.

WAR DIARY
or
INTELLIGENCE SUMMARY.
(Erase heading not required)

Instructions regarding War Diaries and Intelligence Summaries are contained in F. S. Regs., Part II. and the Staff Manual respectively. Title pages will be prepared in manuscript.

Place	Date	Hour	Summary of Events and Information	Remarks and references to Appendices
BELLOY	11/2/17		The following Officer was the recipient of the Croix de Guerre. 2nd Lieut T. BONNER	
	11/2/17	8h.	Relieved 123rd Regiment (French) Ground hard and frozen; trenches in good condition though not revetted	
	12/2/17	6h.	D Coy moved up in close support to 7th Bn N. F. Work: Latrines & sanitary arrangements improved, and trenches cleared Enemy artillery quiet during day and night; village occasionally shelled with 5-9's. No casualties	

WAR DIARY or INTELLIGENCE SUMMARY

Army Form C. 2118.

Place	Date	Hour	Summary of Events and Information	Remarks and references to Appendices
BELLOY	13/2/17		Trenches and dugouts cleared, and draining commenced in BOYAU BOUCHET. Enemy artillery shelled village area N 21 A occasionally with 5.9.	
		7 pm	D Coy returned to this sector.	
	14/2/17		Trenches cleared, owing to frozen state of ground, revetting could not be commenced but material was carried up to ARGONNE TR and BOUCHOT TR in preparation for when thaw commences.	
		11 am 1 pm	Area N 21 A behind village heavily shelled with 5.9. & occasionally during day & night. "C" Coy cookhouse blown in.	
		6 pm	"C" Coy moved up in support to 5-K.N.F. TR de HURES. No casualties.	

Army Form C. 2118.

WAR DIARY
or
INTELLIGENCE SUMMARY.

(Erase heading not required.)

Instructions regarding War Diaries and Intelligence Summaries are contained in F. S. Regs., Part II. and the Staff Manual respectively. Title pages will be prepared in manuscript.

Place	Date	Hour	Summary of Events and Information	Remarks and references to Appendices
BELLOY	15/9/17	8 am	Work and preparations for revetting C. 76 now commenced. ARGONNE TR. & BOUCHOT TR. Work continued throughout day, and carried by 2 parties of 50 from 6.45 N.F. at night, 100 yards in each trench, sides sloped, & 2 ft berm abt 60 yards each. Shelling of Area N21 A desultory during daytime increasing towards midnight. 10 Gas shells were sent over & fell near junction TR. du PARC & BOUCHOT	
		4 pm	A French bomb store (near dump) at N21 C 80 exploded causing casualties, and a fire amongst RE material, which took until 4 am in the morning to extinguish. Casualties 1 killed 6 wounded	

A 5834 Wt. W4973/M687 750,000 8/16 D. D. & L. Ltd. Forms/C.2118/13.

Army Form C. 2118.

WAR DIARY
or
INTELLIGENCE SUMMARY.
(Erase heading not required.)

Place	Date	Hour	Summary of Events and Information	Remarks and references to Appendices
BELLOY	16/2/17		Work continued on ARGONNE & BOUCHOT TRS and carried on at night-time by 2 parties from 6th N.F. More material carried up ready for use. "C" Coy commenced work on BOYAU II 1315 sloping sides, materials carried up from BELLOY for their use. Two shells of 5'9" fell in BELLOY during day and night. Much aerial activity and good observation. Casualties 1 wounded.	

WAR DIARY
or
INTELLIGENCE SUMMARY.

(Erase heading not required.)

Army Form C. 2118.

Place	Date	Hour	Summary of Events and Information	Remarks and references to Appendices
BELLOY	11/24/17	8am	Work continued on ARGONNE & BOUCHOT, about 300/350 yds in each trench done with about 150 yds 2' 6" berm dug. Work carried on by 2 parties from 6th N.F. at night. BOYAU II BIS. "C" Coy worked on tho. sides cleared, duckboards repaired and laid. The following RE material carried up from BELLOY to ARGONNE & BOUCHOT 800 long pickets 15 coils wire, 50 sheets expanded metal & 100 trench boards. Our trenches now show signs of falling in owing to thaw.	
	7th to 12th		Enemy m/guns fired bursts occasionally in village day & night gas shells & 5.9" fell near P.C. SAVOY from direction BARLEUX death Vullets fell near P.C. SAVOY from direction BARLEUX No Casualties	

Army Form C. 2118.

WAR DIARY
or
INTELLIGENCE SUMMARY.
(Erase heading not required.)

Instructions regarding War Diaries and Intelligence Summaries are contained in F. S. Regs., Part II. and the Staff Manual respectively. Title pages will be prepared in manuscript.

Place	Date	Hour	Summary of Events and Information	Remarks and references to Appendices
BELLOY	18/4/17		ARGONNE TR. 50 yards revetted, 200 yds cleared of mud, Channels cut under duckboard	
			BOUCHOT TR 60 feet revetted	
			TR de HURES 70 yds one side revetted	
			MARCHAL TR 50 wooden stakes driven in	
			BOYAU 2 BIS 200 yards relaid, 50 yds new duckboards laid	
			TR au PARC Channels cut under duckboards draining	
			Materials carried up to various trenches for work. 2 rolls rabbit wire, 100 posts 6', 68 pickets, 34 duckboards, 170 pickets, 50 duckboards 27 trenchboards	
			Activity. Occasionally shelling in area. Heavy shelling between	
	11.30	11.30 am and noon near junction SOUVILLE and BOUCHOT TR with 5.9 & 4.2 s H.E and shrapnel	
			2 men wounded.	

Army Form C. 2118.

WAR DIARY
or
INTELLIGENCE SUMMARY.
(Erase heading not required.)

Place	Date	Hour	Summary of Events and Information	Remarks and references to Appendices
N4 A to T4 A	20/9/17		Resumed work on trenches, left bay sector much improved. Reconnoitred overland route to P/C Hedevaux, wire & tape laid. Centre & right Coys work delayed owing to heavy 26 trench boards laid. 4 Handpumps carried from HEDEVAUX to BDANLOUP. Our 18/Coy fenced in enemy wire from 2 hr till dusk. Two patrols from Centre & right Coys were out to report on enemy wire. A sap was discovered towards our lines finishing at T4 A 97. German wire extended from T4 A 91 to T4 A 83 & then its T4 A 85, practically continuous. Sap showed signs of heavy shelling 2 feet of water. Enemy artillery shelled TR ANNAMITES with 5.9s all day & up retaliation also TR MARCHAL junction DANLOUP.	
		7.35 pm	Short barrage on above trenches also 8.30 pm. Fuel Nails 40 fires in ravine 9 pm, & occasionally m/g fire do. TRANNAMITES. No casualties	

Army Form C. 2118.

WAR DIARY
or
INTELLIGENCE SUMMARY.

(Erase heading not required.)

Place	Date	Hour	Summary of Events and Information	Remarks and references to Appendices
N 34 A to T 4 A	9/2/17		Majority of C.Ts in almost impassable condition, over knee deep in places. Left sector fatigue carrying sent to dump for pumps & duckboards. Commenced pumping TR MARTIN. Enemy shelled vicinity junction B. DAMLOUP and TR MARCIPAL with 5.9° heavily between 9.30 & 10.30 am also N 38 D centre occasionally. Two patrols sent out from left & centre coys report ground very soft and greasy. Report enemy sentries 30 yards apart. Our wire in good condition. No casualties.	

Army Form C. 2118.

WAR DIARY
or
INTELLIGENCE SUMMARY.
(Erase heading not required.)

Place	Date	Hour	Summary of Events and Information	Remarks and references to Appendices
N34A to T.H.A	19/9/17	8 pm	Relieved 5th Northumberland Fusiliers. 3 companies front + support	
	20/9/17	8 am	Work continued on ARGONNE, BOUCHOT, MARCHAL TRS. TR de HURES, BOYAU II BIS, 30 yds new revetting done in each	
			Activity occasional shelling BOUCHOT TR near junction SOUVILLE	
			No casualties	

WAR DIARY or INTELLIGENCE SUMMARY

Army Form C. 2118.

Place	Date	Hour	Summary of Events and Information	Remarks and references to Appendices
N34A to T4A	22/2/17		Work continued clearing trenches, front line much improved by pumping. C Ts still bad. Laid 600 yds duckboards from N27c95 to N33 B05 or trans routs. 20 yds TR MARCHAL cleared & trench boards laid. Bridge erected over Trs MURES for or trans routs. 20 yards TR SPEGEL cleared trench boards laid. Our Hows. & 18 prs were firing from 1 hr on enemy's wire. 2 patrols out at midnight. Right & centre orgs. Dragport going along Sap @ T4 A87. discover m/g positions at T4 A83. Rifle grenades @ T4 B 28. 2 m/c trench wire in front of our TR SPEGEL & TR COULOUR. 1 patrol from B Coy left N34 D11 enemy wire intact. Patrol worked 50 yds N. wire very thick. Enemy holding post mortars T4B N34D60. Enemy front delivered N34 D93. Enemy artillery very quiet. Shells & trench mortars TR ANNANITES occasionally at night. m/g fire or near N33D Central. Enemy has 2 barrage lines 100 yards W TR ANNANITES, and TR MARCHAL & TR DANLOUP. NO casualties	

Army Form C. 2118.

WAR DIARY
or
INTELLIGENCE SUMMARY.

(Erase heading not required.)

Instructions regarding War Diaries and Intelligence Summaries are contained in F. S. Regs., Part II. and the Staff Manual respectively. Title pages will be prepared in manuscript.

Place	Date	Hour	Summary of Events and Information	Remarks and references to Appendices
N34 A to T4 A	23/4/17		Work continued clearing & pumping trenches 200 mm duckboards laid on overland track. C.T's still waterlogged. Our howz. & 18 pdrs were all day on enemy line at points T4 B04 N34 D8+6+ T4 B16. 5 platoons were out between midnight & 3am. 1 gap in wire 10 yds wide found at T4 B04 + T4 B16. Capt. @ T4 A81 confirmed. also m/g post T4 A83. Listening post suspected @ N34 D60 + fresh at N34 D73. Enemy artillery quiet during day but at 7.55pm enemy opened barrage on our front line & enthro m/g fire, also trench mortars & night very dark, & communication with centre Coy became cut, they called fr artillery retaliation in case of attack by enemy by phoning up on S.O.S. repeated from Headquarters, our artillery opened barrage 30 secs. after S.O.S. sent up, and enemy fire soon died out about 8.20 to/light - trench mortar activity during night also m/g fire. 3 casualties 1 killed 2 wounded (1 accidentally)	

A5834 Wt. W4973/M687 750,000 8/16 D. D. & L. Ltd. Forms/C.2118/13

WAR DIARY
or
INTELLIGENCE SUMMARY.
(Erase heading not required.)

Army Form C. 2118.

Place	Date	Hour	Summary of Events and Information	Remarks and references to Appendices
N 34 A to T 4 A	24/2/19		Work continued on all trenches, dugouts, & huts in this sector, cleaning & draining. 95 duckboards laid on new track. Bridge built over trench @ N 33 D 1.3 Our artillery continued to cut enemy wire @ N 34 D 8.6 with good results. 3 Patrols out report wire at T 4 B 0.4, gap 10 yds wide; but wire 1' high. Lamp signalling from Ployrus Wood reported at 6.30 pm. Enemy attitude very active. Been sniping many trench mortar and rifle grenades on TR ANNAMITES, report little shelling except light barrage on - do - at 8 pm to 8.15 pm About 30 5 9" about area N 33. B 33 One man wounded	

Army Form C. 2118.

WAR DIARY
or
INTELLIGENCE SUMMARY.
(Erase heading not required.)

Instructions regarding War Diaries and Intelligence Summaries are contained in F. S. Regs., Part II. and the Staff Manual respectively. Title pages will be prepared in manuscript.

Place	Date	Hour	Summary of Events and Information	Remarks and references to Appendices
N34 A to T4 A	25/1/17 to 26/1/17	6 am to 6 am	Work in trenches, posts, dugouts &c continued TRS SPECIAL CRABE, SALMON, MARSHAL wire left, dugouts now in good condition. CTs still bad in places. Patrolling all night done by bays, enemy front line held by sentry groups 30 yards apart, very nervous, occasional bursts of m/g fire. 6.30 pm to 7.30 enemy trench mortars TR ANNAMITES retaliation by artillery silenced him, again repeats 5.30 am 26/1/17. Enemy artillery very quiet, occasional field guns on ANNAMITES & only 4 G's - 9G's. 3 Germans aeroplanes over our lines, 2 returning towards HORNY Duckboard track, length done now from N29C 54 to N33D 64. No casualties	

Army Form C. 2118.

WAR DIARY
or
INTELLIGENCE SUMMARY.
(Erase heading not required.)

Instructions regarding War Diaries and Intelligence Summaries are contained in F. S. Regs., Part II. and the Staff Manual respectively. Title pages will be prepared in manuscript.

Place	Date	Hour	Summary of Events and Information	Remarks and references to Appendices
N34 A to T4 A	20/2/17		Work on trenches continued:- ANNAMITES, CALNOY, SPECL TPS sunken road from BERNY to ESTREES - CARBONNEL ROAD reconnoitred and found in good condition. Ration able to be brought to N33 D 200 yards from Bn H.Q. saving a journey of 1200 yds for ration parties. Enemy shelled TR. ANNAMITES during the day with 5-9a and at night with trench mortars & rifle grenades, latter silenced by our 18 pdrs	
	21/2/17	12n	Relieved by 4th East Yorks Regt. and proceeded to FOUCAUCOURT in CORPS. reserve Day devoted to Bathing of men, inspection of feet & issue of clean clothing. Lieut 6.6. GIBSON reported to duty from leave to England No casualties	

Army Form C. 2118.

WAR DIARY
or
INTELLIGENCE SUMMARY.
(Erase heading not required.)

Place	Date	Hour	Summary of Events and Information	Remarks and references to Appendices
FOUCACOURT	28/2/17		Battalion Employed in cleaning equipment etc., feet washing. Lectures were given to Officers & N.C.Os on the fitting of the new small box respirator, with which the Battalion is about to be equipped. A working party of 1 Officer & 24 men was provided at night to work on the 60 centimetre railway near BERNY DUMP. No casualties.	

Army Form C. 2118.

WAR DIARY
or
INTELLIGENCE SUMMARY.

(Erase heading not required.)

Instructions regarding War Diaries and Intelligence
Summaries are contained in F. S. Regs., Part II.
and the Staff Manual respectively. Title pages
will be prepared in manuscript.

Place	Date	Hour	Summary of Events and Information	Remarks and references to Appendices

CONFIDENTIAL

WAR DIARY

of

4th BATTALION NORTHUMBERLAND FUSILIERS

From 1st March 1917 to 31st March 1917.

VOLUME 3.

WAR DIARY
or
INTELLIGENCE SUMMARY.

(Erase heading not required.)

Army Form C. 2118.

Place	Date	Hour	Summary of Events and Information	Remarks and references to Appendices
FOUCAUCOURT	1/3/17		Working party of 8 groups consisting of 1 N.C.O. and 8 men each was provided by the Battalion to erect wire entanglements for the support line - a length of 2 miles is to be erected by the 119th Infantry Brigade. 2/Lt EMERY M.F. is in charge of this party. Companies 100(?) assisted in the morning and were inspected by the C.O. in the afternoon.	TEXT
	2/3/17		The same strength of working party was sent out for wiring. The remainder of the Battalion commenced training, and took baths at BOIS ST MARTIN. All other ranks available in the Battalion were fitted with the small box respirators and passed through a gas chamber to test their respirators. The remainder of the day was devoted to completing the equipment and clothing of the Battalion. The wiring party was sent out again consisting of the same number of N.C.O.'s and men.	TEXT
	3/3/17			TEXT

WAR DIARY or INTELLIGENCE SUMMARY

Army Form C. 2118.

Place	Date	Hour	Summary of Events and Information	Remarks and references to Appendices
FOUCAUCOURT	4/3/17		March. Working Party found – Batt. Church Parade 10 a/m – Baggages – General Orders inspected. The Batt. in Billets at 3 p.m. Operatic Orders issued 4/h. m.	
FOUCAUCOURT	5/3/17	9 a/m	The Batt. paraded in full marching order & marched to Bayonvillers – via main AMIENS Rd. (about 7 mls) & encamped near tents over & occupied at Bayonvillers – & the aft. by inspection took place.	TNT TNT
BAYONVILLERS	6/3/17		Reveille – Arm drill & harnessing – Aft.Cav.Inspection. Routine same as on previous day – Aft. devoted to attention of feet of A & B Coys. Inspection of Lev. Kathay located.	TNT TNT
"	7/3/17		Routine same as 6th & 7th inst. – Feet Inspection & lectures for remainder of the day.	TNT
"	8/3/17		Instructions for proceeding day issued. The R.A.M. paraded at 8:45 a/m & this morning was moved up to WAREWEZE-BRANCOURT (about 2 mls) & later over hill of T.S.F. Tr.2 over being occupied – the camp composed of huts was very incomplete – Medical R.E. were installed for work & work was commenced soon afterwards.	TNT TNT

WAR DIARY or INTELLIGENCE SUMMARY

Army Form C. 2118.

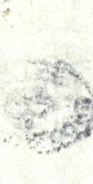

Place	Date	Hour	Summary of Events and Information	Remarks and references to Appendices
WARFUSÉE	10/3/17	9.30 a/m	Training & early morning parades commenced from this date. Batt. Parade & inspection - ofts camp & equipment etc. had been thoroughly cleaned. Close order drill practised.	
	11/3/17		Brigadier General recd D.S.O. took over command of 149th Brigade from this date.	
	11/3/17	10.30 a/m	Church Parade Service. 10f Inspections of to Parade Service in Brigade Centre. Brigade Recreational Training scheme was put into practise from this date - the inter-bty football match commencing.	
	12/3/17	9.30 a/m	Batt. Parade. Inspection of bty shelters - the whole moving into sections & specialists for this date. The whole moving being divided to specialist training. Ofts Large inspection & Recreational Training took place. Ballroom for Bry(?) & flight practise & competitions were commenced. Routine same as 12. most officers lecture at Brigade Centre 6 p.m. night.	
	14/3/17		Routine & training as on day previous.	
	15/3/17		Large working party of 950 O.R. found at 9 a/m for work in village &c. ga/h until orders from Town Major. Only men given this instruction was able to be continued on this bty.	
	16/3/17		Special training continued - ofts aft. By Marades Recreational Training for all from Bty Staff Rres-cwt, morning roues & football	

Army Form C. 2118.

WAR DIARY
or
INTELLIGENCE SUMMARY.
(Erase heading not required.)

Place	Date	Hour	Summary of Events and Information	Remarks and references to Appendices
WARFUSÉE	17/3/17		Specialist Training continued during morning on an previous days. Afternoon Coy Inspections & Football match - 12th Round of Inter-Batt round took place at Mathissen Myrs A.S.C.	
"	18/3/17	2.15pm	Coy inspections during morning. C.O's Rural Parade Service at Brigade Centre.	
"	19/3/17	9.30pm	Batt. Parade. Specialist Training continued except on Sy. which did a practical scheme of Platoon attack etc. Series of Brigadier General's Officers & N.C.O's of Brigade at 5:30pm in Brigade Conference Tent.	
"	20/3/17		Training continued. Two Coys doing general training from Flemant with practice of Artillery Formation upon deployment. Its other doing a practical open warfare scheme.	
"	21/3/17		Routine as on previous day. Two Coys doing a 2nd musketry & Much Discipline etc.	
"	22/3/17	6 P.M.	Lecture by D.C.L.I. Officers & N.C.O's (remainder practice of open order work & deployment) morning & Routine as on previous day - General Training of the Coys which did mixed passive day - other two Coys did a short must practice, deployment & Musketry on Musketry & Discipline etc. Lecture was given by M.G.O. of Brigade Bomb Officer on Rifle Grenades work - rifle - ammunition & fire etc.	

WAR DIARY
or
INTELLIGENCE SUMMARY.
(Erase heading not required.)

Army Form C. 2118.

Instructions regarding War Diaries and Intelligence Summaries are contained in F. S. Regs., Part II. and the Staff Manual respectively. Title pages will be prepared in manuscript.

Place	Date	Hour	Summary of Events and Information	Remarks and references to Appendices
WARFUSEE	22/3/17	9.30 a.m	Batt. Parade & Inspection by General Wilkson (50th Divis.). Field day followed - Bttn going out on a route march - Deploying & advancing from Artillery formation.	TNT
		2.30	Coy. Inspections	
		6 p.m	Lecture for Officers by O.O.G - by Majr. Roth	TNT
"	23/3/17	8.30	Batt. Parade - Field Day - an open order attack practised from main WARFUSEE - VILLERS CARBONNEL Rd to S.E. side of Bois d'Achiet - afterwds. they take up & consolidated on hill found outside HAMEL.	TNT
		5 p.m	Coy Inspections. 5 p.m lecture by Capt. Duke to Officers F/L.Co. A Coy. succeeded on a B.C. scheme - R. & C. Coys Paradrey a Coy & dug the man, attd Coy. attended O.S Baths at WARFUSEE.	TNT
	24/3/17		Coy. Inspections during morning - R.C. & Non-Conf. Church Parade	TNT
		2.15 pm	C. of E Parade Service in Recreation Hut (Brigade) A.I.P. Brigade Cross Country Run - Ten mins in clos. company & ope. 5th Reg. 7pm/t.	
		6.15 pm	Lecture by C.O. to Officers.	TNT

Army Form C. 2118.

WAR DIARY
or
INTELLIGENCE SUMMARY.
(Erase heading not required.)

Place	Date	Hour	Summary of Events and Information	Remarks and references to Appendices
WARFUSEE	26/3/17		Division Field day arranged for to-day was cancelled owing to bad weather. Morning was spent in giving lectures in the huts and attending to general economy Daily inspections and clothing parade in the afternoon. 2 N.C.O.s and 28 men sent as working party to R.T.O. WARFUSEE for unloading supplies. TMF	
	27/3/17		Field Forms Scheme carried out by the Battalion in the morning between HAMEL and WARFUSEE. Every $\_$ 100 yards Pt lot - ions worked alone by billet during the firing and Artillery of 2 N Co.s and 2 D. were harassed by the Battalion Q.M., N.T.O., WARFUSEE for unloading supplies	
	6 pm		Major W. ROBB M.C. lectured to all officers officers and Sgts. on consolidation. TMF	

Army Form C. 2118.

WAR DIARY
or
INTELLIGENCE SUMMARY.
(Erase heading not required.)

Instructions regarding War Diaries and Intelligence Summaries are contained in F. S. Regs., Part II. and the Staff Manual respectively. Title pages will be prepared in manuscript.

Place	Date	Hour	Summary of Events and Information	Remarks and references to Appendices
WARFUSEE	28/8/17	9.45	The 149Inf. Brigade were inspected by Lieut-General Sir W.P. Pulteney K.C.B. KCMG, D.S.O. commanding III Corps. The Batt. marched past and then proceeded on a Route March via CERISY with practice of Deployment.	TMJ
"	"	7.30p.m.	The Batt. practised a night attack on the ground between WARFUSEE & HAMEL.	TMJ
"	29/8/17	9.30p.m.	The C.O. inspected all Coys. in fighting order during the morning The Batt. proceeded by march route to BOUTILLERIE via VILLERS-BRETONNEUX, LONGEAU & CAGNY, a distance of 11½ miles & were billeted in BOUTILLERIE for the night 29/30th.	TMJ
"	30th			
BOUTILLERIE	31st	9.30p.m.	The Batt. proceeded by march route to COISY via AMIENS and POULAINVILLE a distance of 12 mls. & were billeted there.	TMJ

CONFIDENTIAL WAR DIARY

of

1st Battalion Northumberland Fusiliers

from

April 1st to April 30th 1917

VOLUME — 3

Army Form C. 2118.

WAR DIARY
or
INTELLIGENCE SUMMARY.
(Erase heading not required.)

Place	Date	Hour	Summary of Events and Information	Remarks and references to Appendices
COISY	Apr. 1	8 a.m.	B.Coy paraded to BELVUE to take part in Brigade scheme under G.O.C.	
		10 a.m.	Remainder of Batt. paraded - Close order drill.	
		2 p.m.	Church Parade Service in front of Chateau COISY. 9 A.B.	
"	2		The 149th Inf Brigade resumed their march.	
		8.30 a.m.	The Batt. Command moved to BEAUVAL at 10.1 a.m. - The car-road winding west of front was reached at 10.1 a.m. - The starting Villers-Bocage. BEAUVAL was reached at 12.35 p.m. 9 A.B.	
BEAUVAL	3rd		The 149th Inf Brigade resumed its march northward. The Batt. marched to BOUQUEMAISON via DOULLENS, a distance	
		9.15 a.m.	of 8½ mls. BOUQUEMAISON was reached at 12.30 a.m. 9 A.B.	
BOUQUE- MAISON	4th		The Month of the Brigade northwards was continued	
		6.55 a.m.	The Batt. marched to SIBIVILLE via FREVENT & SERICOURT - a distance of 8 mls. The start point being 5.0 p.m. start of cross roads West of Church BOUQUEMAISON. SIBIVILLE was reached about 9 a.m. 9 A.B.	
SIBIVILLE	5th		Kit inspection was held during afternoon.	
		9.30 a.m.	Coys paraded and intensive steeplechasing - the being allotted to each	
		2 p.m.	Coys [illegible] intensive [illegible] two platoons [illegible] under the head of O.C. for apprentices equipping A.S.L.	

WAR DIARY
INTELLIGENCE SUMMARY

Army Form C. 2118.

Place	Date	Hour	Summary of Events and Information	Remarks and references to Appendices
SIRIVILLE	6-	9.30 a/m	Batn Parade. A & B Coys practised an open-warfare attack reducing a salient. C & D Coys doing detached order Drill & Fire Control.	
		11.15 a/m	C & D Coys practised an open order scheme annul out previously by A & B Coys — the latter two Coys during interval rifle drill Gas-Control.	
"	7th	9.30 a/m	March of the 144th Brigade (Inf.) was continued eastwards. The Batn paraded 10 yds short of starting point, which was passed at 10 a/m. At this level crossing on SIRIVILLE-MONCHEAUX Rd. the Batn. marched to MAIZIERES via MONCHEAUX-MONTS-en-TERNOIS & GOUY. MAIZIERES was reached by 12.50 p/m — the distance being 7 mls. During aft. by inspections were held.	
MAIZIERES	8-	9.30 a.m.	The Battalion paraded on the main AMBRINES ROAD and marched via AMBRINES - SIVENCHY-le-NOBLE to BEAUFORT arriving there at 11.30 a.m. At GIVENCHY-LE-NOBLE orders were received to send one company to AGNES-LEZ-DUISANS to report to R.S.O. at Railhead to load Stores, and one company to BEAUMETZ-LES-LOGES to report to R.S.O. at Railhead to load Stores. A Company was sent from (BEAUFORT) to	

WAR DIARY
or
INTELLIGENCE SUMMARY.
(Erase heading not required.)

Army Form C. 2118.

Instructions regarding War Diaries and Intelligence Summaries are contained in F. S. Regs., Part II. and the Staff Manual respectively. Title pages will be prepared in manuscript.

Place	Date	Hour	Summary of Events and Information	Remarks and references to Appendices
	9/4/17	9.30am	AGNEZ-LES-DUISANS at 2pm and B Company to BEAUMETZ-LES-LOGES at the same time.	Ref. Sheet LENS 1/100,000
BEAUFORT			Do	TALT.
			All officers did an Outpost Scheme on the Ground between BEAUFORT and MANIN under Lt Col. B.J. SIBSON DSO — C and D Companies were exercised in a tactical Scheme on the same ground under Major W. ROBB M.C. TALT.	
		2pm		
	10/4/17	8am 1am	Orders received that the 149th Infantry Brigade would move during the day. less A Company The Battalion paraded outside BEAUFORT Church and marched via AVESNES-LE-COMPTE — HAUTEVILLE to WANQUETIN, arriving there at 5 p.m. The Battalion was accommodated in Nissen huts. T.A.L.T.	do
		3 p.m.		
WANQUETIN	11/4/17	10am 6/4	C and D Companies carried out bayonet training and a short march. The Battalion paraded at 6 p.m. and marched via WARLUS — DAINVILLE — ARRAS to RONVILLE CAVES (on the South side of ARRAS)	Ref. 51 B

A5834 Wt. W4973/M687 750,000 8/16 D. D. & L. Ltd. Forms/C.2118/13

WAR DIARY
INTELLIGENCE SUMMARY

Army Form C. 2118.

Place	Date	Hour	Summary of Events and Information	Remarks and references to Appendices
WANQUETIN	14/4/17		Arriving there at midnight Guides were met at 9.27 a.m. & from 151 Bde. Guides were relieved by 150th Infantry Brigade at AGNEZ-LEZ-DUISANS and met the remainder of the Battalion, less B Company at WARLUS. Packs were stored at WANQUETIN, cash Sundries, Very lights, Grenades, flares were issued to the men before starting and carried on the man from WANQUETIN. A motor lorry took the stores (grenades etc) to A and B Companies and brought their packs back to WANQUETIN. Every man carried a blanket rolled in a waterproof sheet. Shoes felt heavily during the greater part of the march. A Company after issuing their stores & loading their packs on the motor lorry proceed to join the Battalion at RONVILLE CAVES arriving there at 10 a.m. Stores were issued on the following Scale — Sandbags 4 per man. Flares 2 per officer and man. No 5 Mills Grenades 40 per Lewis Gun Section. No 20 Italia Grenades 40 per Rifle Grenade Section. Very Lights 4 (2 white) per officer. officer's Servant C.S.M. and (2 green) Platoon Sgt	Sheet 51 B.S.W
RONVILLE CAVES	14/4/17	1 a.m.	The 1st Line Transport was stationed at the CITADELLE, near ALT	

WAR DIARY
INTELLIGENCE SUMMARY

(Erase heading not required.)

Army Form C. 2118.

Place	Date	Hour	Summary of Events and Information	Remarks and references to Appendices
RONVILLE CAVES	12/4/17		Lt.Col. GIBSON, Major ROBB and 2/Lieut WILSON reconnoitred the ground in the area of TILLOY-LES-MOFFLAINES and TELEGRAPH HILL during the afternoon. B Company marched from BEAUMETZ-LES-LOGES	Ref Sheet 51B S.W.
		9/4m	and joined the Battalion at 9 p.m.	TAIT
	13/4/17	11 a.m.	Officers from Headquarters and each company reconnoitred the route from RONVILLE CAVES to the HARP (near TELEGRAPH HILL)	
		1 p.m.	Major ROBB reconnoitred the route from RONVILLE CAVES to VANCOURT	
		5 p.m.	The officer and men detailed to remain behind when the Battalion went into action marched to ARRAS where they took billets.	TAIT
— " —	14/4/17	3:30 am	The Battn. moved from RONVILLE CAVES to N end of THE HARP. Coys marched up by routes previously reconnoitred by Coy. Comrs. On arrival at 7h. NE, whose positions the Battn. were subjected to Shells over, had not moved to Bodn-Lay in war of the HARP. At 5:30 p.m. the Battn. started to move into THE HARP(N), but during the move orders were received to move to the COJEUL SWITCH of South.	

A 5834 Wt.W4973/M687 750,000 8/16 D.D.&L.Ltd. Forms/C.2118/13

Army Form C. 2118.

WAR DIARY
or
INTELLIGENCE SUMMARY.
(Erase heading not required.)

Instructions regarding War Diaries and Intelligence Summaries are contained in F.S. Regs., Part II. and the Staff Manual respectively. Title pages will be prepared in manuscript.

Place	Date	Hour	Summary of Events and Information	Remarks and references to Appendices
THE HARP SOUTH.		8 p.m.	of the HARP in N.7.A. After 5th N.F. had moved forward from above positions the Bn moved in, during the afternoon MONCHY-LE-PREUX which was visible from THE HARP & TELEGRAPH HILL was heavily bombarded & then attacked by 3rd Bav Regt but although the attack was at first successful, our troops drove them out of the West end of the village.	
	15–4–17		Bn. some positions in HARP (S) & COJEUL SWITCH.	
	16th	9 p.m.	Order was received to "Stand to", which was done until midnight when the Bn. stood down again; the cause of this was the enemy had counter attacked on WANCOURT TOWER, driving the same 7th NF. were entering & established himself there.	
Bn vicinity of M.G.C. H.Q.	17th	4 p.m.	The Batt moved forward. The C.O. went in advance to Bde H.Q. N.15.d.4.4 & met the new head direct observation (moving by platoon: owing to the fact that the enemy got down on Bn they could. Both H.Q. went to the M.G.C. dug-out, a long ½ way between THE HARP & Bde H.Q.	
		12 p.m.	A counter attack was made with artillery bombardment upon WANCOURT TOWER by 7 N.F. This was completely successful & deprived the enemy of his one means of direct observation on to ground in rear of WANCOURT.	

C.J.A —

A5834 Wt.W4973/M687 750,000 8/16 D.D. & L. Ltd. Forms/C.2118/13

WAR DIARY
INTELLIGENCE SUMMARY

Army Form C. 2118.

Place	Date	Hour	Summary of Events and Information	Remarks and references to Appendices
WANCOURT		4.15 pm	Orders were received from Bde to move forward with two coys in the BROWN LINE just behind WANCOURT, two coys further forward and in support of 5th NF in the LONE BANK in N.23 d. of N.24.C. HQ arrived & digged in the Bank road to CEMETERY behind WANCOURT. Coys were reported in their counter. Casualties during extry 1.O.R. killed & 1.O.R. wounded.	
"	18th	11.30 am	Order came through from the Bde to "Stand to." This came about from the shortening of a prisoner captured this morning near WANCOURT TOWER who said that Reserves had been brought up during the night & that the enemy were going to attack at 2 pm today (English time?pm). This in the end amounted to nothing more than that the enemy had counter-and a relief. This had already been known before and our artillery had heavily bombarded & caught the enemy's relief. The enemy consequently shelled all morning pretty heavily to-day.	
"		11.30 pm	Orders were received from Brigade that the Brigade would be relieved by the 150th Bde to-morrow & that the Batt would be relieved by the 5th Yorks in the BROWN LINE (South) & would move to the HARP (North)	
"	19th	12.30 pm	All this those orders were received that the previous order standing to for two coys of 5th NF would be cancelled & for the Batt to relieve 5th NF in the front line & that two coys of 5th NF would remain in support with this Batt. Two Batt HQ had been established in WANCOURT for the Batt in the front line. Three the 5th NF took R.Q.A. attack at 3 am. Batt HQ moved from WANCOURT at 3.30 pm and joined them in

Army Form C. 2118.

WAR DIARY
or
INTELLIGENCE SUMMARY.
(Erase heading not required.)

Instructions regarding War Diaries and Intelligence Summaries are contained in F.S. Regs., Part II and the Staff Manual respectively. Title pages will be prepared in manuscript.

Place	Date	Hour	Summary of Events and Information	Remarks and references to Appendices

which joint orders were issued to Coys for utey of the Road in the forof-line. This being so ordered at 8 p.m., guides being received from 5th NF at cross roads that nite, was carried out with Seasualties only 1 OR killed 4 OR wounded. The dispositions of Coys was as per sketch (inset).

L = Lewis gun which covered area between ourselves and 13th Div.
Z = Farm.
X = HANCOURT TOWER
N = 90 yds between our right and 30 Div. On night of 19th April this was only a trench 2ft deep, was on newcarel the same night by 30th Div.

MAP Reference.
51B-SW
N.23 D.
N.24 C & D.

Army Form C. 2118.

WAR DIARY
or
INTELLIGENCE SUMMARY.
(Erase heading not required.)

Instructions regarding War Diaries and Intelligence Summaries are contained in F. S. Regs., Part II. and the Staff Manual respectively. Title pages will be prepared in manuscript.

Place	Date	Hour	Summary of Events and Information	Remarks and references to Appendices
WANCOURT.	20th	—	Produced by quiet day. The LONG EMBANKMENT was shelled during the morning by 5.9" "hows" 7.15 men of 5th N.F. were hit. Orders were received for the relief of the Bde by 150 & 13 Bde. They	
		12 p.m.	5th N.F. moved (less the 2 coys in support with us) back to HARP (South). This left in alone & our H.Q. Bde guard.	
		8 p.m.	Relief by 3rd A.I.F. commenced at 8 p.m. Guides were sent to chosen roads No. 22 & 74 for coys in the front line and for coys in support in completion of relief of B coy in LONG BANK, both the 5th N.F. coys departed for THE HARP (South). Batt. was relieved by 11.40 p.m. and proceeded by coys to THE HARP (North) - no casualties were suffered during the relief. The Bde had now moved back and Brigade H.Q. were so established at HETSAS STREET. RONVILLE. (G.34 d 8.8)	
THE HARP. NORTH	21st	—	The Batt had received orders that the Bde would change places with the 151st Brigade in THE CAVES RONVILLE	
		2 p.m.	The Batt moved from THE HARP (North) to the CAVES RONVILLE & changed places there with 8th & 21. The 5th Borders took over the positions of the Bn in the HARP. HQ officers & staff went to billets in RONVILLE & relief was reported complete at 3 p.m. to Bde at THE FACTORY G.35.A.1.9.	
RONVILLE.	22nd	—	Batt was in position in THE CAVES all day. So far as possible men were re-equipped and all equipment and stores checked.	
	23rd	8 a.m.	St Georges Day. The Batt moved forward again to the O.G. 1.01 Line in M.5.b. and remained there during the day at ½ hours notice. The Batt moved forward at 5 minutes notice at 7.45 p.m. to the BROWN LINE & came under the orders of G.O.C. 151st Bde for Backcap purposes E.y.H.

WAR DIARY or INTELLIGENCE SUMMARY

Army Form C. 2118.

Place	Date	Hour	Summary of Events and Information	Remarks and references to Appendices
WANCOURT	24/4/17	9 am	The Batt. moved forward from the BROWN LINE under the orders of the 151st Infantry Brigade. B Company were sent forward to the front line on the right flank of the 9th D.L.I. and came under the orders of 9th D.L.I. They dug a new trench connected up with the right flank of 9th D.L.I. and occupied it covering party entrenched to Wancourt. No tunnel was obtained on the right flank until 3 p.m. when a slight t[ouch] to its right. The 5th Borders afraid to come forward. 5th Borders who were in rear of three, connecting with B Coy on the left and occupied it at night and dug a trench connecting with at the old British front line North of WANCOURT.	
		1.30 am	A, C, & D Coys 1 Batt. HQR arrived. Their instructions were to [take?] sketch. Rations were brought up to "S.B. Borders" Headquarters in the LONG BANK and brought up to A D HQR by C Company. There was not time to get rations up to B Coy. before daylight so they commenced the second in ration carried on the morn. B Company were reported to continue very heavy shell fire and also [received?] rifle[?], and during the day suffered the following casualties. 2/Lt R. JOHNSON (killed), 5 other ranks killed, 16 other ranks wounded. Their Lewis Guns found good targets at various [ranges?] about 1000 yds. and inflicted several casualties on the enemy. 1 Lewis Gun was [destroyed?] by shell fire.	
		1 pm	The area occupied by the remaining Coys was also subjected to considerable [enemy?] fire which was specially violent from 2.30 am to 7 am & again from 1.30 pm to 2 pm. No direct hits were obtained on the trench and no casualties were sustained in this [area?] During day light	
		2 pm	A party of 10 stretcher bearers and 10 men were sent out to collect wounded &/or [bury?] on the battlefield.	
		3 pm	B Company, under orders received from 9th D.L.I. (2.25 am) sent one platoon to reconnoitre and capture a German trench 600 yds. astride the railway. The platoon captured this trench with 3 casualties and another platoon was sent forward under heavy artillery and Machine Gun fire to help to hold it. Under cover of darkness 1 more platoon of B Coy was sent forward to the trench and 3	

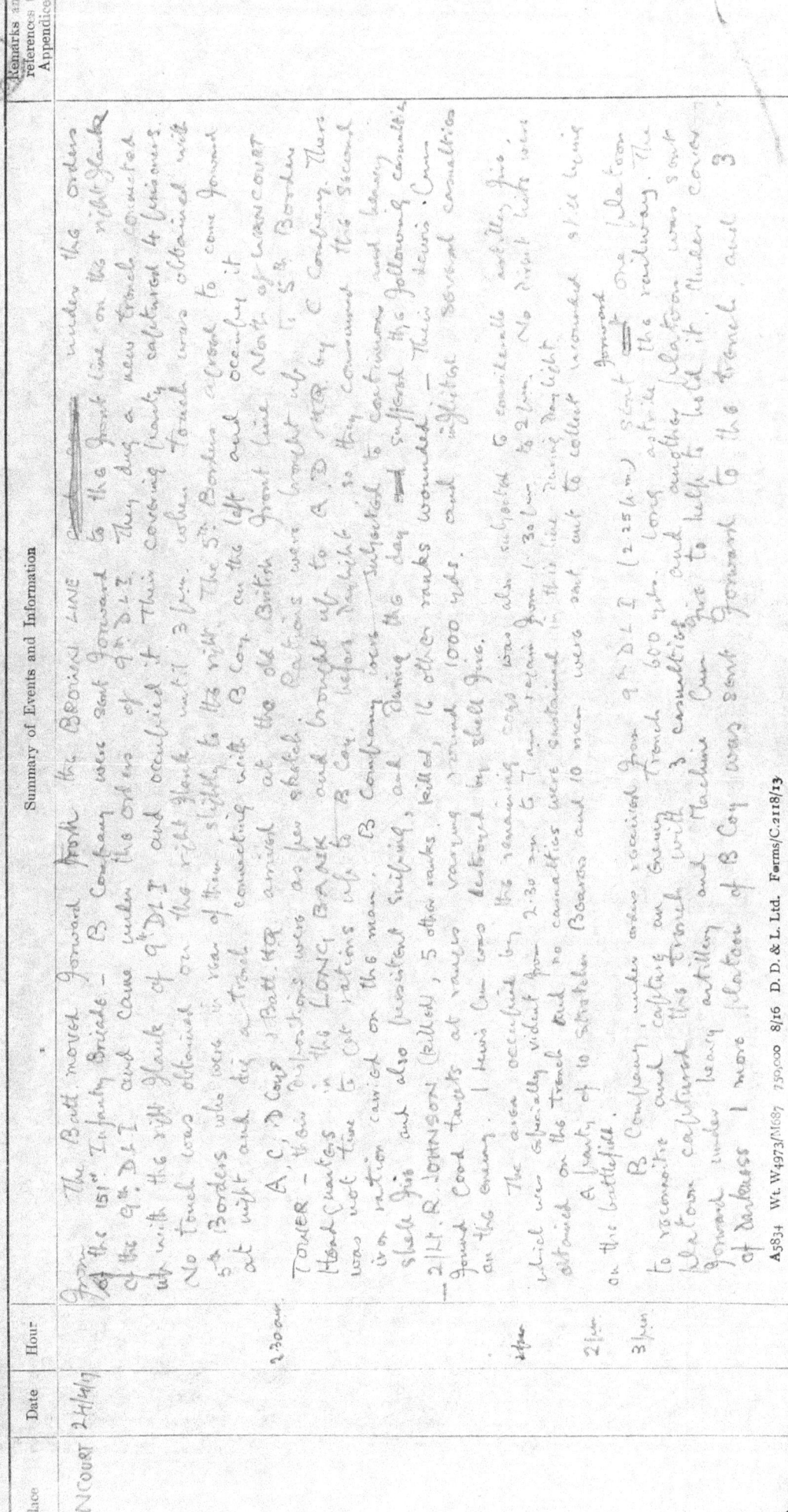

WAR DIARY
or
INTELLIGENCE SUMMARY.

Army Form C. 2118.

Remarks and references to Appendices

Map Reference
Sheet 51 B.s.w.
N. 24
~~N. 19~~
O. 19
O. 20

SKETCH of dispositions of companies (not to scale).

I. 5 a.m. 24/4/17
S = 1 Platoon D Coy.

II. 5 a.m. 25/4/17
F: old German Support line
G: New Brit. H.Q. in dugout

S. 5th Borders
T. 1 Platoon B Coy
U. 5 D.L.I.
V. B Coy H.Q.
W. 5th Borders
X. 9 D.L.I.
Y. 1 Platoon D Coy
Z. 2 Platoons B Coy

T.A.L.T.

Army Form C. 2118.

WAR DIARY
or
INTELLIGENCE SUMMARY.
(Erase heading not required.)

Instructions regarding War Diaries and Intelligence Summaries are contained in F. S. Regs., Part II. and the Staff Manual respectively. Title pages will be prepared in manuscript.

Place	Date	Hour	Summary of Events and Information	Remarks and references to Appendices
WANCOURT	24/4/17		Strong points were constructed, 2 North and 1 South of the railway.	
		8.30 a.m.	Operation orders were received at Batt. H.Q. which informed us that the 15th Division were advancing on our left and 9th D.L.I. would support their advance with rifle and Machine Gun fire. Also that 6th they would find forward patrols to reconnoitre and capture the German trench 300 yds long astride the railway. O.C. 9th D.L.I. detailed B Coy. for this work and captured half the trench as described above.	
		5.22 p.m.	The following message was received from O.C. 9th D.L.I. — A Platoon D Coy. company has just captured German trench Junct O.20.c.7.2. to O.20.c.9.3. killing 4 Germans and taking 3 prisoners including 1 junior officer.	
		9.15 p.m.	Lt. Col. B.D. Gibson and 2/Lt. J.R. Burton went forward to reconnoitre the new position occupied by B Coy. and A & D Coys.	
		10 p.m.	A & D Coys. dug a new support trench between the railway and the colour rise and occupied it. 1 Machine Gun was attached to each company.	
		10.30 p.m.	Batt. HQ. moved to Dugout at (see) old German Gun pits at north end of old German support line between Colour ridge and the railway. C Company remained at the long BANK.	
			TOTAL casualties during the day — 2/Lieut. R. Johnson killed, 2/Lieut. L. Stiff(?) of Hospital, 6 O.R. killed, 26 wounded.	
			B Company lost 2/Lieut. R Johnson (killed by a shell), 5 O.R. killed and 16 O.R. wounded.	

WAR DIARY or INTELLIGENCE SUMMARY

Army Form C. 2118.

Place	Date	Hour	Summary of Events and Information	Remarks and references to Appendices
WANCOURT	25/4/17		B Company had a Quitter day and enemy shelling and sniping were not so persistent. During the day they lost 1 O.R. (killed) and 4 O.R. wounded. Their stretcher bearers worked incessantly under fire, and did a Great deal of work on the Yanks as well as the company.	
		10 p.m	A, D, and C Coys put out a row of knife rests from in front of the new support line for a distance of 230 yards, starting from the railway.	
		11 p.m	The Battalion was relieved — B Company was relieved by 1 company of The 5th O.L.I., A D by One company of the 5th O.L.I., and C Company by one company of 5th K.S.L.I. Relief was reported to complete to 157th Bde. at 11 p.m. On relief Batt. proceeded to the HARP (North) Batt. H.Q. was established there at 1.30 am. On arrival at the HARP (North) the Batt. came under the orders of the 146th Infantry Brigade. TOTAL Casualties During the Day. — 1 O.R. killed 7 wounded (of which 2/Lt FINLAYSON (wounded returned to duty) B Coy lost 1 killed and 4 wounded. 2/Lt W ANDERSON was wounded and admitted to Hospital in ARRAS.	T.A.LT.
THE HARP (NORTH)	26/4/17		During the morning small parties was sent out to collect equipment, arms and accoutrements to complete deficiencies.	
		4 p.m	The Batt. moved by Companies to billets in ARRAS, 200 yds interval being maintained between companies.	
		6 p.m	A billeting party under Major W ROBB was sent by train to MONDICOURT	T.A.LT.

WAR DIARY
or
INTELLIGENCE SUMMARY.
(Erase heading not required.)

Place	Date	Hour	Summary of Events and Information	Remarks and references to Appendices
ARRAS	27/4/17	8.55 a.m.	The Battalion paraded in column of route in RUE JEANNE D'ARC facing the railway and formed up between station and (100) and moved by Tactical Train to MONDICOURT Blankets and packs were carried on this man. Train left ARRAS. Two trains were provided for the Brigade Group. Our train also carried Bn. HQ, 5th North. Fus., 447th Field Coy R.E. and 1/1st Norton. Coll. Aml.	
		3/pm	Battalion detrained at MONDICOURT & were guided from the station by Major in RUSS to billets in the village.	
		10 am	The Battalion Transport proceeded by march route with the remainder of the Brigade Group Transport, via Wanquetin from RONVILLE via ACHICOURT – main ARRAS – DOULLENS Road to MONDICOURT. Distance of 100 kilo. was maintained between Transport of units. Half an hour long was also provided to carry baggage for the Battalion.	
			The following message was received from the 149th Infantry Brigade. "Lieut. General Sir T. D'O. SNOW, K.C.B., K.C.M.G., Commanding VII Corps, called at Bde. HQ, this afternoon in order to heartily thank the Brigade for the work carried out by it during the recent operations". (dated: 27th April 1917).	
				T.A.L.T.

Army Form C. 2118.

WAR DIARY
or
INTELLIGENCE SUMMARY.
(Erase heading not required.)

Instructions regarding War Diaries and Intelligence Summaries are contained in F. S. Regs., Part II. and the Staff Manual respectively. Title pages will be prepared in manuscript.

Place	Date	Hour	Summary of Events and Information	Remarks and references to Appendices
MONDICOURT	28/4/17		The day was spent in reorganisation of companies, cleaning arms, equipment etc. and through inspection's. Indents to complete all deficiencies were forwarded. The following Special order of the day was received. SPECIAL ORDER OF THE DAY by General Sir Edmund Allenby K.C.B. Commanding Third Army. The following message has been received from the Field Marshal, Commander-in-Chief. "The fierce fighting yesterday has carried us another step forward. I congratulate you and all under you on the result of it, and on the severe punishment you have inflicted on the enemy." The Army Commander has replied as follows:- "Chief's message highly appreciated by all ranks of Third Army who are proud of and encouraged by his appreciation." T.A.I.T.	
"	29/4/17		Church Parades were held. An account of the work done by 50th Division during the last town is appended to the Diary. T.A.I.T	E. x 3856

A.5834 Wt.W4973/M687 750,000 8/16 D.D.&L.Ltd. Forms/C.2118/13

Army Form C. 2118.

WAR DIARY
or
INTELLIGENCE SUMMARY.
(Erase heading not required.)

Instructions regarding War Diaries and Intelligence Summaries are contained in F. S. Regs., Part II. and the Staff Manual respectively. Title pages will be prepared in manuscript.

Place	Date	Hour	Summary of Events and Information	Remarks and references to Appendices
MON DI COURT	30/4/17		The day was spent in completing the cleaning up and re-equipment of the Battalion. A statement of the fluctuation in strength during the month is appended to the Diary. T.A.L.	

2nd Lieut R. JOHNSON "B" Coy was killed in action on 24.5.17 & 2 Lieut. W. ANDERSON was wounded on the same day. 2nd Lieut A. FINLAYSON (6 C.H.L.I. attached 4th N.F) was slightly wounded but remained at duty. but total casualties for fortnight ending 27.4.17 were 9 O.R. killed, 41 wounded & 6 missing.

The fighting strength of the unit on 27.4.17 was 44 officers & 867 O.R.

Fluctuation of Strength during month of April.

Fighting Strength on April 1st
45 officers   889 other ranks.

During week ending April 5-1917 Lieut Col F. ROBINSON in Command of 6th N.F was struck off strength & 73. O.R. were evacuated out of Divisional Area

During week ending April 13-1917 5 O.R. were sent to Etaples classified as "P.B". 7 O.R. were transferred to 149th Light Trench Mortar Battery & one man was despatched to Director General of Transportation, BOULOGNE

Capt & Adjt C.G. ARKWRIGHT arrived 10/4/17 & was taken on strength.

During week ending 20.4.17. 7 O.R. arrived & Capt (now Lieut) R. ALLEN having been posted to our Res. Bn was struck off strength.

2 Lieut R C MORTON proceeded to England sick on 8/4/17.

On 22/4/17 2nd Lieut N.S. ROBSON & 33 O.R. arrived nearly all men were previously serving with us & came from 32nd Infantry Base Depot.

50th Division.
G.X. 3856.

TO
All Ranks of the 50th (Northumbrian) Division.
_____

The first tour of the 50th Division in the battle of ARRAS has been completed.

The 151st Infantry Brigade took WANCOURT TOWER on the night 12/13th April, and we handed over a front line one mile further East on the night 25/26th April.

On April 14th the 151st Infantry Brigade advanced, with the object of protecting the left flank of the Division on our right. All attacks failed, and the 151st Infantry Brigade, who advanced a considerable distance, were forced to withdraw.

The 149th Infantry Brigade then took over the line on the night 14/15th April.

From that night until 150th Infantry Brigade took over on the night 21/22nd, the enemy made six attacks on the TOWER. Only one of which was successful.

Of these attacks the 6th Bn. Northumberland Fusiliers repulsed four, and the 5th Bn. Northumberland Fusiliers one.

The 149th Infantry Brigade carried out two attacks on the TOWER, both of which were successful. One attack was made by the 6th Bn. Northumberland Fusiliers and one by the 7th Bn. Northumberland Fusiliers.

The 150th Infantry Brigade took over the line on the night 21/22nd in preparation for a big attack by the whole of the Third Army on the 23rd April.

The attack by the 150th Infantry Brigade was excellently carried out, and some 500 prisoners and 3 guns were captured. Owing, however, to the failure of the Divisions on both flanks, two heavy counter-attacks from the S.E. and along the COJEUL valley drove our men back, and by noon we were back again in our original trenches.

A counter attack was ordered by the VII Corps to take place at 6.0 p.m. This was carried out by two Battalions of the 151st Infantry Brigade, and was completely successful in spite of the fact that the Divisions on either flank again failed. Another 200 prisoners were captured in this attack, and many of our men wounded in the first attack were recovered.

The enemy left on the ground at least three times as many dead as we did.

We captured 3 guns, 15 Machine Guns, Two Medium Trench Mortars, and 12 fish tail trench mortars.

As will be seen by the accompanying Map, the 50th Division, as it did during the SOMME battle, keeps just ahead of the rest of the British line, in spite of the fact that the enemy's artillery is ever so much more severe than it was on the SOMME.

During the period 12th to 26th April our total casualties have been about 2,300.

During the fight on April 23rd we captured 700 unwounded prisoners and some 200 wounded, and the enemy dead on the ground is certainly not less than 300. It is not too much to assume that the enemy wounded amount to at least 1,000.

The total enemy casualties opposite the 50th Division therefore on April 23rd amounts to at least 2,200 as against our 2,300 for the whole period of 14 days, including the fighting on April 23rd.

The Divisions opposed to the 50th Division were the 35th Division and part of the 3rd Bavarian Division.

Prisoners of the 141st, 61st, and 176th Infantry Regiments of the 35th Division were captured during this period, and of the 17th and 18th Bavarian Infantry Regiments of the 3rd Bavarian Division.

The net result of our fight has been that we have soundly beaten the 35th German Division, who rather fancied themselves, and judging by the numbers of Iron Crosses worn by all ranks they must have fought well in previous battles.

The above record speaks for itself without any further commend.

You have all done splendidly.

27th April 1917.   (sd) P.S. Wilkinson   Major-General
                        Commanding 50th Division.

SITUATION at 4.45 a.m. 23.4.17. ....
SITUATION at 10.0 p.m. 23.4.17. ...
SITUATION at 10.0 p.m. 24.4.17.
Ref. Sheet 51b. 1/40,000.

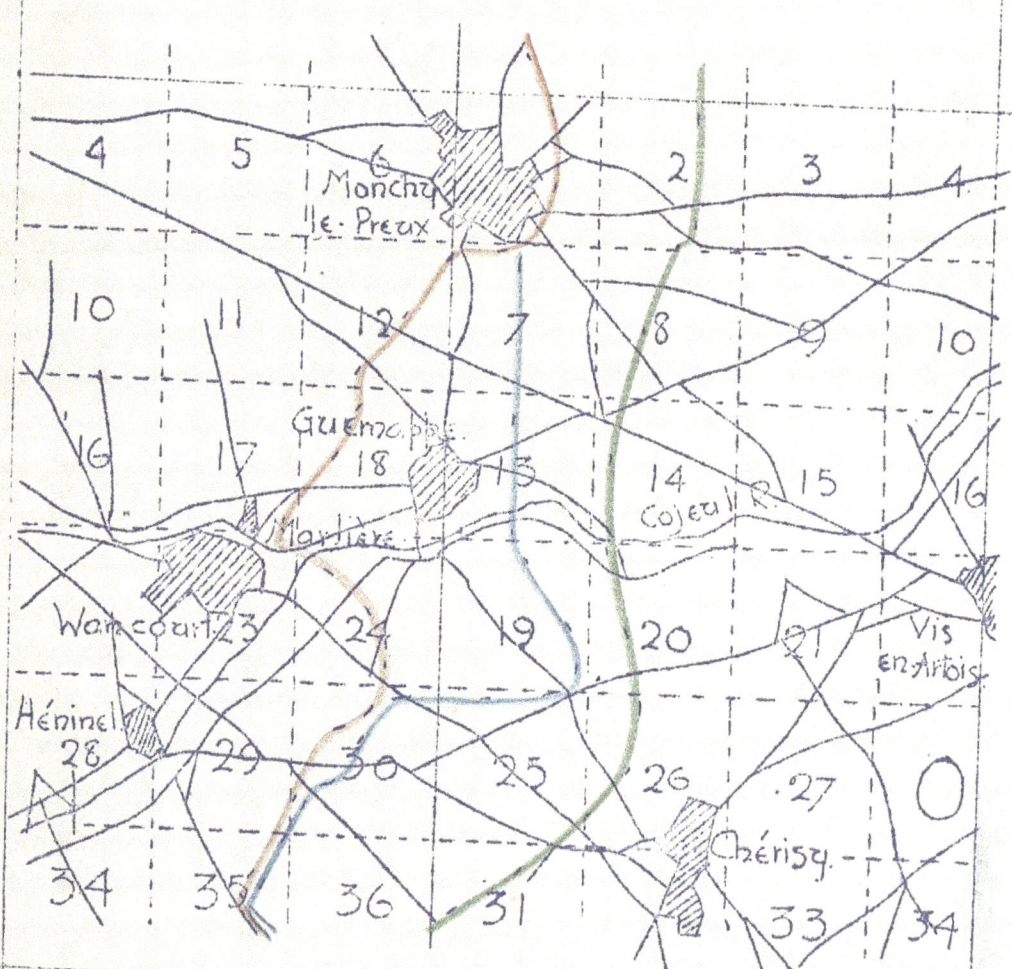

50th. Divn. VII Corps G.C.R.604/429.
G.X. 3859.

G.O.C.,
   50th. DIVISION.

      On the occasion of the Division leaving the line for a well earned rest, the Corps Commander wishes to record his appreciation of the gallant manner in which your men have fought and endured in the recent operations.

      The fighting in your front has been very severe and, as every one knows, your Division outfought and expelled the enemy, inflicting on him heavy loss. The Corps Commander congratulates you personally, and the splendid Division you Command, on the result. He hopes he will soon again have the honour to include the 50th. Division in his Corps.

                              sgd. J. BURNETT STUART,
                                 Brigadier-General.,
26th. April 1917.   General Staff, VII Corps.

=*=*=*=*=*=*=*=*=*=*=*=*=*=*=*=*=

      In reply to a letter sent to our late Corps Commander, Sir William Pulteney, K.C.B., K.C.M.G., D.S.O., describing briefly our doings during the past fortnight, he has written as follows :-

> "My very best congratulations to the old 50th. Division on their magnificent work in the ARRAS fight, there is no doubt they are a top hole fighting lot of fellows, it is grand the way they come up so often"

=*=*=*=*=*=*=*=*=*=*=*=*=*=*=*=*=

      The above are circulated for the information of all ranks of the 50th. Division.

                                       Lt.-Col,
                                 General Staff,
29th. April 1917.   50th. Division.

50th Division.
C.X. 3067.

TO

The Army Commander on the 26th instant called personally on General Wilkinson Commanding the 50th Division, and congratulated him on the way the Division had fought between the 12th and 26th April.

Please communicate this to all ranks.

H. Karslake
Lt-Col.
General Staff.
29th April 1917.   50th Division.

Detail and Trenches revised to 21-4-17.   ETERPIGNY. EDITION 2.

Scale 1:20,000

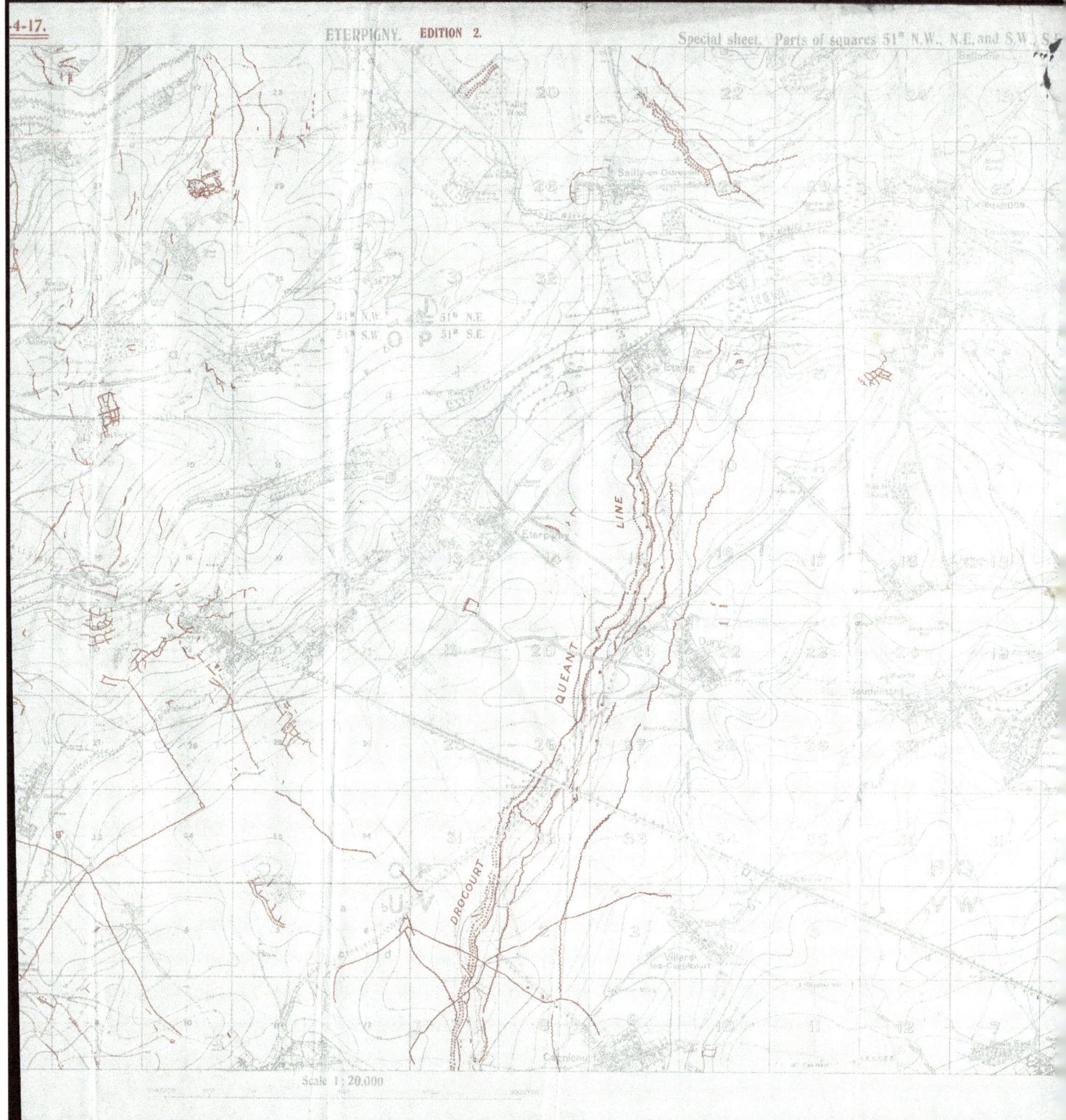

Army Form C. 2118.

WAR DIARY
or
INTELLIGENCE SUMMARY.
(Erase heading not required.)

Vol 22

CONFIDENTIAL

War Diary
of
4th Battalion Northumberland Fusiliers

From May 1st 1917 (inclusive) to May 31st 1917 (inclusive)

VOLUME II

T.A.C. Thompson
Lieut. F.
Lt. Y. No.7 F.

WAR DIARY
INTELLIGENCE SUMMARY

Army Form C. 2118.

Place	Date	Hour	Summary of Events and Information	Remarks and references to Appendices
MONDICOURT	1/5/17	3.1pm	The Battalion marched via PAS and HENU to SOUASTRE (5½ miles) arriving at 4.45pm. Packs were dumped at Mondicourt and men carried blanket wrapped in waterproof sheet on the back of the belt below the haversack. Men were accommodated in Nissen huts, officers in billets.	TA.I.T.
SOUASTRE	2/5/17		The Battalion marched via BIENVILLERS—MONCHY—DOUFFER—HENDECOURT to MERCATEL (12 miles) arriving there at 11.50 a.m. W. Gotha but and roads dusty. Batt. bivouacked in old German trenches N.W. of MERCATEL.	TA.I.T.
MERCATEL	3/5/17		An attack was made by VII Corps. I congratulated with remainder of VII Army. The 14th Division efforts to PUISIEUX—MOIS and 18th Division west of CROISILLE were at first successful but were obliged to Jall back to line of arrival line. Training for Signallers, Lewis Gunners Scouts o N.C.O.s	TA.I.T.
MERCATEL	4/5/17	3pm	Training for officers in work & talking. Received orders to be in readiness to move to SOUASTRE	TA.I.T.

Army Form C. 2118.

WAR DIARY
or
INTELLIGENCE SUMMARY.
(Erase heading not required.)

Instructions regarding War Diaries and Intelligence Summaries are contained in F. S. Regs., Part II. and the Staff Manual respectively. Title pages will be prepared in manuscript.

Place	Date	Hour	Summary of Events and Information	Remarks and references to Appendices
MERICOURT	4/5/17	6pm	Battalion marched via HENENCOURT - DINFER - Moncing BENVILLERS to SOUATRE own accommodation is to same camp as vacated on 2nd May. 4 men fell out on the march. One of whom did not report before marching off on 5/5/17 TMT	
MONDICOURT	5/5/17	7.32 am	Battalion marched via HENU & PAS to MONDICOURT. No men fell out on the march. The afternoon was spent in cleaning equipment etc. TMT	
"	6/5/17	11.45 a.	G.O.C. 149th Inf. Bde. addressed 1/6 and 5th North'd Fus. at MONDICOURT. He congratulated all ranks on the work they had done during the recent fighting and laid stress on the necessity of men learning to make the best use of their rifles, there being a tendency to rely too much on Lewis Guns. Church parades were held. TMT	

A 5534 Wt. W4973/M687 750,000 8/16 D. D. & L. Ltd. Forms/C.2118/13

WAR DIARY
or
INTELLIGENCE SUMMARY.

Army Form C. 2118.

Place	Date	Hour	Summary of Events and Information	Remarks and references to Appendices
MONDICOURT	7/5/17		Training. — Staff Ride under the Brigadier. T.A.L.T.	
"	8/5/17		Training. Chief attention paid to Musketry. Shooting on range. T.A.L.T.	
"	9/5/17		Field Scheme. B 2 Battalions in attack. T.A.L.T.	
"	10/5/17		Training. Route march and practice attack. T.A.L.T.	
"	11/5/17		Brigade Field Scheme. The Battalion fought a Delaying action against the remainder of the Brigade. Regimental Sports were held. T.A.L.T.	
"	12/5/17		Church Parade were held. The Battalion was put through gas test with box respirators. T.A.L.T.	
"	13/5/17		Training. Company and Platoon rifle-shooting competitions. T.A.L.T.	
"	14/5/17		Training. Field Scheme 2w 4th North. Fus. and 6th North. Fus. T.A.L.T.	

WAR DIARY
or
INTELLIGENCE SUMMARY.

(Erase heading not required.)

Army Form C. 2118.

Place	Date	Hour	Summary of Events and Information	Remarks and references to Appendices
MONDICOURT	14/5/17		Training. Field Scheme for the Brigade.	T.A.L.T
"	17/5/17	3.30 p.m	The Battalion marched via PAS and HENU to SOUASTRE, a distance of 5½ miles. One man fell out but rejoined within an hour. Packs were carried on the men, and 1 blanket per man in a motor lorry. The Batt. arrived at SOUASTRE at 5.45 p.m. and was accommodated in huts except the officers who were in billets.	T.A.L.T
	18/5/17	6.2 a.m.	The Battalion marched via BIENVILLERS – MONCHY-AU-BOIS – ADINFER to BOIRY ST MARTIN arriving at BOIRY ST MARTIN at 9.50 a.m. The Battalion was accommodated in shelters and tents. Lunges in the village. The HQ's Infantry Brigade on its arrival at BOIRY ST MARTIN came under the orders of the 33rd Div. The Bg France) 1½ mile march. No men fell out on the march. 10½ miles.	T.A.L.T
BOIRY ST MARTIN	19/5/17	8.30 a.m	Training in the morning. The C.O., Adjutant, and two company commanders reported to 19th Inf.	

Army Form C. 2118.

WAR DIARY
or
INTELLIGENCE SUMMARY.
(Erase heading not required.)

Instructions regarding War Diaries and Intelligence Summaries are contained in F.S. Regs., Part II. and the Staff Manual respectively. Title pages will be prepared in manuscript.

Place	Date	Hour	Summary of Events and Information	Remarks and references to Appendices
BOIRY ST. MARTIN	19/5/17		Bde. H.Q. and with the help of an officer from this Bde. as guide reconnoitred the forward area between CROISILLES and ground 500 yds W of FONTAINE-LES-CROISILLES. T.A.L.T	
ST LEGER	20/5/17	5 a.m.	The Battalion less 108 O.R. Orderov to be left behind when Battalion goes into action, and less Q.M. Stores and 2nd line Transport marched via HAMELINCOURT to ST LEGER. No one fell out During the march. Distance of 200 yds were maintained between coys. H.Q. was established at T.27.D.O.O. (Ref Sheet 51 B.S.W.) at 7.40 am	
		5.15 am	The 33rd Div. to whom our Brigade is attached attacked the HINDENBURG LINE, HINDENBURG SUPPORT LINE between RIVER ROAD and its Exc. HUMP, a strong point in the HINDENBURG LINE just S. of the CROISILLES-HENDECOURT ROAD. The front line was taken with very little opposition, but the support line was not taken. T.A.L.T	
		7.30 pm	Another attack was made on the HINDENBURG SUPPORT LINE in result of an assault front confluent N of the SENSEE river. It was unsuccessful. T.A.L.T.	

Army Form C. 2118.

WAR DIARY
or
INTELLIGENCE SUMMARY.
(Erase heading not required.)

Place	Date	Hour	Summary of Events and Information	Remarks and references to Appendices
ST. LEGER	20/4/17	3.30 p.m.	Received orders to be prepared to move at 1 hr notice. Bombs & other stores drawn and carried on the men as under.— <u>Rifle Grenades</u>. (a) The 2 companies who will take over right half of front line (no. 23 Mills Rifle Grenades per Rifle Grenadier, there being no rifle waster than no. 20 for those companies owing to there range being short (90 yds). The Lewis 3 line is closer to our line on the right than to the left. (b) Remaining Companies Lewitt 5 no. 20 Hales Rifle Grenades per Rifle Grenadier (range 250 yds). (c) Two right companies carried 40 per Platoon (no. 23 Mills with no. carried separately) in 4 buckets per platoon (b) Remaining Companies carried 40 no 5 Mills Grenades per Platoon in 4 buckets per platoon. <u>Very Lights</u>. WHITE All Coys 4 hr Officer, Officer's Servant, C.S.M. Platoon Sgt. RED (SOS) Very scarce — only 4 for 2 right companies and 2 for 2 left Companies. <u>Hand Grenades</u> <u>Sandbags</u> 4 per man <u>Ground Flares</u> (SOS) 150 per Company (for communication to aeroplanes)	T.A.L.T.

Army Form C. 2118.

WAR DIARY
or
INTELLIGENCE SUMMARY.

(Erase heading not required.)

Instructions regarding War Diaries and Intelligence Summaries are contained in F. S. Regs., Part II. and the Staff Manual respectively. Title pages will be prepared in manuscript.

Place	Date	Hour	Summary of Events and Information	Remarks and references to Appendices
ST. LEGER	21/5/17		Training for two hours in morning.	T.R.T.
	22/5/17	5 a.m.	The C.O., Adjutant, and 4 company commanders reconnoitred forward area.	
		8.20 p.m.	The Battalion relieved two Battalions of 19th Inf. Bde. — 2nd Royal Welsh Fusiliers and 5th Scottish Rifles — in the front line. The Battalion moved off from ST. LEGER at 8.40 p.m. with 250 yds. interval between platoons. Each platoon carried 2 picks and four shovels. 2 Twin Stokes Mills being brought into the magazine from a point on the railway S. of CROISILLES — 2 miles. The relief was carried out successfully. Relieving escorts from reported complete to Bde. at 3.40 a.m. 23/5/17. Our dispositions were as per sketch I.	Ref Sheet 51 B. S.W. 1/20,000

SKETCH I
(no scale)

TO FONTAINE–
TO FONTAINE–
LES-CROISILLES

FROM CROISILLES
FROM CROISILLES

SENSEE RIVER

CHALK PIT

A
B

TO BULLECOURT

HINDENBURG LINE
THE HUMP

TO HENDECOURT
TO BULLECOURT

A Coy
B Coy
D Coy
Batt. H.Q.

O.O. OSCAR TRENCH
S. 2' Stokes Mortars
T. Potable enemy support
Q. Bombing Block
C.T. Communication Trench
P. 2 platoons D Coy
X. 2 platoons D Coy
A, B, C Coys. rations brought to this spot
B. D Mtr. rations brought to this spot & Coy HQ

Army Form C. 2118.

WAR DIARY or INTELLIGENCE SUMMARY.

(Erase heading not required.)

Place	Date	Hour	Summary of Events and Information	Remarks and references to Appendices
CROISILLES	22/5/17		Communication by runner was possible by day and night by C.T. (See sketch), but by night it was impossible to communicate with D Coy, by runner in daylight. Telephone communication with A, B, & C Coys. was already established before relief. We ran a wire from D Coy to Batt. HQ. immediately the relief started and by 11.30 p.m. was in telephonic communication with them. There were no casualties during relief. C Coy. got into touch with 5NF but not with 2/5 KOYLI who were obtained on the right, although D Coy sent out 2 patrols for that purpose. Batt. H.Q. was heavily shelled during relief — no casualties. T.A.L.T.	
	23/5/17		Enemy apparently held front line thinly. He seems to have a post with machine gun at road junction (marked T on sketch on previous page). A machine gun fires down the CROISILLES — HÉNDECOURT road from this post — snipers also appear to fire from this point. Infilading fire was obtained from the last night. During the night a company of Lincolns of 33rd Divn. made good progress with A, B, & C Coys. C.T. (see sketch) from A Coy. towards sullest confines of 6th N.F. The C.T. from a new C.T. (sa north) leading towards CHALK PIT was very narrow and wire was lying across it in parts. A party from C Coy cleared this and widened the trench. C Coy HQ. obtained with Batt. on our right flank. D Coy. sent out 2 patrols to find this Battalion. A patrol was sent out from B Company to find NU torel OSCAR TRENCH held by enemy, where the enemy was seen and but was unable to find whether OSCAR TRENCH was held by enemy or not. A patrol was sent out from C Coy to ascertain whether they reported no hostile working on it. A patrol was sent out from C Coy to find but no hostile wire. They reported that wire was in front different to be found but no attempt on enemy wire, being made to obtain it. Enemy trench mortars were active at about 3.30 p.m. near A Coy's Trench about 3.30 p.m. slightly, but caused no casualties.	

Given ...... near

Place	Date	Hour	Summary of Events and Information	Remarks and references to Appendices
	23/5/17	2.15 pm	& 40 of the Enemy were reported to be coming towards our bombing block up Station road in V.13.d and V.14.c. It was thought the enemy might be contemplating a bombing attack, but no action developed. The main objects of our work at night were to make communication by hopfull bomille with D Coy.) and to link up D Coy post and support line with D Coy H.Q. With this object in view, a working party from the Support Battalion (6th N.F.) of 38 men was sent to D Coy. to link up the D Coy defences. They completed that with the exception of about 100 yds from their post his revetments. (see sketch). It was intended to link up A Coy with D Coy by a C.T. A Coy. worked on this also the night 23rd/24th May and dug about 60 yds of it starting from their trench.

Sketch II (no scale)

Z. New C.T. started by A Coy.
V. New CT dug by 6 NF.

Rations were brought up by Transport to places marked on Sketch I and carried up by our companies (except D Coy.), whose rations were brought up by 6th N.F.

Casualties during day. Other Ranks. 1 killed, 1 wounded.

T.A.L.T. | |

Army Form C. 2118.

WAR DIARY
or
INTELLIGENCE SUMMARY.
(Erase heading not required.)

Instructions regarding War Diaries and Intelligence Summaries are contained in F. S. Regs., Part II. and the Staff Manual respectively. Title pages will be prepared in manuscript.

Place	Date	Hour	Summary of Events and Information	Remarks and references to Appendices
CROISILLES	24/5/17	3.30 a.m.	5 prisoners of 225 R.I.R. were captured by B Company. They were brought in at "Staff 6". They informed us that a Tunnel ran between our lines and theirs, an entrance of which was 3 or 5 yds from our parapet and also that a Tunnel ran under our trench not far from. There was found to be a large dug-out with an entrance a few yds from our parapet. The dug-out Tunnel was not found. As they probably have to use snipers kept active. Enemy snipers & several burning bar-bombed men on our front line but caused no casualties. Two wounded Hostile trench mortars again fired during the night 23rd/24th, before had been lying out men of 9th H.L.I. whom we brought in during the night 23rd/24th. They Inform us that the enemy in shell hole in No Man's Land for 4 days. They informed us that the enemy had a string of snipers and a few machine guns in front of his line every night. The relief commenced shortly after dusk. Relief was reported complete to Brigade at 12.20 a.m. 24/5/17. Casualties during relief - Nil. During and after the relief the trench system on our sector was found to be such as only D Coy was accessible in daylight by runner from "K.O.P." In such a way that D Coy was provided in daylight and D Coy lateral communication between A & D Coy was provided in daylight HQ & M from Headquarters of D Coy were all connected up & communication from one to the other were possible in daylight. (See Sketch III)

Sketch III.
(No Scale)

FROM CROISILLES -------- TO HENDECOURT
A5534 Wt. W4973/M687 750,000 8/16 D.D. & L. Ltd. Forms/C.2118/13

—— Work already done
--- New work done on night 24th/25th
···· Road

WAR DIARY
or
INTELLIGENCE SUMMARY.

(Erase heading not required.)

Army Form C. 2118.

Place	Date	Hour	Summary of Events and Information	Remarks and references to Appendices
CROISILLES	24/5/17		On relief Battalion proceeded to SENSEE valley W. of ST. LEGER to same camp as Guards left by us on 22nd May 1917. OTHER RANKS - 2 wounded. The northern side of the SENSEE valley was previously shelled by a high velocity Gun.	T.A.L.T.
ST. LEGER	25/5/17		Between 8.30 am and 11.30 am The day was spent in cleaning and cleaning equipment A working party of 2 Officers & 120 men was sent off at	
		8.40 a.m	8.40 a.m. & carried stores (ammunition etc.) from CHALK PIT to front line (see Sketch I). They returned at 7.30 am having lose 2 (Ormaya & Wic(?)) NCO's. 30 men with 1 Officer in charge of the UP remain. The party was divided into four (parties of 30 men with 1 officer in charge) and one officer in charge of the transport working party, no Coys. Without shelling Casualties occurred.	T.A.L.T.
	26/5/17		Training in morning. — Battalion moved to MOYENVILLE	
		7.30 pm	at 7.30 pm. Q.M. Stores details and Lewis gun limbers — 15 minute interval was maintained between Coys. during the march. No enemy shells out.	T.A.L.T.

Army Form C. 2118.

WAR DIARY
or
INTELLIGENCE SUMMARY.
(Erase heading not required.)

Instructions regarding War Diaries and Intelligence Summaries are contained in F. S. Regs., Part II. and the Staff Manual respectively. Title pages will be prepared in manuscript.

Place	Date	Hour	Summary of Events and Information	Remarks and references to Appendices
MOEUVRE	27/5/17		Cleaning up of areas. W& informed Church Parade was held at 5pm. 33rd Div. attacked TUNNEL TRENCH (Hindenburg Support line) with success. Our Brigade was in Div. reserve still not move. TMT	
MONCHY- AU- BOIS	28/5/17	6.30am	Battalion moved to MONCHY-AU-BOIS. All Transport (including Lewis Gun limbers, March horses) were inspected and proceeded under Brigade Transport officer. Distance of march 5½ miles. Only one man for Out, but has rejoined Battalion within an hour of our arrival. Pack Blankets, in a motor lorry. Battalion was were carried on the men. Accommodated in bivouacs and a very few tents.	T.A.L.T.
	29/5/17		Rain prevented training in morning — Two lorries Mens Canteen Stores started in afternoon — (a) Truck men to be trained to take place of Nos. 1 and 2 if required (b) Football ground and new area questions &	T.A.L.T.
	30/5/17		Training. Brigade Field Classes — inoculation for all in Brigade. In all ranks who have not been inoculated yet began.	T.A.L.T.
	31/5/17		Men off duty after inoculation	T.M.T.

Army Form C. 2118.

WAR DIARY
or
INTELLIGENCE SUMMARY.
(Erase heading not required.)

The following Military medals were granted to men of the Battalion during the month.

No. 200167 Pte. MICHAEL DAVIDSON
No. 201960 " MATTHEW ANDERSON

For conspicuous bravery and devotion to duty near WANCOURT on the 24th and 25th April 1917. Ptes. DAVIDSON and ANDERSON worked practically continuously night and day as stretcher bearers for 48 hours. They attended to and brought in the wounded at 5 different battalions under trench M.G. fire and in constant shelling which caused a number of casualties.

No. 23800 Pte. THOMAS STERLING NICHOL.

For conspicuous bravery and devotion to duty on the 24th 25th April 1917 near WANCOURT. Pte. Nichol was a Company Runner and after all the other runners had become casualties through rifle fire and continued to do the work under M.G. fire and continued smiling. On returning from the line it was found that he had a bullet lodged in his ankle which necessitated his immediate evacuation to hospital though he had not complained or had as long as his work permitted.

WAR DIARY
or
INTELLIGENCE SUMMARY.

Army Form C. 2118.

Place	Date	Hour	Summary of Events and Information	Remarks and references to Appendices
			The following were mentioned in Sir D. HAIG's Despatches, May 1917, for Distinguished conduct:—	
			Lieut W.M. TURNER (Transport Officer).	
			No. 20088 Sgt. L. BELL	
			9007 Pte. B. ADCOCK	

WAR DIARY or INTELLIGENCE SUMMARY

FLUCTUATION in STRENGTH during May 1917

Strength on May 1st. 42 Officers. 820 O.R.
                      44 "   796 O.R.
                      31

	Off	O.R.
Increase		
Drafts. 5th May	-	14
" 11th "	1	17
" 15th "	-	16
" 29th "	4	30
From Hospital	1	43

Decrease
To Hospital
Casualties
(Cmds (Commission) etc.)

Officers Other ranks
   3   107
            1 killed
   1 wounded 3 wounded
            13

7713

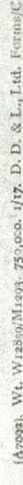

Army Form C. 2118.

WAR DIARY
or
INTELLIGENCE SUMMARY.
(Erase heading not required.)

149/50

Vol 23

CONFIDENTIAL

WAR DIARY

OF

4th BATTALION NORTHUMBERLAND

FUSILIERS

FROM JUNE 1st 1917   TO JUNE 30th 1917

VOLUME 3

Army Form C. 2118.

WAR DIARY
or
INTELLIGENCE SUMMARY.
(Erase heading not required.)

Place	Date	Hour	Summary of Events and Information	Remarks and references to Appendices
MONCHY-AU-BOIS	June 1st to June 17th 1917		Training. The main features of the training were company, Battalion, and Brigade Field Schemes, varying from trench-to-trench attacks to Open Warfare Schemes. Signallers, Scouts, Snipers, Lewis Gunners received special training when opportunity offered, but then always attended Battalion and Brigade Field Schemes. Night patrolling was practised. Officers had special training in Map Reading. — About the middle of this training period, a new organisation was brought in. A fifth company was formed for training purposes, composed of those men who are left behind when the Battalion goes into action. The remainder of each company, after the men for the 5th company had been taken away, was organised in two Platoons and company HQ. — All available officers and other Ranks were inoculated (2nd Dose) on June 6th. —	

Army Form C. 2118.

WAR DIARY
or
INTELLIGENCE SUMMARY.
(Erase heading not required.)

Place	Date	Hour	Summary of Events and Information	Remarks and references to Appendices
MONCHY-AU-BOIS	June 1st to June 17th		Brigade Sports were held on ground between MONCHY-AU-BOIS and BIEN VILLERS-AU-BOIS on June 10th. — General SNOW, commanding VII Corps inspected the Battalion in gasmasks drill at MONCHY-AU-BOIS on June 14th. — On and after 15th June the following working parties were provided by the Battalion.	
	15/6/17		I. 2/Lt. J.A. BURTON and 7 other ranks relieved Town Major (as Town Major) at [8th E. SURREY Regt] and took over duties of Town Major of BOISLEUX-ST-MARC and BOIRY-BECQUERELLE.	Ref/Sheet 51.B.S.W. 1/20,000
	do.		II. 1 N.C.O. and 3 men relieved 1 N.C.O. and 3 men Horse Troughs at S.10.c.3.0.	— do —
	do.		III. 1 N.C.O. and 3 men relieved 1 N.C.O. and 3 men as guard on Horse Troughs at S.10.9.8.2.	BOISLEUX-AU-MONT BOISLEUX-ST-MARC
	do.		IV. 1 N.C.O. and 3 men as Guard on water points	BOIRY-BECQUERELLE

Army Form C. 2118.

WAR DIARY
or
INTELLIGENCE SUMMARY.
(Erase heading not required.)

Instructions regarding War Diaries and Intelligence Summaries are contained in F. S. Regs., Part II. and the Staff Manual respectively. Title pages will be prepared in manuscript.

Place	Date	Hour	Summary of Events and Information	Remarks and references to Appendices
MONCHY-AU-BOIS	17/6/17		V. D Company less detail of 5 E Company, proceeded to NEUVILLE VITASSE to unload Ammunition for Heavy Artillery. They relieved a similar party of 53rd Bde. They also relieved 1 N.C.O. and 6 men of other 53rd Bde. as [?] on Corps Ammunition Dump, MERCATEL. Both parties rejoined the Battalion at HENIN CAMP on 24/6/17.	
			VI. C Company sent 1/Lt. H.B. BELL and 50 other Ranks to BLAIRVILLE to make mining frames. They rejoined the Battalion on 24/6/17. T.A.L.T.	
	18/6/17	7.30 p.m.	The Battalion marched to near BOISLEUX ST. MARC (S.17.c. central Ref Sheet 51 B.S.W.) via ADINFER - BOIRY - ST. RICTRUDE. No men fell out. Distance of march 6½ miles. Battalion accommodated in tents and a few huts. Marched in to camp 10.15 p.m.	

WAR DIARY
INTELLIGENCE SUMMARY.

(Erase heading not required.)

Army Form C. 2118.

Place	Date	Hour	Summary of Events and Information	Remarks and references to Appendices
Huts BOISLEUX-ST-MARC. S.17.c. A)h+5)B.S.W.	18/4/17 to 24/4/17		Training. Special training for Lewis Gunners, Signallers, & Scouts.	TM.D
	24/4/17	2 p.m.	The Battalion moved to camp 500 yds N. of HENIN & became 1st Reserve Battalion 5th Inf. Brigade. The 5th Inf. Brigade held the line the 6th in support, while the 7th was in 2nd reserve Battalion.	TM.D
	24/5/17 to 29/4/17		Training. Reconnoitring forward areas by Officers. Musketry on Rifle Range. Special training of Lewis Gunners, Signallers, Scouts, Bombers &c. continued.	TM.D

Army Form C. 2118.

WAR DIARY
or
INTELLIGENCE SUMMARY.
(Erase heading not required.)

Instructions regarding War Diaries and Intelligence Summaries are contained in F. S. Regs., Part II. and the Staff Manual respectively. Title pages will be prepared in manuscript.

Place	Date	Hour	Summary of Events and Information	Remarks and references to Appendices
C'toy in EGRET TR				
A Coy EGRET TR	28/6/17		The Battalion relieved 5" NORTHD FUSILIERS in support line Relief commenced at 12.30 p.m. The Battalion proceed by half platoons at five minutes interval via HENNEL and FOSTER AVENUE. Casualties during relief NIL. Relief completed by 4.30 p.m. Disposition of companies was as per attached map.	
B " EGRET LOOP				
C " " in BUZZARD TRENCH				
P. 3 - EGRET TRENCH			Battalion Transport Park too far away. Roads up to battalion front too —	
D-5 AT THE NEST				
BATT. H.Q. THE NEST	29/6/17		A fairly quiet day. The Battalion dug a new trench at night from WREN LANE to DEAD BOSCHE SAP (see map). The idea of this was to establish ourselves in this line so as to prevent the enemy getting observation over our line. The trench was dug to an average depth of 4 feet good elevation over the enemy rear areas and commanders in EGRET TRENCH in which there was an O.P. We also constructed another O.P. in EGRET TRENCH.	
			Enemy shelled EGRET TRENCH and EGRET LOOP from 6-30 f.m. to 7-0 p.m. & caused one casualty. (1 O.R. wounded)	
	30/6/17		Another fairly quiet day. The enemy shelled EGRET TRENCH and EGRET LOOP from 3 to 3-30 a.m. & from 10-45 a.m. to 11-15 a.m. obtaining two direct hits on EGRET TRENCH one of which killed two men of "A" Company.	
			Officers reconnoitred the Right Sector with a view to relieving 4" YORKS Regt. and arranging our frontage	

WAR DIARY or INTELLIGENCE SUMMARY

Army Form C. 2118.

Place	Date	Hour	Summary of Events and Information	Remarks and references to Appendices
	30/6/17		"B" Company relieved one Company of 6th Northd Fusiliers between WREN LANE and COALS TRENCH. Relief complete by 11.30 p.m. Remainder of relief took place in the early morning of July 1st. Weather conditions poor & front trenches in muddy condition.	

Army Form C. 2118.

WAR DIARY
or
INTELLIGENCE SUMMARY.

Vol 24

CONFIDENTIAL

WAR DIARY

of

4th Battalion Northumberland Fusiliers.

From July 1st 1917 (inclusive) to July 31st (inclusive)

VOLUME III

Army Form C. 2118.

WAR DIARY
or
INTELLIGENCE SUMMARY.
(Erase heading not required.)

Place	Date	Hour	Summary of Events and Information	Remarks and references to Appendices
FRONT LINE opposite CHERISY	1/7/17 to 5/7/17		Fairly Quiet. CURTAIN TRENCH was subject to Artillery Fire & in enfilade from VIS-EN-ARTOIS & was occasionally a very unhealthy spot, especially at its junction with Sunken Road in O.31.c. (see map attached) On the evening of July 1st the enemy shelled this area very heavily but it was noticeable that end day his artillery activity lessened. Snipers and Machine Guns did not cause us much annoyance. Observation. An O.P. with a double loophole was established at the junction of LARK LANE and STORK TRENCH and from there a good view could be obtained of the enemy's back areas immediately behind FONTAINE and CHERISY for a long way back - to the DURG-HENDECOURT Road. A fine view could also be had from HORSE SHOE SAP. WORK. The main feature of work done in the past line was the amount of work done on existing and new trenches.	See attached Map No. 1

Army Form C. 2118.

WAR DIARY
or
INTELLIGENCE SUMMARY.
(Erase heading not required.)

Place	Date	Hour	Summary of Events and Information	Remarks and references to Appendices
FRONT LINE New CHERISY	1/7/17 to 5/7/17		**WORK** A. Digging 1. The new trench which we dug from CABLE TRENCH to WREN LANE was deepened and widened 2 foot of a centrum held this trench. The trench was called NORTHUMBERLAND AVENUE in our honour. 2. SWIFT TRENCH was cleaned out and generally improved, especially the South end marked K on Map No. 1 3. HORSE SHOE SAP. cleaned out and给 - bays cut between CABLE & R.E. 4. CURTAIN TRENCH deepened and widened daily. TRENCH at LARK LANE. A party of 20 men reported daily to R.E. In this work in addition to the work we did on this front trenches. Authority given to reported BTE each night for the same work. 5. D Coy. carried rations up for A.S.C. Corps each night. 6. 2/Lt G.E. CHARLIE WOOD with a few men carried out a daylight and night patrol to investigate enemy encroaching HORSE SHOE SAP. The ground is in a very bad condition - much of it all communication roads & ground signs of fighting. There were also burial dead Germans still lying there in a very bad state of decomposition. The daylight patrols had to be carried out by crawling forward from WREN LANE as this land was very exposed to enemy's view.	

Army Form C. 2118.

WAR DIARY
or
INTELLIGENCE SUMMARY.
(Erase heading not required.)

Instructions regarding War Diaries and Intelligence Summaries are contained in F. S. Regs., Part II. and the Staff Manual respectively. Title pages will be prepared in manuscript.

Place	Date	Hour	Summary of Events and Information	Remarks and references to Appendices
			7. SALVAGE. A considerable amount of salvage was collected and sent down to the Transport lines.	
			8. WIRING. About 600 yds. of concertina wire was reinforced but out in front of our sector. There was no wire worth speaking of when we went up to the front line — by the end of 4 days we had wired the whole front from the HENINEL-CHERISY Road to HORSE SHOE and HORSE SHOE SAP was wired all round. The two front Companies — A and B Coys — provided covering parties for wiring. C Coy did the wiring. The Pioneer Platoon* and every available man of E and D Coys carried up wire and iron pickets from Dump near ROOKERY.	* See next Section
			ORGANISATION: On the 108 men left behind, a Pioneer Platoon of 50 men under an officer was formed to do special work. The remainder (74 O.Rs) was left at Transport lines where training was carried out. Only 20 Officers went into action.	
			CASUALTIES. 3rd July ------- 3 O.R. wounded 4th July ------- 3 O.R. wounded 5th July ------- 1 O.R. wounded	TOTAL 9 officers (including one in support) O.R. 2 killed 9 wounded

T.M.T.

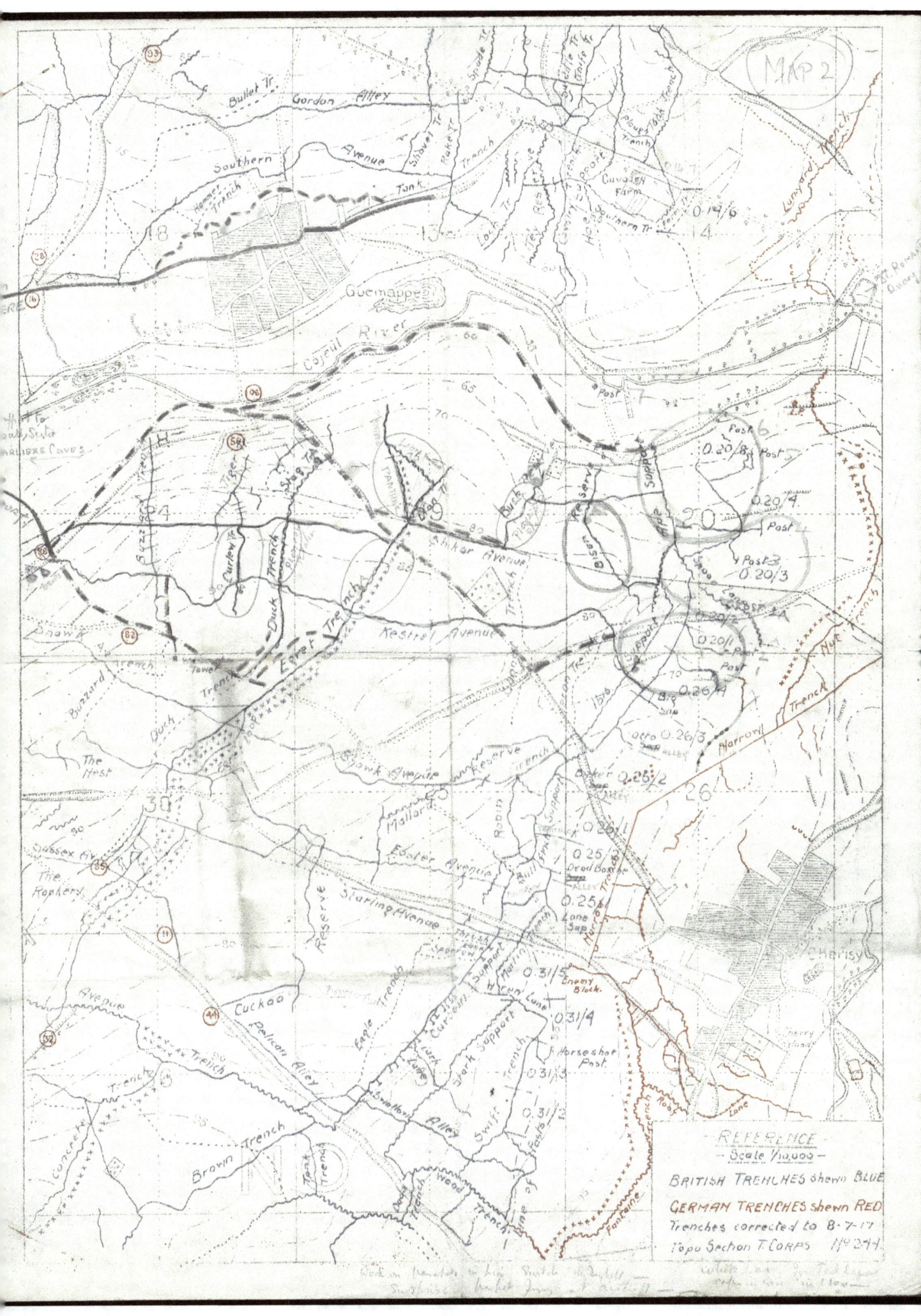

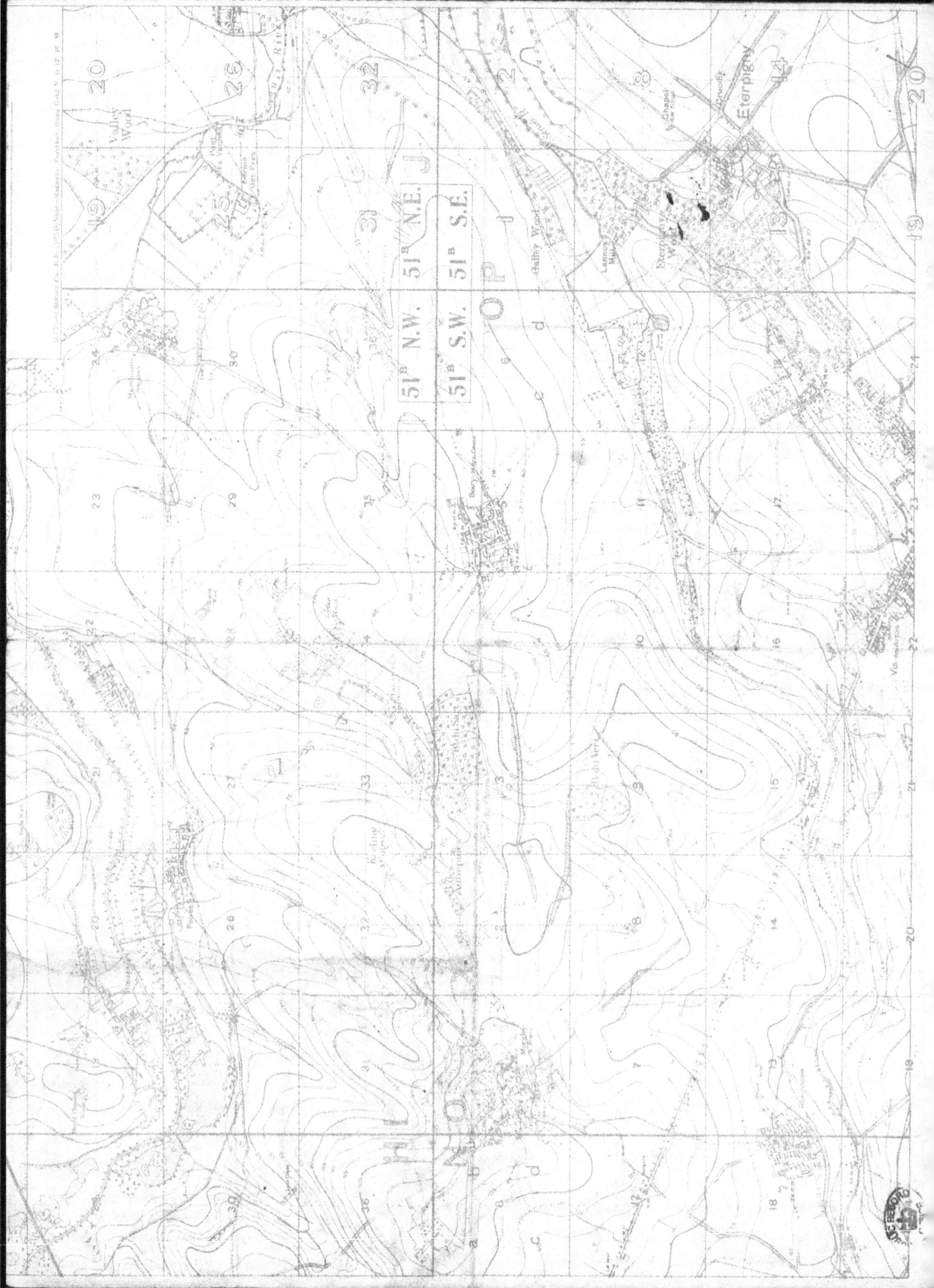

WAR DIARY
or
INTELLIGENCE SUMMARY.
(Erase heading not required.)

Army Form C. 2118.

Instructions regarding War Diaries and Intelligence Summaries are contained in F.S. Regs., Part II. and the Staff Manual respectively. Title pages will be prepared in manuscript.

Place	Date	Hour	Summary of Events and Information	Remarks and references to Appendices
FRONT LINE near CROISILLES	4/7/17 to 5/7/17		**GAS.** On night 4th/5th July, one of our Gas cylinders was burst and the bar escaped & was blown in direction of Enemy's lines. The cylinder was on our front line parapet. No one was affected by this incident except a working party which was out in front. They were slightly gassed, but apparently the detonator of the cylinder had not been exploded. In after-effects they received no ill effects. — by 2nd Notts Fus. **RELIEF** The Battalion was relieved on the early morning of the 5th July on relief proceeded to our old camp at HENIN, then becoming Brigade Reserve.	2LT
HENIN	5/7/17 to 10/7/17		Re equipment. Training, cleaning up and working parties. Working parties provided by the Battalion during this time were:—	NOTE:— 1 Group = 8 men under an NCO or Senior NCO to Office or Senior NCO in Serpt note Guns 3 Coys.
			1. 6th July ——— 5 groups — work on Mealt Dugouts in ECOST LOOP.	
			2. " " ——— 2 groups — VII Corps Dump. BOISELLES Jr. STRN. R.E. loading up trains with R.E. material & proceeding to HENIN Dark for units to unload	
			3. 7th July ——— 6 groups ——— do ——— (cp in no. 1.)	
			4. 8th July ——— do ——— do ——— do	
			5. " " ——— do ——— Improvement of MONSTER AVENUE between Left Battn HQR. and BULLFINCH TRENCH	
			6. 9th July ——— do ——— do	

Army Form C. 2118.

WAR DIARY
or
INTELLIGENCE SUMMARY.
(Erase heading not required.)

Place	Date	Hour	Summary of Events and Information	Remarks and references to Appendices
HEAUN	8/7/17	7. 9th July	wok - same as no. 1.	
	9/7/17	8. "	---- do ---- same as no. 2.	
NEUVILLE VITASSE	10/7/17 to 19/7/17		During this time the Battalion was in Divisional Reserve. Very few working parties had to be supplied and this was thought an opportunity for Training. The present programme of training was:— 7 — 7.30 am. Saluting and Squad & Platoon Drill without arms. 9.30—10.15. Physical Drill & Bayonet Fighting. 10.15. lecture by company officers. 10.30—11. Musketry. 11—12. Platoon training (including Bombing) under platoon Commander. 12—12.30. Company Drill. 2—3. Daily Instructions, Handling of Arms, Gas Drill, lectures, & communicating, shooting drill for NCO's	DLG DLG

Army Form C. 2118.

WAR DIARY
or
INTELLIGENCE SUMMARY.
(Erase heading not required.)

Place	Date	Hour	Summary of Events and Information	Remarks and references to Appendices
NEUVILLE VITASSE	10/7/17 to 19/7/17		WORK. Daily during the time the Battn was in Div. reserve a party of 2 Lt men constructed barbed wire concertinas, 40 per day under supervision of an Officer. WORKING PARTIES	
	11th July		(A) — 1 Officer and 25 men to work for 146th Fd. Coy R.E.	
	12th July		(B) — 1 N.C.O. and 12 men to work for 50th D.A.C. (loading bricks)	
	13th July		(C) — 1 Officer and 30 O.R. to work on rifle range near Camp.	
	14th July			
	15th July		(D) — 2 Groups to work for 56th Div. R.E. (loading material at trains and proceed to Henin Surtt to unload)	
	do		(E) — 1 N.C.O. and 12 men to work for 56th Div R.E. (work on shelters at HENIN SUR P).	
	16th July		(F) — Same as (E).	
	do		(G) — 3 Groups to work for 146th Coy R.E. on construction of tanks for Battn.	
	17th July		(H) — Same as (E)	
	do		(I) — Same as (G)	
	18th July		(J) — Same as (G)	

W.B.

WAR DIARY
INTELLIGENCE SUMMARY.

Place	Date	Hour	Summary of Events and Information	Remarks and references to Appendices
NEUVILLE VITASSE	18/7/17		Capt J.A. HERRIOT took over command of the Battalion Vice Lt. Col B.D. GIBSON D.S.O. to Hospital Sick.	DHG
FRONT LINE NO EN-ACTAS Sector	19/7/17		The Battalion relieved the 6th D.L.I. in the front line in the night of 18/7/20.	DHG
	19/7/17 to 23/7/17		During this tour of four days the enemy's artillery was not often but with the exception of one occasion which is described below the enemy's fire was not concentrated at any time but its shelling was not severe and the enemy's trench mortars were not subject to much artillery fire and communication trenches. Observation. We had 2 O.P.'s one at junction of DHWAN AV & BISON Tr & one at O.20.a.15.15. from the first a good view of the ground N. of the control was obtainable from the latter a good view of enemy's lines immediately in front of the line.	DHG

Army Form C. 2118.

WAR DIARY
or
INTELLIGENCE SUMMARY.
(Erase heading not required.)

Instructions regarding War Diaries and Intelligence Summaries are contained in F. S. Regs., Part II. and the Staff Manual respectively. Title pages will be prepared in manuscript.

Place	Date	Hour	Summary of Events and Information	Remarks and references to Appendices
FRONT LINE (cont)	12/4/17 (cont)		**SNIPING.** There has been a fair amount of sniping on both sides. We claim some kills one for Pte S/S SPOOR 1ANE.	
			WORK. A large amount of work was done (1) The support company and Pioneer Platoon worked on dug-outs and trenches under R.E. supervision.	
			(II) The garrison of the forward posts worked on improving the posts.	
			(III) The garrison of trenches worked on the trenches they occupied in the posts.	
			(IV) **WIRE** Except for a little wire in front of the posts there was very little done. In front of our sector when we went in there was the main line run up to strengthen the existing wire but to make a continuous line of wire in front of the posts. This work was not completed.	
			PATROLS Patrols went out every night and trouble back in during the night.	
			1. Enemy sat in front of no 1 post so regularly held a rifle.	
			2. Enemy to wire encountered near Coucelles Salient 10.15pm They attempted to get an covered position for enemy working parties.	

WAR DIARY
or
INTELLIGENCE SUMMARY.
(Erase heading not required.)

Army Form C. 2118.

Place	Date	Hour	Summary of Events and Information	Remarks and references to Appendices
PATROLS (cont)			3. No enemy seen. Found in vicinity east of SPOOR LANE	
			4. Enemy wiring in front of NUTTRENCH is 5ft high no wire in front of NO-MANS-LAND S. of/the return in this area. No trip wire found between B my no. 1 Pat and enemy sap – this is no obstacle.	
			Wire in front of enemy trench thicker O/C company sector returned cool but not seen.	
			5. No evidence of Gottfried Shell holes as posts in left company sector	
			6. Southern Branch of COLOUR Reconnoitred and no enemy met with	
			7. Enemy machine gun fired from low ground W. of BAROMETER PASSAGE QUARRY	
			RATIONS H.Q. returns to Sunken road N. of STAG TRENCH Reserve Platoon, Right & Centre I-Platoon Coy. To Junction of DUCK N. Left Coy to <del>the</del> Eron roads A.26.a.	
			CASUALTIES 2/Lt MAIN wounded. 2 O.R. killed 10 O.R. wounded DKG	

WAR DIARY or INTELLIGENCE SUMMARY

Place	Date	Hour	Summary of Events and Information	Remarks and references to Appendices
FRONT LINE	23/7/17	3.10 am	**RAID.** At 3.10 am enemy attempted to raid No 2 Post evidently with intention of getting identifications. Two 5/10 Group succeeded in working round the left flank and coming into the C.T. between Sap and front line. The Second party made a frontal bombing attack, throwing bombs at our own to the Post into the C.T. belaying owing to the prompt action taken by the N.C.O. in charge. Two men in rear were killed and the second party were driven off with bombs, the enemy leaving two dead and some of our party were wounded.	
	Night 23/7/17 to 24/7/17		The Battalion was relieved by the 58th N.F. and on relief proceeded to Suffolk camp Dickebusch arriving about 4 am. 2	
	24/7/17 to 28/7/17		Enemy attitude [quiet]. Capt Cliff Jenkins was took over Pioneers rated for R.E. to be attached to the company whilst on what of Silvercorn Pioneer Platoon on RESTRAIN, one company on making ERRETRANSON ford one Company on LON Se making.	

J.A. Cook Lieut Col

Army Form C. 2118.

WAR DIARY
or
INTELLIGENCE SUMMARY.
(Erase heading not required.)

Instructions regarding War Diaries and Intelligence Summaries are contained in F. S. Regs., Part II. and the Staff Manual respectively. Title pages will be prepared in manuscript.

Place	Date	Hour	Summary of Events and Information	Remarks and references to Appendices
SUPPORT AREA	24/1/17 & 25/1/17		RATIONS HQ Pioneer Platoon & 1 company in CURIOS Tr. to HQ. MOEUVRE company to MARLIERE CAVES. Remainder to have from of ZION Tr. and railway. OBSERVATION 1 O.P situated at WESTERN AV. at D.19.c.50.25. CAUSALTIES 1 O.R killed. 1 O.R wounded. RELIEF The Battalion relieved 5th N.F. in HQ front line, Dehors. gave to before the 6th N.F. relieved the Battalion in Support. O.J.G.O.	
FRONT LINE	Night 25/1/17 & 26/1/17		Attitude of enemy — Suites of their hergering town. Enemy switching a distinctly more pronounced air. Stokes Hoffer gave more at night on suspected working heading to No mans - land. WORK. (i) Working parties of R.E. & 1 Co. of 4th Hussars Regt. (ii) wiring of front line almost completed. (iii) Suffolt dry unused trenches is out between BISON and 13.5 Trench. (iv) Fireplaces & posts of resistance in front line worked on.	

WAR DIARY or INTELLIGENCE SUMMARY

Army Form C. 2118.

Place	Date	Hour	Summary of Events and Information	Remarks and references to Appendices
N.V.L.	3/1/17 4/5/17		(4) Sgt dug southwards for about 30 yds from elbow of 6 landing to No 1 Post with a view to establishing a flank post on the right. Posts sapt dug from No 6 Post northwards to protect valley. PATROLS were sent out all night except on our & rebel(?) (i) No enemy in SPOON LANE. (ii) Enemy sent offshoots to 1 Post still held strongly at with No plan... (iii) Enemy sent forward single men into its Could be [seen?] by Very Lights. (iv) Enemy attack on Train tunnel efforts left Company Sector between spun attempted on M.3 May CASUALTIES 1 O.R. killed, 6 O.R. wounded. RATIONS up in last town RELIEF The Battalion was relieved by 5th H.L.I. and on relief proceeded to Brig Reserve at NEUVILLE VITASSE DHG	

WORKING PARTIES SUPPLIED BY 4 Bn. NORTH'D FUSILIERS.

PERIOD 19th — 31st July 1917.

Groups	Place of Parade	Time and Date	Report to representative of	Work to be done and Locality	Tools	Haversack Rations	Work till
3	Junction of APE Support and Jungle Alley	10-0 a.m. 20/7/17	2nd/Lt. Pottle, 7th F. Co. R.E.	Deepening and widening APE Support	1 Shovel and 1 Pick per man	No	2-0.0.m
1	Junction of BISON Reserve and Jungle Alley	10-0 a.m. 20/7/17	2nd/Lt. Baldwin 7th Fld.Co. R.E.	Clearing spoil from Mined dugout in BISON Reserve.	No	No	2-0.0.m
4	Junction of APE Support & Jungle Alley	10-30 a.m. 21/7/17	2/Lt Pottle 7th Fld.Co. R.E.	Deepening and widening Jungle Alley.	1 Shovel and 1 Pick per man	No	2-30 a.m
1	Junction of BISON Reserve & Jungle Alley	10-0 p.m. 21/7/17	2nd/Lt. Baldwin 7th Fld.Co. R.E.	Work & carry dugout for M.G.C. in BISON Reserve	No	No	2-0 a.m.
4	Junction of APE Support and Jungle Alley	10-30 a.m. 22/7/17	2/Lt Pottle 7th Fld.Co. R.E	Deepening & revetting APE Support.	1 Shovel and Pick per man	No	2-30 a.m
½	Junction of BISON Reserve and Jungle Alley	8-0 a.m. 22/7/17	2/Lt Baldwin 7th Fld.Co. R.E.	Work on deep dugout for M.G.C. in Bison Res.	No	No	2-0/a.m
½	-Do-	2-0 p.m. 22/7/17	-Do-	-Do-	No	No	8-0 p.m
½	-Do-	10-0 a.m. 23/7/17	-Do-	-Do-	1 Shovel and 1 Pick per man	No	2-0 a.m.
2	Junction of ELKAR and ALBAYROSS	5-0 a.m. 24/7/17	No. 1 Section, 181 Tun.Co. R.E.	Mined Dugouts in BUCK and BISON TRENCHES.	No	Yes	—

- 2 -

GROUPS	PLACE OF PARADE	TIME AND DATE	REPORT TO AND REPRESENTATIVE OF	WORK TO BE DONE AND LOCALITY	TOOLS	HAVERSACK RATIONS	WORK TIME
2	JUNCTION OF SHIKAR AND ALBATROSS	1·0 P.M. 24/7/17	No.1 SECTION, 181. TUN.Co.R.E.	MINED DUGOUTS IN BUCK AND BISON TRENCHES.	No	YES	—
12	-DO-	9·30 P.M. 24/7/17	-DO-	-DO-	No	No	—
1	WANCOURT CHURCH	9·30 P.M. 24/7/17	2/LT POTTLE (7TH F.Co.R.E.)	Carrying to PIPE SUPPORT	No	No	2 CARRIES
4	-DO-	10·0 P.M. 24/7/17	2/LT. BALONIN 7TH FLD.Co.R.E.	Carrying for deep dugout in BISON RESERVE	No	No	-DO-
1	-DO-	10·0 P.M. 24/7/17	-DO-	Carrying for M.G. Tunnel in GERMAN DUGOUTS near BUCK RES	No	No	-DO-
4	-DO-	9·45 P.M. 24/7/17	2/LT SLATTERY 7TH FLD.Co.R.E.	Reclaiming GUEMAPPE-CHERISY ROAD	1 SHOVEL PER MAN	No	2-15 A.M.
1	JUNCTION OF SHIKRA & ALBATROSS	5·0 A.M. 25/7/17	No.1 SECTION 181, TUN.Co.R.E.	Mined dugout in BUCK AND BISON TRENCHES.	No	YES	—
1	-DO-	1·0 P.M. 25/7/17	-DO-	-DO-	No	YES	—
6	-DO-	9·30 P.M. 25/7/17	-DO-	-DO-	No	No	—
1	WANCOURT CHURCH	9·30 P.M. 25/7/17	2/LT POTTLE. 7TH F.Co.R.E.	Carrying up to PIPE SUPPORT	No	No	2 CARRIES
1	-DO-	9·45 P.M. 25/7/17	2/LT BALONIN 7TH F.Co.R.E.	Carrying for M.G. dugout in Tunnel in BUCK RESERVE	No	No	2 CARRIES
5	-DO-	9·45 P.M.	2/LT SLATTERY 7TH FLD.Co.R.E.	Reclaiming GUEMAPPES-CHERISY ROAD.	1 SHOVEL PER MAN	No	2-15 A.M.

- 3 -

GROUPS	PLACE OF PARADE	TIME	REPORT TO REPRESENTATIVE OF	WORK TO BE DONE AND LOCALITY	TOOLS	HAVERSACK RATIONS	WATER BOTTLE FULL
2	MAPLELEAF DUMP	1.0 a.m. 26/7/17	Lieut. 7th FIELD Co. R.E.	General R.E. Stores	No	No	—
1	Junction of SHIKAR and ALBATROSS	5.0 a.m. 26/7/17	No.1. Section 181 Tun. Co. R.E.	Mined dugouts in BUCK and BISON TRENCHES.	No	Yes	—
1	—Do—	1.0 p.m. 26/7/17	—Do—	—Do—	No	Yes	1
6	—Do—	9.30 p.m. 26/7/17	—Do—	—Do—	No	No	1
5	NANOURM CHURCH	9.45 a.m. 26/7/17	2/Lt. SLATTERY 7th F. Co. R.E.	GUEMAPPE–CHERISY ROAD reclaiming of	1 SHOVEL PER MAN	No	2-15 PM
1	—Do—	9.30 p.m. 26/7/17	2/Lt. POTTLE 7th F. Co. R.E.	Carrying of R.E. SUPPORT	No	No	2 cans
1	Junction of SHIKAR and ALBATROSS TR.	5.0 a.m. 27/7/17	No.1 SECTION 181 TUN. Co. R.E.	Minor dugouts in BUCK and BISON TRS.	No	Yes	1
1	—Do—	1.0 p.m. 27/7/17	—Do—	—Do—	No	Yes	1
6	—Do—	9.30 p.m. 27/7/17	—Do—	—Do—	No	No	1
2	Junction of APE SUPPORT and SPOGA LANE	10.0 a.m. 28/7/17	2/Lt. BALDWIN 7th FLD Co. R.E.	Reclaiming J.13.15 SUPPORT	1 SHOVEL PER MAN	No	2.15 am
5	Junction of APE SUPPORT and SHIKAR AV.	10.30 p.m. 28/4/17	2/Lt. POTTLE 7th F. Co. R.E.	Reclaiming APE SUPPORT	100	No	2.30 am
2	Junction of APE SUPPORT and SPOGA LANE	10.0 a.m. 29/7/17	2/Lt. BALDWIN 7th F. Co. R.E.	Reclaiming J.13.15 SUPPORT	1 SHOVEL AND 1 PICK PER MAN	No	2.15 am

- 4 -

Groups	Place of Parade	Time	Report to representative of	Work to be done and locality	Tools	Rifles	Work Time
2	Junction of Ape Support and Spoor Lane	10-0 A.M. 29/9/17	2/Lt. Baldwin 7th F. Co. R.E.	Reclaiming IBIS Support	1 Shovel and 1 Pick per man	No	2-15 a.m.
5	Junction of Ape Support and Shikar Avenue	10-30 a.m. 29/9/17	2/Lt. Pottle 7th F. Co. R.E.	Reclaiming APE Support	-do-	No	2-30 A.m.
5	Junction of Ape Support and Shikar Av.	10-30 p. 30/9/17	2/Lt. Pottle 7th F. Co. R.E.	Reclaiming APE Support	-do-	No	2-30 a.m.
2	Junction of Ape Support and Spoor Lane	10-0 p.m. 30/9/17	2/Lt. Baldwin 7th F. Co. R.E.	Reclaiming IBIS Support	-do-	No	2-15 a.m.

WAR DIARY
or
INTELLIGENCE SUMMARY.
(Erase heading not required.)

Army Form C. 2118.

Instructions regarding War Diaries and Intelligence Summaries are contained in F. S. Regs., Part II. and the Staff Manual respectively. Title pages will be prepared in manuscript.

Place	Date	Hour	Remarks and references to Appendices

SHEET 51B.S.W. Squares O & front opposite Wyatt T. & U.

Scale:- 1:20,000.

Vis-en-Artois

Chérisy

Fontaine-lès-Croisilles

Fontaine Tr.
Enemy Post
Hot Pot
Hook
Egret
Lark Lane
Sea Lion Lane
Wheat Lane
K. Castle Tr.
Captain
Snipers
Dead Cow
Marrow
TRENCH
Foster Avenue
Starling Tr.
Cuckoo
Pelican Tr.
Avenue Tr.

WAR DIARY
or
INTELLIGENCE SUMMARY.

Army Form C. 2118.

Vol 25

CONFIDENTIAL

War Diary.
of
1st Battalion Northumberland Fusiliers
From August 1st 1917 inclusive to August 31st inclusive.

VOLUME IV

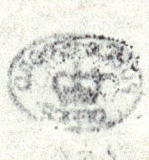

Army Form C. 2118.

WAR DIARY
or
INTELLIGENCE SUMMARY.
(Erase heading not required.)

Instructions regarding War Diaries and Intelligence Summaries are contained in F. S. Regs., Part II. and the Staff Manual respectively. Title pages will be prepared in manuscript.

Place	Date	Hour	Summary of Events and Information	Remarks and references to Appendices
NEUVILLE VITASSE N19b71.92. Batt.Hq.?	1/8		The Batt. having moved into B. de Reserve from the left Batt. Sector Pt. sub- (Battalion) Sector of Vis-en-Artois the previous night i.e. 31/7/18. morning was devoted to cleaning of equipment and clothing. The weather during the four days in B.de Reserve was wet so no actual parade could take place save those of clothing in 2nd inst. and bathing on 1st inst. (morning) the dug-outs situated in the Trenches E of the cross-roads N20 a17 Neuville Vitasse, occupied by the Coys were in a wet and uncomfortable condition. Some 150 or 200 lengths of duckboarding were procured & placed in the dug-outs & Trenches which considerably added to the comfort of occupation. The following working parties were formed during this period	By/M/gr 5/3 S.W.
	August 3rd & 4th		1NCO & 12 men at 9a/m to Div. Bath Neuville Vitasse to construct tanks in connection with appliment from Bath, under R.E.	

WAR DIARY or INTELLIGENCE SUMMARY

Army Form C. 2118.

Place	Date	Hour	Summary of Events and Information	Remarks and references to Appendices
NEUVILLE VITASSE	4th	6.30 p.m.	The Batt. proceeded by Platoons to the camp M24d2.8 authorities when the 7th W. Rd. became R.d. Divisional Reserve.	
Camp M24d 2.8	5th	10 a.m.	Church Parade on Parade ground with the 6th Northumberland Fus. was held. Q. coy. inspection in the afternoon.	
Def. Sheet 51cSW 1:10,000	6th		Regtl. Batt. parade was held at 9.15 a.m. — the remainder of the morning being devoted to Training in Bayonet fighting, General Mounting & duties; Company Drill; Gun teams Drill opened fire on many of 6th "Specialist training" Coy offices	
	10th		from 11 a.m. to 12.30 p.m. The range was available on 7th & Co.d & 8th a Lewis Gun Competition was fired and Platoon Musketry Competition consisting of two practices — i) Grouping & ii) Application, were also fired. Early morning parade of the was held daily from 7 a/m to 7.15 a/m when an & Platoon drill was practised for Platoon competition in Tirmont & drill.	
	11th	9.30 p.m.	Regmt Sergt. Major's Parade was held prior to the Ceremonial Parade	

WAR DIARY or INTELLIGENCE SUMMARY

Army Form C. 2118.

Place	Date	Hour	Summary of Events and Information	Remarks and references to Appendices
NEUVILLE-VITASSE Camp M24 d 2.8.	11	11.45—	Reg. Rec. held at 11.45 a/m at which the S.O.C. 149th Inf. Bde Brigadier General presented medals to the following recipients:- M.M. to Sgt PITTENDRY. The G.O.C. also judged the drill turn-out of "A" Coy "2008509 He PEARSON R.Platoon and presented the prize-cup to the winning l/c CLARKS. "20817 "Mc CLURE R. Platoon together with two huge cups for "B" Coy 200574 Sgt SPINTLE R. Platoon Musketry Competition & Lewis Gun Team 1207920 Pte ANDERSON M. 1204607 "NICHOLAS Competition. Results as below:- No 3. Platoon 1st Drill, 1st Marchpast & Turnout Competition. No 2 " 1st Shooting Competition. No 1 " L.G. Team 200442 l/cpl HEALEY — L.G Competition Team The remainder of the day was devoted to Sport. The reg's Football Team won the inter-Cpl Scothall.	
	12	10 a/m 1.15 p/m	Church Parade held on Batt Parade ground. "D" Coy moved off to the trenches Pt B Co Sect - R.R Batt.	

Army Form C. 2118.

WAR DIARY
or
INTELLIGENCE SUMMARY.
(Erase heading not required.)

Instructions regarding War Diaries and Intelligence Summaries are contained in F. S. Regs., Part II. and the Staff Manual respectively. Title pages will be prepared in manuscript.

Place	Date	Hour	Summary of Events and Information	Remarks and references to Appendices
NEVILLE-VITASSE Cant. M24d21.8 to	4/5/17		ent. sector & "B" Coy. moved at 1.30 p.m. followed by "C" Coy Bays. at 2/c & 2.30 p.m. respectively. Hdqrs moved at 2.45 p.m. The relief was complete by 7 p.m.	
		WORKING PARTIES	During the period in Div. Reserve the following working parties were found :-	
		5-10"	Daily at 9 a.m. 1 NCO & 12 men to Div. Baths NEUVILLE VITASSE. 7 Daily at	
		5-11"		
		5"	A carg party of 1 Off. 4 NCO's & 30 men who reported to "S" Head Cg R.E. at 0.13.d.9.4. to carry fascicles to pt. 0.20.a.5.8.	
			at 10.30 p.m. Two journeys were made, I suggests being carried pgt 2 men.	
		8"	2 parties (2 NCO's & 16 men) proceeded to ERVILLERS & AYETTE no Hayrakes party in relief of those provided by 1st Divisn.	

Army Form C. 2118.

WAR DIARY
or
INTELLIGENCE SUMMARY.
(Erase heading not required.)

Instructions regarding War Diaries and Intelligence Summaries are contained in F. S. Regs., Part II. and the Staff Manual respectively. Title pages will be prepared in manuscript.

Place	Date	Hour	Summary of Events and Information	Remarks and references to Appendices
FRONT LINE FONTAINE-CROISELLES SECTOR	12/1/16	1 A.M.	"D" Coy was in New Coy Sector on Right of ROTTEN ROW & PUG LANE (taken over from 21st Divn). "C" Coy from ROTTEN ROW (inclusive) to Junction of Pat. 3rd Coy sector out at 3 (inclusive) & SWIFT SHOOT. "B" Coy tied on left Coy sector Pat. 3 to HORSESHOE SAP (inclusive) at WREN LANE (exclusive). "A" Coy & Pioneer Platoon (30 strong) in support of PELICAN LANE, Batn. HQrs in AVENUE TR. The four Coy Bases on the whole quiet except Pack Bosch Heavy T.M. firing from NW corner of FONTAINE Wood on centre (C) Coy Rd. Frosts. Shir manually opened at Sten 70 - once along appt. once along enemy front about 10.30 p.m. 9f own machgfl reported to Batty. of W. Stens & did not cause trouble on night of 15/16. Night of 15/16. was active. No. 2 a/m up at usual time - much light shells, MG Qns & TM fidentin (above named) was directed against left Coy. sector. Much post observed. No possess near Pat. 19 (C Coy) & Pat. 15 (B Coy) - Moment observed & enemy opened out at 600 & 1000 yds Ranges with effect. Much cleaning of gun & rifle bombs was done & over 350 duckboards laid about the front line. The weather was fair & dry - Relief carried out on 14.9.15.3 inst. An exchange of the formerly took out our night by 5 army super infanticide of trench artillery enemies.	

WAR DIARY
or
INTELLIGENCE SUMMARY.
(Erase heading not required.)

Army Form C. 2118.

Place	Date	Hour	Summary of Events and Information	Remarks and references to Appendices
SUFFOLK FONTAINE- CROISILLES & ACHERY Sects	16th to 26th	2p.m.	The Scout Cy i.e. 'D' Cy was relieved by a Cy of 3rd NF & proceeded to EGRET LOOP trench into support area. 'C' Cy who relief proceeded to the Nest to stem Batt Hq & moved at 4.30 p.m. 'B' Cy & 'A' Cy proceeded to EGRET TR. & MALLARD TR.) Cr.180 Reserve Tr. respectively. Working parts of 200 odd were furnished each night for R.E's. Work went on dug-outs under construction & support tr. improvement of trench - dugout & checkerboard revetments &c. On the night of 19/20th all available work (some 300 men) was supplied for work on the greats no. they cut at night. Sea p.h.m. & 2 a.m. I returned chilly normal) took place about EGRET LOOP North end of EGRET TR. & Support Areageneral - round about 9-10 p.m. & in the evening the FOSTER AVENUE was often received by bursts of 77 mm.	

Army Form C. 2118.

WAR DIARY
or
INTELLIGENCE SUMMARY.
(Erase heading not required.)

Place	Date	Hour	Summary of Events and Information	Remarks and references to Appendices
Suffolk Area	16/4/20		The Bn. furnished the uncommissioned working parties during the period 16/4/4T	
"El Nad"	17th		4 groups at N30.b.2.4	
		6.0 a/m	Report to No 2 Sec La. 181st Tunnel Coy R.E. Motor object	work on Mallard, Chicken Co. HQs & Chicken
			Junction of Esgr & T. Loop with Find Av.	
		2 p.m.	ditto	ditto
		6 "	ditto	
		10 p.m.	"	
	18th		Fourteen groups were furnished at same times as previous day & for same work	
	19th		12 groups were furnished at same times as previous day & same work.	
			5 groups reported at junction of FOSTER AV. & CHICKEN TR. at 5 a/m. 2/m. 10/m. had g.o. p.m. 30 groups at last mused tr. & 1 each at previous times. They reported to 181st Tunnel Cy R.E. numbered in T.M. sapper near SWIFT O 31.d.4.4.	
	20th		4 groups at N30.b.2.4 at 6 a/m to No3 Sec for 181st T. Saclay for work on HALLARD & CHICKEN dugouts. 1 group at SWIFT AV. & CHICKEN TR. at 5 a/m. to same Coy R.E. for work on T.M. emplacements near SWIFT O31.d.4.4	

WAR DIARY or INTELLIGENCE SUMMARY

Army Form C. 2113.

Place	Date	Hour	Summary of Events and Information	Remarks and references to Appendices
FRONT LINE	20/4	2 p.m.	Bn. relieved the 5th North'd Fus. i/l the front line – the four Coys. took up exactly similar dispositions as previous four days. V3 "A"Coy front line left – "B"Coy, "C"Coy, "D"Coy in "B"Coy in support in PELICAN LANE (found R.S. & Piccad. Platn.) The four Coy fronts were considerably quieter than previous four 12/4 of. No attempt of the enemy afford [?] & we managed them entirely on regards patrolling, some prisoners. All TM's (Stokes) were exchanged as in two occasions our artillery replying. The band end of quickly 10th Mai. The weather was fine, with occasional showers. A considerable amount of work was done (particulars) as right. The front system was cleared up & a large no. of german trolls, dug in SWIFT & SWALLOW Tr., PELICAN was cleared. Attacks of WOOD LANE to No.16 Post. Two pillboxes were constructed - one at M.19 B.8.7 & the other between posts No.14 & 15. Part were dug down & cab[?] trompled with dug-out tracks running to enemy. The support Coy in SUNKEN RD. did a cavage of dug outs for C.O. Hq. Comp.[?] empty material for R.E. followers & covered were[?] concentrated aromat[?] the PIONEER Platoon	
HORSE SHOE SAP to PUO LANE				

WAR DIARY
or
INTELLIGENCE SUMMARY.
(Erase heading not required.)

Army Form C. 2118.

Instructions regarding War Diaries and Intelligence Summaries are contained in F. S. Regs., Part II. and the Staff Manual respectively. Title pages will be prepared in manuscript.

Place	Date	Hour	Summary of Events and Information	Remarks and references to Appendices
Battn Reserve 2A Camp Nazasu	24/4	2 P.M	The Relief of the Battn. by the 5th Norfolks commenced. Coy's of the relief proceeded to Battn Reserve Camp at N23a5.9 B&C Coys being on the W. and E of the MAIN NEUVILLE–TRESCAULT Rd. & D Coy. N. of same. 'A' Coy moved from PELICAN SUNKEN RD to CONCRETE Ts as reserve Coy to 1st Batt (fr. out-diates) reg— 5th N.F. The Relief was complete by 4 p.m.	
"	25/4	Night of 23/24 to 24/4	1) Coy. of 9 p.m. 19 gun works on T.M. emplacements near SWIFT No. 3306... 2) Many of 24th Batt. 3 groups ≈ located at 9am & 7th Z. Co. R.E. grs unknown Staff in HINDENBURG LINE pointy worked till 4fm — Both also working Posts were found by selected Coy.	
"	25/4		The morning and afternoon were allotted to baths, cleaning up and cecitly parade during the afternoon.	
"	26-	10.30 a/n	Church Parade was held headed YMCA marker W side of camp.	
"	27"	11 a/n	'C' Coy was inspected by C.O. & O.C. P. & D Coys did not parade being at work. Parades were carried on as [?] forwards	

Army Form C. 2118.

WAR DIARY
or
INTELLIGENCE SUMMARY.
(Erase heading not required.)

Instructions regarding War Diaries and Intelligence Summaries are contained in F. S. Regs., Part II. and the Staff Manual respectively. Title pages will be prepared in manuscript.

Place	Date	Hour	Summary of Events and Information	Remarks and references to Appendices
Billets Reserve Gump N25 a 5.9	24/4/18		Bn. 1 & 3 Coys found working parties Regt. working under RE. The Amnon construction RE. remainder of Bn. on training. Provided such night one 3 groups for work under RE Cap in dug-outs & 1 in the suffer trenches. Some 450 in all. Groups were provided by day & men kept at work. Relieving at 5 p.m.	
HINDENBURG SUPPORT LINE SHAFTS	28		The Battn. moved into Hindenburg support Line & provided work parties as per attached note for 4 days shell, supplies of Cay to "A" similar end of Trench J3, J3, J8 were shot. All men were accommodated in tunnel nine beneath trench. The tunnel on the continuous was in places involved on account of wet or broken shafts. The accommodation was good in many places, two being several baths for the men is some Cay. sector.	
	29		Lt. Lane visited being accompanied by a Staff Myd. Off 2. Went shown the tunnel. On the morning MP. Gen BLACKLOCK & the other Proplets arranged by 16. Bd Exhens.	
	30		See Area Orders were accompanied by 5th on the Staff Rep. All volunteers of Wickers LM Guns mostly up/introduced mounting

Army Form C. 2118.

WAR DIARY
or
INTELLIGENCE SUMMARY.
(Erase heading not required.)

Instructions regarding War Diaries and Intelligence Summaries are contained in F.S. Regs., Part II. and the Staff Manual respectively. Title pages will be prepared in manuscript.

Place	Date	Hour	Summary of Events and Information					Remarks and references to Appendices
			DAILY WORKING PARTIES.					
			STRENGTH OF PARTY	TIME OF PARADE	REPORT TO	PLACE	TIME TO COMMENCE WORK	WORK TO BE DONE	TOOLS	HAVERSACK RATIONS
COY									
A			2.6ft R.O.DR	8pm	174th Tunnelling Coy	Dugouts SWIFT SUP	9pm	Working new dugouts	No	YES thumbnails
B			2.0TR	"	"	"	"	"	"	"
C			1.5ft 2.2 OR	6.30pm	7th Leeds Rgt	LARK TRENCH	9.30pm	Reclaiming LARK TR.	25 shovels 7 picks	No
B			1.5ft 34 OR	15pm	181st Tunnelling Coy	Junction of CUCKOO TR & PIONEER AV. O.28.C.20.05	11pm	Working dugouts	No	YES thumbnails
C			1.5ft 2.5 OR	4am	174th Tunnelling Coy	Dugouts SWIFT SUP	5am	do	No	do
C			9.OR	6am.	181st Tunnelling Coy	Junction of CUCKOO TR + PIONEER AV. O.28.C.W.00	7am	do	No	do
A			10ft 2.5 OR	12 noon	174th Tunnelling Coy	SWIFT SUPPORT	1pm	do	No	do
A			9.OR	2pm	161st Tunnelling Coy	Junction of CUCKOO TR + PIONEER SUPP	3pm	do	No	do
A			9 OR	9am	BATT 1Q	Rest 1TR	9am		YES	No
			9 OR	9am		SHAFT 20	9am	Reconstructing dugouts etc	10 shovels 7 picks	No

30431 8/17

S.N.F. FRONTAGE

17/6/7

1/10,000 Brit & Boch trenches
QUEMAPPE — FONTAINE

Vol 26

CONFIDENTIAL

WAR DIARY of
4th Battalion NORTHUMBERLAND FUSILIERS

From September 1st 1917 (inclusive) to September 30th (inclusive)

VOLUME V.

Army Form C. 2118.

WAR DIARY
or
INTELLIGENCE SUMMARY.
(Erase heading not required.)

Instructions regarding War Diaries and Intelligence Summaries are contained in F.S. Regs., Part II. and the Staff Manual respectively. Title pages will be prepared in manuscript.

Place	Date	Hour	Summary of Events and Information	Remarks and references to Appendices
HINDENBURG SUPPORT LINE	1/9/17	11 a/m	The Batt. was relieved by the 6th North'd Fus who took over all working parties etc 12 noon on Relief the Batt proceeded by ½ platoon to Cross Rds HENIN & thence by Motor to DURHAM LINES CAMP. S.11 a Ref. 57 b S.W. 1/20,000. The accommodation was good - all huts being NISSON ones and Cy lines etc own Cookhouses, Mess Huts, Drying Sheds, Mess Halts including many other buildings.	
DURHAM LINES CAMP S.II A Ref. 57 b S.W.	2/9/17		The morning was devoted to Cy parades of cleaning equipment, arms clothing etc. Daily Inspection were held after dinner t the remainder of the day available for recreation - 4 grounds were set a considerable amt. of work on the Camp - a large Cookhouse & several Cookhouses laid tracks templates for flooring, Ablution Benches & several ducktracks laid trailed.	
	3/9/17	9.30 a/m	Batt Parade followed by 20 min. Batt Drill on ground immediately N. of to cm. trench Northern side of Camp. Remainder of morning was devoted to Training - Rifle Sciences, Drill, Platoon & Cy & Bayonet & Physical Training instruction. The Officers entertained 8 American Officers & other Guests to a Batt. dinner.	
	4/9/17	9.30 a/m	Batt Parade & Drill; the remainder of the morning spent on Cy Training as on 3/9/17. Daily Inspection held in the afternoon Inoculation Sick [unclear] followed. A considerable amt. of work was done on the Camp during the day. [unclear] Ply [unclear] Cookhouse & [unclear] - 1 Cookhouse Stove built, all Latrine seat letts

(A9597.) Wt. W12391/M2193. 75,000. 1/17. D.D. & L., Ltd. Forms/C/2118/14

WAR DIARY / INTELLIGENCE SUMMARY

Army Form C. 2118.

Place	Date	Hour	Summary of Events and Information	Remarks and references to Appendices
DURHAM LINES Camp SHIA	4th		with our tinfoil slabs — were put being freely made & general cleaning up of once round the Camp Hy effected.	
	5th	12.30 pm	The Batt. commenced to move into the flight. Relief Rt Subsection relief of 6 C.O.L.S. 'D' Cy moved off the Lines followed by 'C' Cy at 1 hr. B & D arrived at 1.30 & 3 pm respectively. Hy 3 at 1 pm. The order of Bg to be by an order :— Rt Cy 'D'; Centre Cy 'C'; Left Cy 'B'; Support Cy 'A'; Bison Tr.; Pioneer Platoon (30 strong) in Buck Reserve. Bath. Hy. in STPO Trench. Old Bomb Gunpit & Dugouts working Parties were found as unders :— A Cy 3 guards with R.E. supervision north JACKDOW Tr. D " " " " " " " " " "BUFFALO"	
LEFT Section			The night passed very quietly with exception of some light trench mortaring on the right of Right Coy area of Spoor Lane & Iris Support.	
Right-Sub- Section Front Line			1 Guard worked on revettment of Rt. Cy trenches under R.E supervision from 8.30 am Tues	
	6th		" " " Left " " " " " The day passed quietly — very slight shelling [Turkey?] place of SHIROR Nn about [illegible] 6 B.K.M. Rt. [illegible] Registered always the left upper dug about 9–10 h.m. [illegible] [illegible] gunpits in each Cy street were formed as on night of 5th	

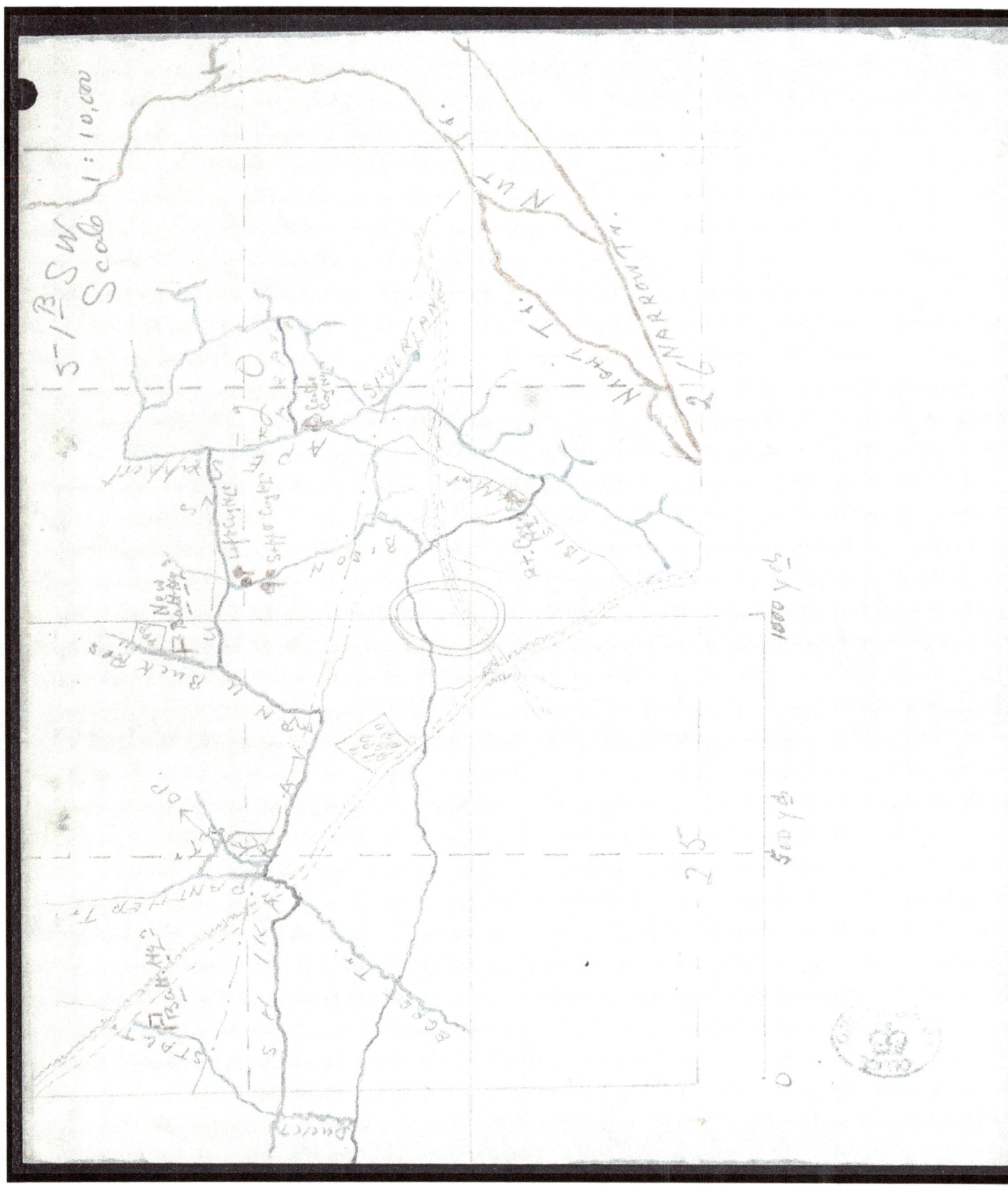

HANF

HANF

WAR DIARY
or
INTELLIGENCE SUMMARY.
(Erase heading not required.)

Army Form C. 2118.

Place	Date	Hour	Summary of Events and Information	Remarks and references to Appendices
Right Sub-Section Left Section Div. Sector	6th Contd		Night of 6/7 - a certain amt. of duckboarding & wiring were done by 'B' & 'D' Coys. Wire was put out into the gap south of SPOOR LANE between the two Coys. sectors. Duckboarding was carried on in SHIKAR AVENUE between APEX Support & BUFFALO front line. Coys. section were employed by revetment, widening deepening etc. under R.E's. More wiring was put out & duckboarding completed along SHIKAR AV. between APEX Support & BUFFALO.	
	7th 8th			
	9th	2 a.m.	Relief commenced by 5th N.F. in order of Centre Coy; Left Coy; Support; Right Coy; was relieved about 6 p.m. KESTREL AV. being used. Coys. proceeded to Support Area:- A Coy in MARLIERE CAVES; B Coy - ERST Trench; C Coy in CURLEW Tr; D Coy in LION & DUCK Trenches; Pioneer Platoon in BUZZARD Tr & H.Q. Back in ALBATROSS LONG BANK. Review of Period in front line. Much excellent patrolling work was done, each Coy sending out one patrol each night in addition to a strong Officer patrol carried out twice by 2/O Davies. This latter was carried out twice unmolested; SPOOR LANE & other pts of the front a useful amt of enemy H.Q. took place, who retaliated & Shelly that area. Enemy trench mortar activity was negligible. Some Minnies relatia for much Shelly that our Artillery carried out on enemy trenches Further on our 9.45 HEAVY TM. in COUNTRY LANE [illegible] [illegible]	

WAR DIARY
or
INTELLIGENCE SUMMARY.

Army Form C. 2118.

Place	Date	Hour	Summary of Events and Information	Remarks and references to Appendices
Support Area Left Section	9th		Wiring of BISON Tr. was carried on until the wiring being continued for 6 yards of DCy - the wire pickets & coils of Barbed wire reached by 5 m. t. That material i.e. screw pickets & coils of Barbed wire was carried up to BISON Tr. For the wiring with on BISON other work consisted of groups in cmdy:- 3 groups BCy LIGHT Dump at 9AM for work on Halon dugouts on BISON under 181st Tunnel Cy. 6 groups CCy at 9.30 AM for work on McShgent behind Buccleuch on under 181st Tunnel Cy. 1 group DCy Coy at 2"TM amm to Front line under 447 Cy RE. 3 "" "" HICK Dump carry north material for 447Cy. Off.n. under 447th Cy R.E. 1 "" "" sept at South COEVRE Valley at	
	10th		A little work was done by C Cy in building timbered shelters & improvement of exits & finishing etc. on item Cy. section At night the same groups were found for work enverlop	
	11th		as on previous night of 9th	
	12th		1 NCO & 10 men at 9.30 AM dymk at 2.0.PM. on 12th additional carry parties for 2"TM am. Btth. & Stokes Amm	
	13 a.		Mining - 6 groups carried out ↓ dummies under 2 IP Durrar for G.C. Coy for RE dumps, HENIN Tam Pit on HENIN - HENINEL Rd Front line Kent lane of 5th NE Tam Front line Rt.[?] out each [?]	
	2.30PM		Relief of 5th	

WAR DIARY or INTELLIGENCE SUMMARY

Army Form C. 2118.

Place	Date	Hour	Summary of Events and Information	Remarks and references to Appendices
Left Section	13th		Disposition of Coys were as previous tour of 4 days in Rt sub-sector — A Coy on the Rt, C Coy centre; B Coy left Coy; B Coy in support on the crassier. Both MG² were in Brick Reserve, the change having been made by 5.30 P.M. on 11th Sept. Night of 13th morning of 14th - 3 groups worked on a reinstatement of Rt & Left Bays' section. Night of 13/14 - an afternoon patrol 1/Offr & 15 OR reconnoitred SPOIL LANE approaching it from Rt Coy	
Right Sub-Section				
Div Section	14th		trenches. Enemy hot E and W SPOIL LANE were held but nightfall the bright to allow of patrol working round the hot. Day caught passed quietly with very little of interest taking place. A minor operation carried out by 50th A.I. took place during the aft & evening. It consisted of a raid on a large part of 3 Coy — Object to enter Boche trenches — secure prisoners, capture equipment, arms, damage & destroy dug-outs & generally harrass the enemy. This confirmed the first phase.	
	15th	4 P.M	Zero time a heavy barrage of corps heavy artillery - 50th D.W RF.A & 12 & 16th Div R.F.A together with much machine gun fire & executed...	

T2134. Wt. W708—776. 50000. 4/15. Sir J. C. & S.

WAR DIARY
or
INTELLIGENCE SUMMARY.
(Erase heading not required.)

of Stokes Mortars, Medium & 4" mortars firing Thermite, this barrage covered all the Sector front & had the desired effect of completely capturing the enemy & the latest & finished of the attack. Our own barrage was at the same time brought down by medium TMs. Two Coys of 9th D.L.I raided the enemy lines East Hufbert from O.26.c.25.10.65. O.26.c.50.70. while on the East our front group of Durry Pigeon fired in further night of 14/15th was used successfully & Batteries and 10.S.R. These dummies were kept up for 40 mins from Zero of the guns opening at Zero time. The Barrage rcvd was completely successful – 32 prisoners being taken – enemy Trenches broken & blown up & several dugouts set fire to. All slight Casualties in our own but 1 enemy were reported by an officer. If staff officers, two per Coy taking up also on the flanks The Casualty the result of this was undoubtedly settled for this work. The enemy arty acted upon at 4.2 p.m being a success the enemy arty shelled at 4.2 p.m being numerously distributed along the whole Sector which evidently.

amount of fire directed on the actual trenches for when its raid was made. The raiders suffered no casualty. Counter barrage lasted for some 3/4 hr. but the enemy shell chiefly satisfied that he had successfully quelled an attack on a large scale, became quieter down & by 5-5.15 p.m. the situation was again normal on our front.

2nd Phase & consisted of a raid in the same place as in 1st Phase - but reaches remained in enemy trenches 10 mins instead of 30 mins as in 1st Phase

1.40 p.m Zero Hour - A second effective barrage on scale as in 1st Phase was brought down on Enemy Trenches - 2 numerous arms on our own front & Raiding Parties effected a safe entry into enemy front trench - the raid was still successful - may dead enemy seen; Ruins; Ruins went on to Supp at Trench & capturing 2 rkrs - 1 T.M. light + 3 prisoners. They suffered slight casualties returning & 2 of the 3 prisoners were killed, while being brought back. Enemy barrage came along with a minute of our own opening & appeared to be rather more concentrated on

WAR DIARY
or
INTELLIGENCE SUMMARY

the Rt. section also the rest was taking place. The same procedure was adopted in repeating all light signals sent up by the enemy.

3rd Phase - consisted of a Gas Attack with Projectors also in the coun locality. This was carried out at 4.3 a.m. 16 inst. some 500 projectors being projected successfully. At the same, gas shells were fired by artillery and 18/dm. fired several rapid bursts for 10 mins. The Attack of the enemy after the second phase had been very quiet - no very lights being sent up in normally until 3.30 a.m. It was however located in E. of SPOOR LANE that midnight many batteries of intense work being in progress between 2 a.m. 13" & 3 a.m. 16 & not until 3.30 a.m. & not until steam. At 3.30 a.m. the situation changed from quiet to normal- the enemy fully up many lights, slight MG fire taking place again; from the 1st phase until 10 p.m. 15/4/17 many of our Spandau breakages withdrawn & the casualties of personnel accumulated in dug-outs. In this way all casualties were reduced to a minimum.

Our total casualties being 1 Officer died of wounds; 1 other 18 wounded; 2 O.R. shell shocked.

WAR DIARY
INTELLIGENCE SUMMARY.
(Erase heading not required.)

Army Form C. 2118.

Place	Date	Hour	Summary of Events and Information	Remarks and references to Appendices
	16th		The damage done to our trenches was considerable - several directs being made in SHIKAR AVENUE, one or two in BUFFALO & APE SUPPORT, also in KESTREL AV. about junction of IBIS SUPPORT & KESTREL AVENUE. All this damage was completely cleared & made good by midnight. Hostile shelling was slightly more evident - one gun shelling SHIKAR AV. & extent BISON Tr. with planting fire 10-1 p.m. Night of 16th a continuous fire was put out in the low ground on left of Pt. Coy.	
	17th		Company of ours & usual 3 groups of Pt. Coy became of left Coy. worked portion of line; Usual 3 groups of Pt. Coy became of left Coy worked under REs on new trench & one patrol was sent out. The dummies were brought in from in front of Post 4. & like to DENT'S DUMP where they were carried back to R.E. dump HENIN by 6 "NF. The Batt. was relieved from the front line by 5 NF. Relief commenced at 3 p.m. 16go proceeded to Reserve Camp in N15 c&d & N21 c. A,B,+D Coys in Sunken Rd N15-d S of WANCOURT-TILLOY Rd; Trench NE of the Rd & in dugouts on WANCOURT TILLOY Rd; HQ 2 & C'Coy in tents & shelters near abrit Bank in N21 a. Relief was complete by 6 p.m.	

WAR DIARY
or
INTELLIGENCE SUMMARY.
(Erase heading not required.)

Army Form C. 2118.

Place	Date	Hour	Summary of Events and Information	Remarks and references to Appendices
Bde Reserve Camp N21a.N15c&d	18th		The morning was devoted to general cleaning of arms equipment – Daily Defectus were held by Coys & incidents for differences of kit, etc. taken.	
	19th		Roy Parade for Rifle Services & inspection was held during the morning. Coys held parades as on 19th inst. The Baths at NEUVILLE VITASSE were available from 2.0 P.M. till 5.30 p.m. all Ranks being marched to the Bath & served with a clean change etc.	
	20th		A draft of 84 other Ranks which arrived at the Detail Camp M29 proceeded to join the Batt. & were posted to Coys. while in Bde Reserve the Batt. provided 4 groups from 9 A.M.–12.30 P.M. & 2–4 P.M. daily for work on the reconstruction of the Camp – Four shelters – dugouts were accepted & 2 completed in the Bank N21a – while B, D & P Coys commenced drains in their own lines & head and led duckboards.	
	21st	10 a.m	The Batt. was relieved from Bde Reserve by 5 Yorks Regt. & proceeded by Platoons to Camp A DURHAM Lines. G.S.11.a.	

Place	Date	Hour	Summary of Events and Information	Remarks and references to Appendices
Nissen Hut Camp CAMPA. DURHAM LINES SH.C.	21st	3 P.M.	B & C Coys proceeded to FICHEUX for work on Horse-Standings & hutments etc. Gun Artillery wrote quarter. 1 group from A Coy - relieved a similar group of 5th Yorks Regt. at SOUTHAMPTON Siding - by 12 noon for similar work etc.	
"	22nd		Working parties according to attached table were found by th Batt.s from 22nd to 25th inclusive	
		9.30 P.M.	All available ranks paraded for 2 hr. Rifle Team Drill-Salute etc. Saw 12 O.R. use the Outside Gun Patch in its camp & samples were made with messing munly clean Groundsheets, loose filled, turny letters of Nissen huts & covering of thick Heavy cement as floor of other to trenches.	
	23rd		Routine of working parties.	
	24th		As on previous day.	
	25th	6.30 P.M.	B & C Coys returned from FICHEUX having been relieved by 6th NF who	

Army Form C. 2118.

WAR DIARY
or
INTELLIGENCE SUMMARY.
(Erase heading not required.)

Instructions regarding War Diaries and Intelligence Summaries are contained in F.S. Regs., Part II. and the Staff Manual respectively. Title pages will be prepared in manuscript.

Place	Date	Hour	Summary of Events and Information	Remarks and references to Appendices
CAMP A	25th		Troops were all working parties from 6pm 25th inst.	
DURHAM LINES	26th	7.30-7.45 am	Batt Parade - Musketry Drill without Arms. Officers NCO under RSM.	
BOISLEUX au MONT S11 a		9 am	Batt. Parade in Drill Order :: The Range at M24a-M23b. was used by Coys as under; D Coy 9.30 am; A Coy 10.30 am; B Coy 1.30 pm C Coy. 2.30 p.m.	
		9.30-10.30 am	A Coy. Platoon Drill, Musketry & intell. of arm	
		9.30-11-0 am	B & C Coy " " "	
		11-11.30 am	Batt Parade for B & C Coys	
			Daily Inspection of Field under Coy. arrangements	
	27th	7.30-7.45 am	Batt. Parade - Musketry Drill without Arms - Officers NCOs under Adjt. RSM for Arm Drill etc as on 26th inst. Two Coys. used the range. Remainder of the Batt - carrying on Training.	
	28th		Routine as on 27th inst. Eighteen Coy proceeded to the Ralli Boiry-Becquerelle.	
	29th		The Batt relieved the 9th D.L.I. in the front line of the Right Section of Div. Sector Rt. sub-section	

WAR DIARY
INTELLIGENCE SUMMARY
(Erase heading not required.)

Army Form C. 2118.

Place	Date	Hour	Summary of Events and Information	Remarks and references to Appendices
DURHAM LINES	29th	12.15 A.M.	Bn. A. & D. Coys. proceeded by light Rly. from DURHAM LINES to TONBRIDGE Station HENIN, thence by march route via HINDENBURG Supp. line, CONCRETE Tr. to front line of Bn. sub-section.	
S.11.0. S.6.S.W.		1.15	B & C Coys. proceeded by light Rly. from DURHAM LINE to TONBRIDGE E STA. Y. thence by route to the line. The order & disposition of Coys. as follows:- Right Coy:- Ribbon - Tank - Dodo Tce. 'B'Coy. Centre Coy:- Hood Lane & Swallow Tr. 1st AVENUE als. 'A' Coy. Left Coy:- Swift Support, PIONEER ALLEY - HORSE SHOE SAP - D Coy. Support Coy. ('C' Coy) & Pioneer Ribbon shelter - a chalky hole PELICAN DUKE Rd. Batt. Hqrs in AVENUE Tr. Relief was complete by 4.45 p.m. The remainder of the day might passed without any event worthy of mention - attitude of enemy remained quiet. Hostile shelling was negligible. Some sniping was done with good effect wherever heads shewn. Enemy put up 2 Red Balloon opp. left Bn. front - that settler fell behind his line in accurate T. in the second our travellers permitted to our tower line slightly forward.	

Rt. Sect.
Rt. Sub Sect.
W.16. 21 b.
031 b 75.15.

WAR DIARY
INTELLIGENCE SUMMARY

Army Form C. 2118.

Place	Date	Hour	Summary of Events and Information	Remarks and references to Appendices
R/Section Per-Sub-Sector A1a 23.50. 63186 75.15			in, finally falling in No man's land. A strut on chassis at 6.15 A.M. Enemy aeroplane chopped slowly until fired at when it fell rapidly, coming down in ROTTEN Row at 40-60yds in front of our No 4 post. Nothing followed these suspected land shots. On night of 29/30 & 30/1st each Coy sent out 2 patrols – one normally before midnight & one after dark. The second one had orders to recon before dawn. Owing to the seldom cleaness of the night & dull moonshine, patrols trying large extent distance were impracticable. Some wiring was done between again. Renewed & the light neglcted. Our trenches during this spell are the best Bat. has held (Arthurs), mainly during its service in the full in France. The trench – C.T. & star huts also except being neither duckboarded & well drained. The dug out accommodation was excellent & permitted of the line being held short during the dy & a maxm and post by been just to all posts.	

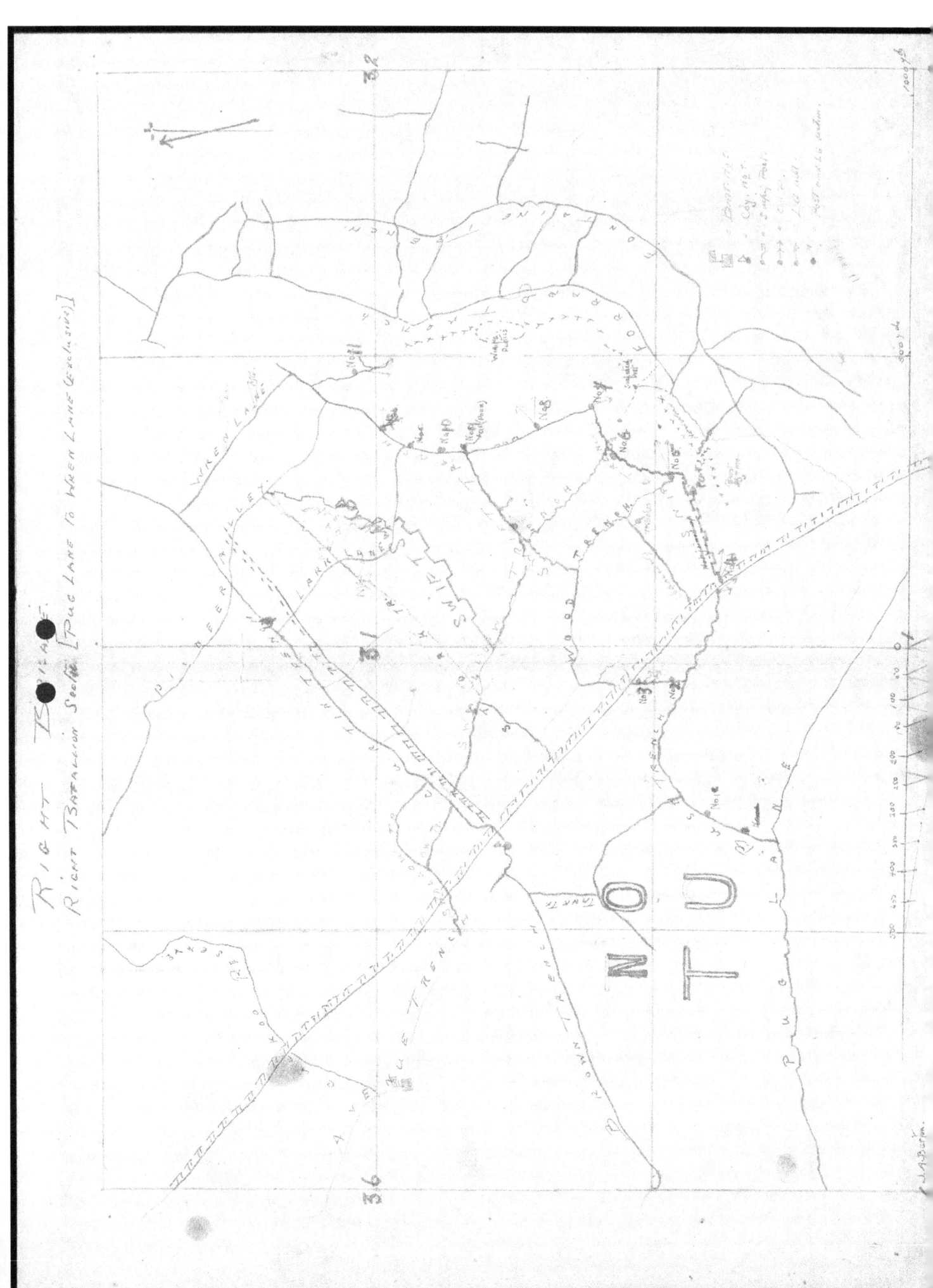

WAR DIARY
or
INTELLIGENCE SUMMARY.
(Erase heading not required.)

Army Form C. 2118.

Place	Date	Hour	Summary of Events and Information	Remarks and references to Appendices
FRONT LINE W. of CHERISY	Oct 1st to Oct 14th		A quiet tour in the front line with nothing of particular interest to report. Work consisted of wiring the front line and improving trenches. A party of 1 Officer and 30 O.R. was left back at the Transport lines and brought up at night for special patrolling work. This scheme tried before, and find it a good one. A Pioneer Platoon for special work was formed from men out of each company - total 1 Officer and 50 O.R. This scheme was also found to work well on several occasions. The Pioneer Platoon was attached to the company in Reserve. The Battalion was relieved in daylight by 7th GORDONS (51st Division) who had recently come down from the fighting round YPRES. — On relief the Battalion marched via HENIN to BOISLEUX-ST. MARC (DURKAR LINES Camp G-).	
	Oct 15th	2 p.m.	The Battalion proceeded by march route via BOIRY ST. RICTRUDE and AYETTE to COURCELLES-LE-COMTE, where they encamped in huts.	

WAR DIARY
INTELLIGENCE SUMMARY

Army Form C. 2118.

Place	Date	Hour	Summary of Events and Information	Remarks and references to Appendices
COURCELLES LE COMTE	Oct 5th to Oct 17th		A period of hard Training with a view to offensive operations in the YPRES area. Commencing with Platoon Training, Company & Battalion training was organised and on Oct. 14th a Brigade assault practice took place. Every effort was made to make this practice realistic, troops assembling on a taped line by night and assaulting at dawn. A barrage of Stokes Mortars was fired at zero hour for 3 minutes and flares were lit during the operations to act barrel assaulting as co-operating Candidates. Was practised to the extent of blessing trenches a width of 4'6" Companies attacked on a platoon frontage in lines of sections, the leading line extended when they came under heavy M.G. fire. Each platoon was given a definite objective, the first platoon taking the first objective, the second platoon leaving through them took the second objective, the third platoon to third objective, and the 4th Platoon being a reserve in the hands of the company Commander & to be employed for consolidation, counter attacks or to	TMG

WAR DIARY
or
INTELLIGENCE SUMMARY.

Army Form C. 2118.

Place	Date	Hour	Summary of Events and Information	Remarks and references to Appendices
COURCELLES LE-COMTE			Company Commander considered most efficient. The Battalion attacked as a 3-company group (300yds) with 1 company in Reserve in the hands of the Battalion Commander. Training in Offensive action was carried out on the above lines. Bayonet fitting & rangefinder were also indulged in, and conference between officers and N.C.O.s in the evening. The weather was not too strenuous and rather hampered Training.	
	Night 17/18 Octr		The Battalion moved by rail to CASSEL, entraining at MIRAUMONT station and detraining at CASSEL. (a) One company with 1 cooker entrained at 2.30 a.m. & Train left 4.5 a.m. (b) Remainder of Battalion with 1st line Transport, baggage supply wagons entrained at 6.30 a.m. Train left 8.15 a.m.	Ref. Map HAZEBROUCK sheet 5a. 1/100,000

WAR DIARY
INTELLIGENCE SUMMARY
(Erase heading not required.)

Army Form C. 2118.

Place	Date	Hour	Summary of Events and Information	Remarks and references to Appendices
ARNEKE	18/10/17		After detraining at CASSEL the Battalion marched to ARNEKE where we stood (whilst there) for two nights.	M.T.
	19/10/17		A quiet day. Orders received at 3 p.m. to be prepared to move eastwards to-morrow 20th inst.	M.T.
	20/10/17		Battalion marched off at 10 a.m. and passing through LEDRINGHEM – WORMHOUDT – HERZEELE – HOUTKERQUE arrived at a camp between PROVEN and HOUTKERQUE at 4 p.m. Battalion in tents, except one company who were in Nissen huts. A halt was made on the march from 12.30 p.m. to 2.15 p.m. when the men had Dinners. The axle broke on one of the cookers – probably through carrying too many rations on it [being ab? 3 cookers, 2 coys rations were put on one.] The Battalion marched well and no one fell out.	M.T.
PROVEN	21/10/17		Church Parades. – C.O. and four company Commanders reconnoitred the forward area. Companies practised the attack formation.	T.M.G.

WAR DIARY
or
INTELLIGENCE SUMMARY.
(Erase heading not required.)

Army Form C. 2118.

Place	Date	Hour	Summary of Events and Information	Remarks and references to Appendices
PROVEN	23/9/17	10 am	Orders received to move forward.	
		8.20 pm	Battalion (less Details of officers DR to be left behind and Transport) marched to PROVEN station where they entrained at 9 am. Detrained at BOESINGHE on the YSER CANAL bank, and from there marched Southwards along the CANAL BANK to HULLS FARM (bivouacs and tents).	
			Details of officers DR left out of action proceeded by march route to DUBLIN CAMP on the WOESTON-PESALHOEK Rd. Transport proceeded by march route (Brigaded) to CHEAPSIDE FORT area near HULLS CAMP FORT. Company officers and Signals Intelligence officers reconnoitred the forward area.	
HULLS FARM	24/9/17		Details left DUBLIN CAMP & proceeded by train to BOLLOZEEL NW of CASSEL. The Battalion was equipped in preparation for offensive	TMG

Operations. — The following is a list of what men carried into action.
S.A.A. — 170 rounds per man, except Rifle Grenadiers who carried 120 rounds, & Signallers, Runners, Lewis Gunners who carried 50 rounds.
Rifle Grenades. 8 per Rifle Grenadier. (4 in each carrier Sandbag pattern).
Sandbags. 2 per man.
Flares. (for communication with aero(planes). 500 distributed amongst Battalion.
S.O.S. cartridges. 42 distributed among officers & NCO's.
Fighting order with entrenching tool carried below the belt in front of the body — no haversack — pack on the back containing: —
2 "Tommy" Cookers (solidified alcohol).
2 days rations.
Emergency ration.
Spare water bottle.
1 pr Dry Socks.
Waterproof cape or sheet.
M.G

Army Form C. 2118.

WAR DIARY
or
INTELLIGENCE SUMMARY.
(Erase heading not required.)

Instructions regarding War Diaries and Intelligence Summaries are contained in F.S. Regs, Part II. and the Staff Manual respectively. Title pages will be prepared in manuscript.

Place	Date	Hour	Summary of Events and Information	Remarks and references to Appendices
HULLS FARM		5/am	Battalion moved forward into action 578 strong. 20 officers and OR.	
			RELIEF – Relieved 11th Bn. SUFFOLK REGT s. of HOUTHULST FOREST @ Route via RAILWAY STREET (Duckboard Track as far as about 200 yds W. of PASCHAL FARM, where (we met Batt.) (a) Guides provided on scale of 4 per company, and 1 for Batt. H.Q. had never been N. of the Railway (BOESINGHE – STADEN railway) and therefore none of them were able to guide our men – In spite of that relief was completed by 2.30 am (b) Dispositions as per attached sketch (A). – 5th Bn. North Fn. were on our left, and 4th/5th Bn. LOYAL NORTH LANCS Regt. on our right. Touch on our right could not be obtained owing to nearby ground – (c) Casualties during relief – Nil, except for a few men who were struck in the third's subsequently lost their way – Operation Orders for the attack received from	
LUT 29/9/17 8.31 am				
HQ U 12 R44				

WAR DIARY
INTELLIGENCE SUMMARY.
(Erase heading not required.)

Army Form C. 2118.

Place	Date	Hour	Summary of Events and Information	Remarks and references to Appendices
LINES — A+(1/12)144	25/9/17	2 pm	Brigade.— Sent our operation order to companies [see Appendix D] Communication with front line was extraordinarily difficult on account of (i) Route to front line under Direct Observation and there was no cover except shell-holes. (ii) A wire could not therefore be laid, nor visual signalling established. (iii) Incessant shelling especially on the line running along the Road N.W. and S.E. of TRONQUILLE HOUSE, which appeared to be our enemy barrage line. In spite of the difficulty, two Runners found their way to the front line Constantly, although they indeed at least 50 yds. beyond our position in the direction of the enemy and were only just stopped in time. All operation orders were received safely. Our own Hostile shelling front line company were constantly shelled by	TB24

Army Form C. 2118.

WAR DIARY / INTELLIGENCE SUMMARY.

(Erase heading not required.)

Instructions regarding War Diaries and Intelligence Summaries are contained in F. S. Regs., Part II. and the Staff Manual respectively. Title pages will be prepared in manuscript.

Place	Date	Hour	Summary of Events and Information	Remarks and references to Appendices
LONE. (R 1/12.d.4.)	25/4/17	7 pm	Our own Howitzers, and one casualties resulted. — Batt. HQ. moved forward to TAUBE FARM. R.A.P. moved to POSCHOL FARM, from OLSO HOUSE.	
nr TAUBE FARM		7pm to 9am	Between these hours companies moved forward to the position of assembly. FORMATION:— The formation for the attack was twice altered in 12 hours. — The first intention was to attack on a 3-company frontage, each company being on a [platoon frontage] in depth (4 waves). — After relief it was found that on account of the swampy state of the ground on our right flank there would only be room for a two-company frontage. The C.O. reported this to Bde. (See Appendix B). — When this tape was laid, it was found that there was only sufficient room for a one-company frontage. — One company was accordingly in the front line on a	

WAR DIARY
or
INTELLIGENCE SUMMARY.
(Erase heading not required.)

Army Form C. 2118.

Place	Date	Hour	Summary of Events and Information	Remarks and references to Appendices
LINE HQ at THIEPVAL "			one platoon frontage, one company in rear of the right company of the Battalion on our left (Towedge in between our front line company and the company on their left when the attack started) and one company in reserve about 700 yds behind our front line company (on a two platoon frontage) and one company under the Battalion Commander at TAUBE FORT and TRANQUILLE HOUSE. ASSEMBLY. The leading wave was laid by 2/Lieut. J.A. BURTON. Successfully. Companies assembled in shell hole line tending to the formation described above. A cross fire of talc was laid to show the Division between the 4th & 5th North'd Fus. (HOT FOOD with tea) was carried up in tanks (packed tightly with hay) to the 4 companies on the assembly position.— OBJECTIVES. (As laid down in Operation Orders (see Appendix A). The first platoon were given the 1st objective, the	WHT

WAR DIARY
INTELLIGENCE SUMMARY.

Place	Date	Hour	Summary of Events and Information	Remarks and references to Appendices
LINE — in all TAUBE FARM			Second Platoon to the Second objective, third Platoon to first objective, the fourth Platoon in reserve in the hands of the Company Commander to be used for counter-attack or consolidation according to the tactical situation. The system of "Leap frog" i.e. Platoons leaving through each other & further objective had been practised & decided upon. Battalion reported in position for the attack.	
		4.5am		
		5.40am	THE ATTACK. Zero hour 5.40 am. — At zero the Battalion moved forward to the attack in conjunction with the Batt. 5th North'd Rs. on the left and 4/5th LOYAL NORTH LANCS on the Right (57th Division) in Good order and were all clear just before the enemy's barrage was put down. BARRAGE consisted entirely of shrapnel which was quite useless against line of concrete huts, which was our first objective. — In addition to this rain	TMS

WAR DIARY
INTELLIGENCE SUMMARY

Army Form C. 2118.

Place	Date	Hour	Summary of Events and Information	Remarks and references to Appendices
LINE H.Q. at TAUBE FARM.			fell heavily and the conditions of mud were frightfully appalling. Our attack was held up about 50 yds. W. of the line of MORS and Machine Gun fire and sniping were so severe that any movement of any kind was quite impossible. Battalions are at points noted on the attack. — INFORMATION owing to the difficulties above & difficulty of getting information back was extremely difficult.	
		8.50	Wire received from Brigade saying Wounded F.O.O. reports just objective taken & men advancing well to the 2nd objective. — This information was wrong. 2/Lt. Wood came down wounded reported casualties heavy & attack held up in front of MORS.	
		8.50	2 Runners sent up to front line to get information. These runners did not return. —	TWC

T.J.134. Wt. W708-776. 500000. 4/15. Sir J.C. & S.

Army Form C. 2118.

WAR DIARY
or
INTELLIGENCE SUMMARY.
(Erase heading not required.)

Instructions regarding War Diaries and Intelligence Summaries are contained in F.S. Regs., Part II. and the Staff Manual respectively. Title pages will be prepared in manuscript.

Place	Date	Hour	Summary of Events and Information	Remarks and references to Appendices
LINE H.R. TAUBE FARM		11 am	2/Lieut. BURTON was then sent up to reconnoitre. It confirmed the news that the attack was held up about 100 yds from the huts.	For and Ranges Sgt Offensive C =
		1 pm	Sgt THOMPSON returned from the front line and confirmed report of 2/Lieut BURTON and casualties were very heavy. Sun tan was unknown later by Capt. J.V. GREGORY. The substance of all this information was sent on to Brigade by pigeon Special Signalling (LUCAS LOT (P)).	Munro C
		10/4	Two Platoons of Reserve Company under 2/Lieuts PEDDIE and SCOTT to consolidate our original line if held before the attack.	
			The following is a list of points noted in the attack.	M.G.

WAR DIARY
or
INTELLIGENCE SUMMARY.
(Erase heading not required.)

Army Form C. 2118.

Place	Date	Hour	Summary of Events and Information	Remarks and references to Appendices
LINE Hd at TAUBE FARM			1. 2 Machine Guns were attached to the Battalion in the attack. They went forward with the support company (in rear of 5th Northd Fus) did excellent work. 2. 2 Stokes Mortars were to be attached but did not succeed in getting ammunition forward. 3. Communication to Brigade exceptionally valuable and wonderfully maintained under a heavy barrage by the Bde Signalling Officer (Lieut Wd Erg Clarkson) and the other Signallers. Runner to 6 & 5th North Co almost continuously maintained. Visual Brigade also kept up although the Lanthorn crashed over 3 times, and pigeons. 4. Wounded Officers. Although Strength in officers wounded an very light, movement in the forward line was checked by Machine Gun Sniping. 5. Liaison. Lieut W.B. Hicks acted as liaison officer between 62nd Div on Brigade the Brigade on our right. MH	

WAR DIARY or INTELLIGENCE SUMMARY

Army Form C. 2118.

Place: LOOS

Liaison with 1/5th Local North Lancs maintained through S/North Rs, who had an officer from 1st Battalion with them —

6. Rations and Mr brought up by Daventort in these conditions. Men must carry 2 days rations with them; also 2 Tommy cookers.

7. Kit is laid down appear its best, though many loads will probably be thrown away.

8. Method should always be carried up to the trenches the night before the attack — also RUM.

9. Guiding officially difficult owing to scarcity of landmarks. Obvious landmarks, such as a railway, or dayleuo on the enemy naturally concentrate his artillery on them. We suggest a double line of pickets with plain wire on them. This is not conspicuous and very helpful.

TMG

WAR DIARY
INTELLIGENCE SUMMARY.
(Erase heading not required.)

Army Form C. 2118.

Place	Date	Hour	Summary of Events and Information	Remarks and references to Appendices
HQ (LINE) TUBE YPRES	25/4		The Battalion was relieved by 4th YORKS REGT. and on relief proceeded to via RAILWAY STREET (Northern track) to ROE CROSS ROADS and Straight job were amongst whole places by (ADLL) & carts on men coming down from the line. Guide team to camp.	
			CASUALTIES.	

			OFFICERS. 2/Lieut. D.A. SMITH. Killed 2.
			Killed 2/Lieut. W. RUDDY
			died of wounds 2/Lieut. R.O.B. SIMPSON Died of wounds 1
			Wounded 2/Lieut. G.E. CHARLEWOOD
			  2/Lieut. A.W.F LEARY Wounded 5
			  2/Lieut. H.B. BELL
			  2/Lieut. J.R. RUDDOCK
			  2/Lieut. R. WOOD	

			Missing 2/Lieut. R.G. ROGNER and 2/Lieut. H. STOBBS. Missing 2. TOTAL. 10.	

Army Form C. 2118.

WAR DIARY
or
INTELLIGENCE SUMMARY
(Erase heading not required.)

Instructions regarding War Diaries and Intelligence Summaries are contained in F. S. Regs., Part II. and the Staff Manual respectively. Title pages will be prepared in manuscript.

Place	Date	Hour	Summary of Events and Information	Remarks and references to Appendices
LINE HR-M			Casualties	
TAUBE FARM			Killed — Wounded — Missing — TOTAL	
			36 — 156 — 74 — 256	
"	27/4/17	2/-	Battalion entrained at BOESINGHE - Detrained at ONDONK from there marched to CARIBOU CAMP (huts).	
CARIBOU CAMP	28/4/17		Re-organisation, re-equipment.	
"	29/4/17		ditto. 2/Lt W.H. NICOLSON and 50 OR went to WHITEMILL ELVERDINGHE there they were attached to 463th Field Company R.E. for work.	
"	30/4/17		Re-organisation, re-equipment. 2/Lt W.F.R. ESSEX and	
"	3/4/17		ditto. 48 OR sent to be attached to 157th M.G. Company as Carrying party.	

MG

WAR DIARY
or
INTELLIGENCE SUMMARY.

APPENDIX B A

OPERATION ORDER No 1 A.
=

1. The 149th Inf. Bde. will attack on the morning of the 26th inst. 4th N.F. on the right, 5th N.F. in centre and 7th N.F. on left. 57th Div. are attacking on our right, with 4th/5th LOYAL NORTH LANCS as their left battalion.

2. The Battalion will attack on a 3-company frontage each company being on a platoon frontage. A Company on Right, B Coy. in centre and D Coy. on left. C Coy. will be in Reserve on a 2-platoon frontage.

3. (a) Platoons will leap-frog and capture and consolidate the objectives already given them i.e. FIRST WAVE to HUTS, SECOND WAVE to line V.2.c.1.6 – V.2.c.5.1. THIRD WAVE to Final Objective V.2.a.3.0. to V.2.b.1.5.5. (b) Reserve Company will move forward

with attacking waves to a point approximately 250 yds W. of the Huts.

C Coy will detail parties to obtain touch with Batt. on their Right at the following points.
(c) Concrete Shelter at V.8.a.1.8.
(d) ——— to ——— at V.2.c.4.1.
(e) ROAD BRIDGE at V.2.D.0.6.

4. Two M.G's will accompany 4th wave of B Coy.
5. Two Stokes Mortars will be attached to C Coy and will be available to give at any strong points holding up the attack.

6. Barrage will begin to creep forward at ZERO + 8 minutes and will creep at the uniform rate of 100 yds in 8 min. throughout. Lifts will be at 50 yds at a time.

7. Tapeing out of the assembly trench will

WAR DIARY or INTELLIGENCE SUMMARY

Army Form C. 2118.

be carried out under an officer from Batt. HR. One line of tape will be laid from Railway Embankment to a point V.1.a.0.2 to V.7.c.6.5. Two guides will be left at the end of this tape. A Railway Embankment to start length of tape will be laid at right angles to Assembly tape to mark the left of D Coy. Short lengths of tape will be laid at right angles to Assembly tape every 30 yds to mark company frontages. The Assembly tape marks position of leading wave.

B, D, C, D Coys. will more forward & assemble positions at 11 pm. D on right, each company providing its own covering party. B Company will withdraw to Assembly tape at Upper Completion of Assembly will be notified by code word AREAS sent by runner to Batt. HR. Contact aeroplane will be flying

MG

WAR DIARY
or
INTELLIGENCE SUMMARY.
(Erase heading not required.)

Army Form C. 2118.

Place	Date	Hour	Summary of Events and Information	Remarks and references to Appendices
			O/C Coys. front at Zero + 1 hr. 30 min. and at ZERO + 3 hours. Leading Troops will show brass positions to contact aeroplane only when called for (a) by CLAXON horn (b) by Servin White Very Lights. Dropped from the Plane. 10. R.A.P. will be at MASCHEUL FORM 11. PRISONERS. 1 man as escort to 5 Boches. Batt. H.Q. or 12. Reports will be forwarded to Batt. H.Q. or once in the first hour after ZERO TAUBE FORM as frequently as possible and always 13. Batt. H.Q. will open at TAUBE FARM at 7 hrs. To.night 14. ZERO will be after full of the Barrage. This of this will be notified later when synchronised. Watches 15. General confirms learning patrols SSD Malpulsr 16. Orchards Dawned at 1:30 Copy to - C.O., A, B, C, D.	

WAR DIARY
or
INTELLIGENCE SUMMARY.
(Erase heading not required.)

Army Form C. 2118.

Place	Date	Hour	Summary of Events and Information	Remarks and references to Appendices
			CORRIGENDA OPERATION ORDER No 1 A	

1. Owing to the muddy state of the ground on the right of our attack, it has been decided to attack on a 2 company frontage instead of a 3-company frontage. B, C, D Coys will have instructions exactly as laid down in O. no 1 O.

2. A Coy will NOT go to the Reserve Trenches but will move from TRANQUILLE HOUSE to TAUBE FARM at 9 p.m. 6-w/EN infantry will be the Batt. Reserve.

3. Rations and men will be brought up to within 1 Guide per Coy. to be at TAUBE FARM at 11 p.m. to guide company parties.

4. Acknowledge.

Issued 21.2/—.

Copies to Coy A, B, C, D.

Hugh Stuart
Capt/Adjt

WAR DIARY
or
INTELLIGENCE SUMMARY.

(Erase heading not required.)

Place	Date	Hour	Summary of Events and Information	Remarks and references to Appendices
			APPENDIX B	
			L.T.3 C.O's report. — From reports received from 11th SUFFOLKS the right of my Batt front is a swamp. Even if it is possible to assemble the right company I do not consider they would be able to advance but would have to be dug out. Therefore with your permission to attack with 2 companies only in the front line, one in Support and to keep the 4th Company in Reserve in TRONVILLE HOUSE area. Conditions on rest of the front are such that if a man steps off a firm piece of ground into the slightest hollow he has to be dug out. There are very few firm pieces of ground away from the Railway and Route.	
			(?) Appendix C. MESSAGES during the action.	
			L.T.19 Trinet 12.20am — Wounded officer left company reports attack on both VID held up by many machine Guns about 150 yds W. of NUTS. Right Company held up in same position. Right company of SEED (5th N.F.) held up on same line — Impossible to work round flanks owing to swamp on Right and Machine Guns on left. MAR There are company still in Reserve in TAUBE FARM and TRANQUILLE HOUSE area and I do not propose to make another frontal attack with this company, as it is appears	

WAR DIARY or INTELLIGENCE SUMMARY

Army Form C. 2118.

Place	Date	Hour	Summary of Events and Information	Remarks and references to Appendices
Suzanne			Unable to obtain a reliable report. OOO The Officer states that HUNS are very little developed and full of Machine Guns. OOO Unless pressure return to the contrary I will move Reserve Company up tonight at dusk to take on a rearranged front line. OOO Am investigating this matter information will reach later. OOO Movements found very Broady and casualties very heavy in wounded Officers company to VESUVE.	South PIGEON Sentrance to VESUVE
		AT 20 Timed 12.40pm. In continuation of my AT19 I am unable to reach front line companies owing to M.G. fire and Sniping from HUNS and concrete emplacements S. of HUNS. OOO There is not the slightest doubt that to little attack is less ut. too. to 150 yds W. of HUNS OOO I am much of ascertain infantry position of troops on my right but they do not appear to have advanced far from where we are now. To estimate casualties.	— do —
		AT 21 Timed ? A very reliable Sgt. has just brought back a report from front line ORR He states that 5D of our men - 2 officers are lying about 100 yds W. of Middle HUNS. OOO Remainder of B Coy, I think are casualt. OOO 3rd about 300 OOO Boch prisoners have been lying low when our line advanced their OOO Boches have also sniped majority of wounded. They tried to get back. Attack started in excellent order and was clean of Boch barrels.	
		Won't cause learn - a few men succeeded in reaching HUNS but have not come back. Remainder caught by M.G. fire from HUNS and both flanks. OOO our flares are in France of large barry to get our wounded in tonight with both stretcher. It is figured about to warm from stretcher.	

Vol 2

CONFIDENTIAL
WAR DIARY
OF
4th BATTALION NORTHUMBERLAND FUSILIERS
FROM NOVEMBER 1st to NOVEMBER 30th 1917

VOLUME III

Army Form C. 2118.

WAR DIARY
or
INTELLIGENCE SUMMARY.
(Erase heading not required)

Instructions regarding War Diaries and Intelligence Summaries are contained in F.S. Regs., Part II and the Staff Manual respectively. Title pages will be prepared in manuscript.

Place	Date	Hour	Summary of Events and Information	Remarks and references to Appendices
CARIBOU CAMP	1/4/17 to 8/4/17		The Battalion remained at CARIBOU CAMP during this period, carrying out carrying parties as follows:— 1 Officer and 50 OR working for 446th Field Company R.E. on erecting shelters in Support Line 1 Officer and 50 OR attached to 6th NORTHUMBERLANDs for carrying duckboards, etc. to the line. 40 OR daily for work on draining and improving A.S.C. camp. A Lewis Gun Guard with 2 Lewis Guns was maintained at CARIBOU CAMP for anti-aircraft purposes.	ELVERDINGHE ON BANK area (Shot APPROACH S.A. 1/100,000)
YSER CANAL BANK Near BOESINGHE	9/4/17		The Battalion moved forward into Support at MARSOUIN FARM with Batt. H.Q. on YSER CANAL BANK near BORD CANTEWORT (near BOESINGHE). We suffered a party of 1 Officer and 40 OR to carry hot food up to 6th NORTH'D Fus. in right gyfl to. All the food arrived safely to the front line Battalion. Casualties during tour — NIL	

WAR DIARY

Army Form C. 2118.

Place	Date	Hour	Summary of Events and Information	Remarks and references to Appendices
WHITE MILL CAMP, BLENDECQUES	10/4/17 to 12/4/17		The Battalion moved back into Reserve Area on the morning of the 10th. On 13th the Battalion moved by Train (less Transport, which moved by road) to SERQUES area, about 4 miles N. of ST. OMER. — Billeted in scattered billets in ZUDROVE. —	
ZUDROVE	12/4/17 to 30/4/17		Training. — Draft of 1 Officer and 80 O.R. arrived 14/4/17, including several men of previous Service in France. Organisation of 4 coys. 4 platoons, 4 sections (section in each of Lewis Gunners and Riflemen and 2 Sections of Rifle Grenadiers). All Headquarter Transport, R.E. Personnel accounted in their companies. — Recreational Training every afternoon — all men turned over to Play games & sports after Dinner — no Trumpet & in the afternoon. Platoon training from 19/4/17 to 24/4/17. — One whole day of Musketry on a lark range. Your practices of Company Table 93 Part III Mun Reg were completed by double drenched strength	

WAR DIARY
or
INTELLIGENCE SUMMARY
(Erase heading not required.)

Army Form C. 2118.

Place	Date	Hour	Summary of Events and Information	Remarks and references to Appendices
ZUDROVE	13/4/17 to 30/4/17 cont.		of the Bn. Platoon & Coy training, in accordance with XVIII Corps Notes, during the mornings. Recreational training in the afternoons. On 26th/25th men from the Bn. took part in cross country race (Brigade), twenty seven came in either scheduled time. On 28th Bn. beat Bde HQ in tug of war. On 29th Bn. beat 9th &21 (Div Semi final) at football. The tactical Bn paraded by command, the field de Manœuvre being NEM. R23.29.30 about 278 St. Victor sur Ternoise in the matter. The Brigade sports, at the Olympia ground, 130. & J Pte HQ provided 4 ouveniers (1 prize). DOUBLE MARATHON. stood 2nd in the BANTAMS, at this and 3rd at TUGS OF WAR. Formed first class group.	
"	1st			
"	2nd			

E. Curving D/
Major
for North & Gen.

CONFIDENTIAL

WAR DIARY

4th Northumberland Fusiliers

December 1917

Volume III

WAR DIARY
INTELLIGENCE SUMMARY.
(Erase heading not required.)

Army Form C. 2118.

Place	Date	Hour	Summary of Events and Information	Remarks and references to Appendices
LA RONVILLE	Dec 1 to Dec 17		On Dec 1st Battalion moved from ZUDROVE to LA RONVILLE in order to obtain a better training ground. Training — Special attention was paid to the organisation of the platoon and the section, each man being made to know the name of his section commander, platoon commander etc. — Understudies appointed to all commanders, right down to the section commander. Every effort was made to train Lewis Gunners to replace casualties in the recent fighting but this G.C. was not time to complete this. One whole day was spent on the Range completing classification practices. During this time the C.O. and company commanders reconnoitred the forward area in DISCHENDALE into a view to taking over that sector.	
	Dec 18th to Dec 19th		Move to forward area. — Bulk of Battalion	
(A Ronville)				

WAR DIARY
or
INTELLIGENCE SUMMARY.
(Erase heading not required.)

Army Form C. 2118.

Place	Date	Hour	Summary of Events and Information	Remarks and references to Appendices
			Proceeding by road on 3 Xmas days' journey commencing Dec 10th. Remainder of Transport proceeded by rail from ST OMER on 11th and the General by rail from WATTEN on the same day. The whole Battalion (including Transport) arrived at BRANDHOEK (BRIDGE CATO) on the afternoon of 11th.	Apf
BRANDHOEK	14/12/17		The Battalion moved forward through YPRES to the Sulphart Barracks area. Remained here till 16/12/17. During this time all officers, platoon Sjts reconnoitred the route to the forward area.	M.G
HUTS (east of POTIJZE)	16/12/17 17/12/17		The Battalion relieved 6th NORTH'D FUS in close support to the new HAMBURG (see Map) — Front line held by 5th NORTH'D FUS on Left and 6th NORTH'D FUS on Right. Two of our Companies carried rations, water and hot food to the two Battalions, two companies being in reserve to counter-attack should MANCHESTER be	P

WAR DIARY
or
INTELLIGENCE SUMMARY

Army Form C. 2118.

Place	Date	Hour	Summary of Events and Information	Remarks and references to Appendices
Loos (Sill-ul)	18/19 Dec		Taken by the Enemy. Arrays of this companies were keeping their covering Group. At the HARLEM Sector. We send to Reserve Company. After the Coy left, his Battalion men forward from that trench to support the left Battalion & they commenced strenuous where possible — Work was also done in constructing shelters in our own area — under R.E. supervision, and 1 Sergeant of N.C.O. and 8 men each worked on covering withdrawal and laying a new duckboard track to CREST POST. D.O. daylight Dawn and casualties were light. Considering that ration parties walked through moderately G.T. with - a fog which was generally shelled by the enemy. Both casualties during the Dawn. Other Ranks SK[tch 13 wounded. 2 the Battalion (less Two Coys.) On the evening of 19th Dec. Two Coys. remained up under orders of 8th D.L.I. made to subscribe to this good task. was relieved by 8th D.L.I. The remainder of the 20th aft. who have relieved the...	

WAR DIARY or INTELLIGENCE SUMMARY

Army Form C. 2118.

Place	Date	Hour	Summary of Events and Information	Remarks and references to Appendices
BRANDHOEK	24/9/17 to 26/9/17		Battalion at POTIJE	AHL
			Busses took enough to convey the Battalion to from POTIJE to Reserve Area at BRANDHOEK on 20th inst. Rev arrived late, Battalion marched half way to BRANDHOEK. When troops arrived, the Battalion was very tired. Two days spent in which time 2 coys had baths & their clothing and blankets disinfected. —	
			On Dec 23rd 3 coys proceeded to POTIJE and provided about 200 men on 23rd, 24th for working parties HR and 1 coy remained at BRANDHOEK until 25th when they went round to join the Battalion at POTIJE. The company at BRANDHOEK also had baths and clothes & blankets disinfected. Battalion tubs taken to complete Battalion the disinfection. —	
				TMG

Army Form C. 2118.

WAR DIARY
or
INTELLIGENCE SUMMARY.
(Erase heading not required.)

Instructions regarding War Diaries and Intelligence Summaries are contained in F. S. Regs., Part II. and the Staff Manual respectively. Title pages will be prepared in manuscript.

Place	Date	Hour	Summary of Events and Information	Remarks and references to Appendices
POPNE	25/10/17		Battalion was in this camp. Fine day. Inspections all day & watched fatalities was observed. It being known.	
WIPPERS (CAMP)	26/10/17		letter to renew the till we came out of the line.	MLG
SEINE	27/10/17		On afternoon of 26th Battalion proceeded to SEINE this becoming Battalion in Reserve under orders of 150th Inf Bde. No held the line for the event of a hostile attack our company was told off to man the Bellevue switch line (see map) the other 3 coys from yard for support or counter attack. A this direction of Bde. a Bn.	
		7.50p	S.O.S. sent up by Divison on our Left went up Aided by coys of left Battalion at CREST FARM Batt. stood to in readiness. Enemy but hostile shelling died down. Every apparently quiet. Men rested at 8.30p.m. Down a practice barrage.	MLG

WAR DIARY
or
INTELLIGENCE SUMMARY.
(Erase heading not required.)

Army Form C. 2118.

Place	Date	Hour	Summary of Events and Information	Remarks and references to Appendices
SAME	26/10/17		D Coy's Lewis Gun - The coy started to man Beluvue switch line in case of counter attack. Word that this line stood only of long line was put out. Battalion also organised a party of 3 officers and 150 O.R. to carry for the wounded coys who were consolidating front position. Returned to 30 Y.R. on 28th. N. saw of our coys in the front line. Casualties during these 2 days. "Hatter" 29th SMO NOPTER MC wounded at duty. 1 OR killed 6 OR wounded.	
	29/10/17 to 30/10/17		On evening of 28th relieved 5th Yorks in the front line. left Oxton Butt First company moved off at stemin and relief was completed by 5:30 p.m. without much casualty. 2 O.R. were wounded after relief complete.	
	31/10/17		D Coy's Lewis Gun with the exception of Little Barrage gun has to fire at 26/10/17 was put down at 6 a.m. 31/10/17. Started the 6:45 am. Own casualties during	

WAR DIARY
or
INTELLIGENCE SUMMARY.
(Erase heading not required.)

Army Form C. 2118.

Place	Date	Hour	Summary of Events and Information	Remarks and references to Appendices
			The Barrage only succeeded to 1 CR moved Telephone communication with all coys was lost when the first few rounds of the Barrage. — Rations were carried up by Coy pack transport. R. Feed corp who carried Coy supply (to united Bde who was in support. Hot Grub was in huts stripped up to carried data radiator	
			WORK Bright moon light and snow on the ground. Uneventful day worsing after front trenks being carried out Patrolly was also active on the account.	
			AMMUN w/GRENADE Quiet on the whole sector.	
			NEXT [?] In shelter subsistence/gully with wire all long. In Nuclear ([?] open EXIST copse around the GARDENS were active at night. Rations wood bought up on Jany. brought by Bn shelter on ground to mule. An excellent sledge was studded up to mule of Soups Stave was brought up in this way from mortar for loving by Reserves Bn	

WAR DIARY
or
INTELLIGENCE SUMMARY.
(Erase heading not required.)

Army Form C. 2118.

11. Counter Attack for ....
12. Hostile (a) Battery
      (b) Machine Gun } active at ....
      (c) Trench Mortar
13. Reinforcements wanted as ....
14. I estimate my present strength at .... rifles.
15. Add any other useful information here :—

Time .... m.

Date .... 1917.

Name ....
Platoon ....
Company ....
Battalion ....

(A). Carry no maps or papers which may be of value to the Enemy.

(B). Give no information if captured, except the following, which you are bound to give :—

    Name and Rank.

(C). Collect all captured maps and papers and send them in at once.

No. 27.   MESSAGE MAP.   German Trenches Corrected to 24-10-17.

Scale 1:10,000.

MESSAGE FORM.

To :—   No.

1. I am at.................... (Note :—Either give Map Reference or mark your position by a 'X' on the Map on back.

2. I have reached limits of my Objective.

3. My Platoon / Company is at.................... and is consolidating.

4. My Platoon / Company is at....................and has consolidated.

5. Am held up by (a) M.G. / (b) Wire at....................(Place where you are).

6. Enemy holding strong point ....

7. I am in touch with....................on Right / Left at............

8. I am not in touch with ....on Right / Left.

9. Am shelled from....................

10. Am in need of :—

11. Counter Attack forming at ....

12. Hostile (a) Battery / (b) Machine Gun / (c) Trench Mortar active at ....

13. Reinforcements wanted at

14. I estimate my present strength at............rifles.

15. Add any other useful information here :—

Name....................

Platoon....................

Time............m.   Company....................

Date............1917.   Battalion....................

(A). Carry no maps or papers which may be of value to the Enemy.

(B). Give no information if captured, except the following, which you are bound to give :—

Name and Rank.

(C). Collect all captured maps and papers and send them in at once.

Army Form C. 2118.

WAR DIARY
or
INTELLIGENCE SUMMARY.
(Erase heading not required.)

WA 30

CONFIDENTIAL
WAR DIARY
OF
1/4th BATTALION NORTHUMBERLAND FUSILIERS

1st January — 30th January 1918.

VOLUME 4

Barnes Lt.

Army Form C. 2118.

WAR DIARY
or
INTELLIGENCE SUMMARY.
(Erase heading not required.)

Instructions regarding War Diaries and Intelligence Summaries are contained in F. S. Regs., Part II. and the Staff Manual respectively. Title pages will be prepared in manuscript.

Place	Date	Hour	Summary of Events and Information	Remarks and references to Appendices
Passchendaele Ridge	Jan 1918		The 4th Bn Northumberland Fusiliers were relieved by the 5th Borders	
			151 Brigade on extreme left of 50 Divisional front & moved out of the line into billets & camps near YPRES.	
WHITBY CAMP YPRES.	12/1/18		The Bn. Battalion found two companies to YORONTO CAMP, BRANDHOEK	
			found parties back to Divisional rest.	
BRANDHOEK	13/1/18		from TORONTO Camp the battalion moved by rail to ABEELE	
			Thence into billets in the WATOU area, also training of young NCOs under R.S. Major.	
WATOU area BELGIUM	13/1/18 16/1/18		During this period the training of the Battalion mainly consisted in Company training. Specialist training. "Gas."	
WATOU area & TILQUES area	18/1/18		The battalion again moved into the Tilques area, from STEENVOORDE	
			GODEWAERSFELDE & WIZERNE and into billets at ST MARTIN-au-LAERT	
ST MARTIN-au-LAERT	18/1/18 27/1/18		The battalion remained in Tilques area except whilst training in Range practices, Specialist training, Company training & tactical schemes.	
ST MARTIN AREA & ST MARTIN AU LAERT	27/1/18		from ST MARTIN, battalion into forward area YPRES, entraining at WIZERNE detraining at ST. JEAN	
			from thence into ALNWICK camp, POTIJZE, less acting as Corps working battalion	

Army Form C. 2118.

WAR DIARY
or
INTELLIGENCE SUMMARY.
(Erase heading not required.)

Place	Date	Hour	Summary of Events and Information	Remarks and references to Appendices
ALNWICK CAMP ST. JEAN.	29/1/18 & 30/1/18		Each day between these dates from 9.0 a.m. to 1.0 p.m. the battalion provided three companies to work under C.R.E. in VIII Corps works. This consisted in carrying & digging Strong Points. Also one officer and 50 O.R. worked on loading. Any other available men were employed in improving the camp, especially in draining.	

Army Form C. 2118.

WAR DIARY
or
INTELLIGENCE SUMMARY.
(Erase heading not required.)

Vol 31

31

CONFIDENTIAL

WAR DIARY
of
4th Northumberland Fusiliers

— Vol IV —

FEBRUARY 1918.

Thos Thompson
Colt.
4th No'thd Fus

Army Form C. 2118.

WAR DIARY
or
INTELLIGENCE SUMMARY.
(Erase heading not required.)

Instructions regarding War Diaries and Intelligence Summaries are contained in F. S. Regs., Part II. and the Staff Manual respectively. Title pages will be prepared in manuscript.

Place	Date	Hour	Summary of Events and Information	Remarks and references to Appendices
ALNWICK CAMP POTIJSE.	1/2/18	2/pm	--- The Battalion left ALNWICK CAMP and proceeded to billets in YPRES for night 1/2nd. --- Three companies worked on the Army Reserve Line during the morning under Supervision of VIII Corps. This work was taken over by Tr. North on completion of Day's work. TMT	Sheet 28 1/40,000
YPRES	2/2/18		--- The Battalion proceeded by Light-Railway (60 cm. gauge) to BRANDHOEK. Regimental Transport proceeding by road. Three Trains consisting of 9 trucks each were provided. Two Gr. (personnel and one Gr. (vehicles). Each truck held 30 men. TMT	
BRANDHOEK	2/2/18 to 6/2/18		--- The Battalion on arrival at BRANDHOEK became Divisional Reserve. These four days were spent in reorganisation, re-fitting and all men had baths. TMT	
BRANDHOEK	6/2/18	2.30pm	--- The Battalion moved forward into Support at SEINE and Came under orders of Suffolk Brigade [151st Inf. Bde.] for three days. — TMT	

Army Form C. 2118.

WAR DIARY
or
INTELLIGENCE SUMMARY.

(Erase heading not required.)

Instructions regarding War Diaries and Intelligence Summaries are contained in F. S. Regs., Part II. and the Staff Manual respectively. Title pages will be prepared in manuscript.

Place	Date	Hour	Summary of Events and Information	Remarks and references to Appendices
SUPPORT at SEINE	6/2/18 to 9/2/18		While the Battalion was at SEINE the following work was carried out. 150 O.R. carried dugout material daily to CREST FARM under orders of 171st Tunnelling Company. 50 O.R. [unclear] trucks of R.E. material from SEINE Dump to WATERFIELDS. Remainder of Battalion were employed in cleaning up the SEINE area and Salving. MG	Ref. Sheet ZONNEBEKE 1/10,000
FRONT LINE	9/2/18 to 12/2/18		At 5pm 9/2/18 the Battalion ceased to be under the orders of 151st Inf. Bde. and came under the orders of 148th Infantry Brigade, relieving 2/6th MANCHESTER Regt. 66th Division in the front line from D.17.1.9 to D.23.c.7.9. This portion of the line had not previously been held by our Brigade. It consisted of :— 1. A line of posts on the PASSCHENDAELE ridge — BROODSEINDE. This line was held by two Companies "A" or	

Place	Date	Hour	Summary of Events and Information	Remarks and references to Appendices
FRONT LINE	9/2/18 to 12/2/18		the Right holding 6 posts and 'B' on left holding 7 posts). The posts were held by 1 N.C.O. and 6 men by night. The reflecting relief were carried out before dawn and after dusk.	MAP 'A'

1 N.C.O. and 6 men by night, 1 N.C.O. and 3 men by day and
out before dawn and after dusk.

WORK. The main work was wiring in front of these posts,
the men on duty at night carrying up their own material. The
wire was put up 75 yds in front of the line of posts. It is therefore that should the enemy endeavour to precede an attack
with artillery preparation, a separate concentration of fire
would have to be made on the wire and the posts. All
wiring was done from right to left and three belts of wire
were made 10 feet thick and knee high. Both posts and
Companies put up about 80 yds apron wire under these conditions
during the tour.

2. Main Defensive Line, on the Reverse slope of the
BROODSEINDE — PASSCHENDAELE Ridge consists of
six strong points and was held by our company ('D') who
left one platoon in Reserve at DARING CROSSING. Our counter-
attack on their s support posts only.

WORK. The main work of the company was

WAR DIARY or INTELLIGENCE SUMMARY

Army Form C. 2118.

Place	Date	Hour	Summary of Events and Information	Remarks and references to Appendices
FRONT LINE	9/2/18 to 12/2/18		the improvement of the Support front. Parapets and traverses were strengthened and training and sanitary arrangements were made. 3. One Company (C) was held in Reserve in vicinity of DARING CROSSING at disposal of Battalion Commander for counter attack on any part of the Battalion front. This company carried rations and R.E. material to the other two companies and provided a daily party for patents work in its area. PATROLS were sent out on night 9th/10th and 10th/11th with the object of (1) locating the enemy. (2) Reporting on state of ground in front of our line. On the first night patrols reconnoitred ground to our line. On the second night in front of our lines and on the second night up to a line drawn through the Eastern ends of DAIRY and DAISY woods. No enemy were encountered or located and the ground was found to be very cut up by shell fire and waterlogged. CASUALTIES 6/2/18 to 12/2/18: 1 officer wounded at duty. 1 OR wounded at duty. 3 OR killed 4 OR wounded.	Map 'A'

MKS

WAR DIARY
or
INTELLIGENCE SUMMARY

Army Form C. 2118.

Place	Date	Hour	Summary of Events and Information	Remarks and references to Appendices
WHITBY CAMP POTIJE	12/2/18		The Batt. was relieved before dawn on 12/2/18 and proceeded to WHITBY CAMP, POTIJE, half-a-day being spent at SEINE.	Maj. A.
	12/2/18 to 16/2/18		In Brigade Reserve at WHITBY CAMP. Time spent in cleaning up, refit and baths. Three Jerv. Rau were paid to men's food which were bathed out rather hostile. On 14/2/18 Batt. provided parties of 6 officers and 150 O.R. to work on Army Reserve line under supervision of VIII Corps.	DLG
Suffolk SEINE	16/2/18 3pm to 19/2/18		Batt. proceeded to support area at SEINE, relieving S^d Norf. Fus. One Company (A) occupied SUFFOLK area and one Yorkswide for the defence of Bde. Reserve line (Map W) They Company worked on wiring Bde. Reserve line and in 3 days completed 350 yds of wire 10 feet thick. (C) Coy. carried out wiring in front of the main Dragon position and completed 350 yds from to rear thick during the 3 days.	DLG

WAR DIARY
INTELLIGENCE SUMMARY

Army Form C. 2118.

Place	Date	Hour	Summary of Events and Information	Remarks and references to Appendices
SUPPORT SERRE	16/2/18 to 19/2/18		Remaining two coys. provided between them 2 Officers 100 OR Carrying Dugout material to CRESTFALLEN Jn "7" Tunnelling Coy. 1 Officer and 50 OR. to construct strong points in new defences under R.E. Supervision.	
FRONT LINE	19/2/18 to 22/2/18		The Bull. relieved 6th N.F. in front line before dawn on 19/2/18, and held the same portion of line as last time WORK. In continuation of work done during last tour all front line posts were completely protected by wire (that wire can not as far out as 75 yds. from the posts. The heel. Tunnel Dugout at no. 9 front (See Map A) was protected for all round defence by wire but was in a circle round it. (42 as. long). PATROLS were sent out on night 20th/21st and 21st/22nd with the object of ① Reporting on state of ground with a view to advancing gun line ② Locating enemy gun line. The ground was found to be in a	

Army Form C. 2118.

WAR DIARY
or
INTELLIGENCE SUMMARY.
(Erase heading not required.)

Instructions regarding War Diaries and Intelligence Summaries are contained in F.S. Regs., Part II. and the Staff Manual respectively. Title pages will be prepared in manuscript.

Place	Date	Hour	Summary of Events and Information	Remarks and references to Appendices
[FRONT LINE]	19/2/18 to 21/2/18		Consolidated state in the whole of our front beyond a line 100 yds. in front of our posts. No enemy were located though patrols went out on BURMA, RHINE COPSE, and TABLE WOOD. At 9 p.m. 21/2/18 several red lights were burnt up by the enemy opposite to our front. On three suits of guns behind the BODDY FARM Ridge and it appeared that the enemy did not permanently hold the ridge but it seemed possible that listening posts were pushed out by the enemy to listen and direct bursts of M.G. fire on our side of our front when movement or noise were detected. No movement or noise on our side when movement or noise were detected.	SITREE ZONNEBEKE 1/10,000 (MAP A)
FRONT LINE	22/2/18		Relieved by 9th M.L.I., 33rd Divn. on evening of 22/2/18 and on relief proceeded to ST. JEAN CAMP, POTIJZE via Duckboard track to BURRY FARM and thence by light Railway (60 cm. Gauge)	

Casualties 16/2/18 to 22/2/18.
1 Off. died of wounds
1 O.R. wounded

TMG.

WAR DIARY
or
INTELLIGENCE SUMMARY.
(Erase heading not required.)

Army Form C. 2118.

Place	Date	Hour	Summary of Events and Information	Remarks and references to Appendices
YPRES	23/2/18	10 am	Batt. proceeded by rail to WIZERNES and from there by march route to billets in ZUDAUSQUES area.	
ZUDAUSQUES	23/2/18 to 28/2/18		Refitting, organisation, and commencement of training. Half day on Rules on 27/2/18 and demonstration of Rifle and attack given to all officers and N.C.O's on 28/2/18. — A few points noted having the last two tours in the line.— (1) Hot food was brought up by transport at night and heated up again at company cookhouses and then carried forward to the front. The food arrived really hot, but was due to the heating up at coy. cookhouse. (2) A lateral wire (Mains wire on long screw pickets) connecting up front line posts, was maintained. This was found to be essential, especially on dark nights. PMT	

WAR DIARY
or
INTELLIGENCE SUMMARY.

(Erase heading not required.)

Army Form C. 2118.

Place	Date	Hour	Summary of Events and Information	Remarks and references to Appendices
			3. Light Railway was used a great deal for carrying up troops to and from the line and handling being extremely beneficial to getting up men, the economy of hours Transport this ensuring was very to welcome. 4. Salvage. A considerable amount of Salvage was collected and sent to rear dumps by returning ration lurries. A daily party of 10 OR for yet of the line Gunn. non saturation for hunt and disinfection trough in the 5 - Divisional Gun Rank Centre was prepared and erected in most parts. This seems a good scheme as men learn the direction of the enemy, of hosts in their flanks and their Dublin Generally.	MG

149th Brigade.
50th Division.

4th BATTALION

NORTHUMBERLAND FUSILIERS

MARCH 1918

Vol 32

CONFIDENTIAL
WAR DIARY
OF
4th Battalion Northumberland Fusiliers
FROM
1st MARCH 1918 – 31st MARCH 1918

VOLUME III

J. Gregory Captain
Comdg 4th Battalion Northumberland Fusiliers

Army Form C. 2118.

WAR DIARY
or
INTELLIGENCE SUMMARY.
(Erase heading not required.)

Instructions regarding War Diaries and Intelligence Summaries are contained in F.S. Regs., Part II and the Staff Manual respectively. Title pages will be prepared in manuscript.

Place	Date	Hour	Summary of Events and Information	Remarks and references to Appendices
ZOABGQ86	1/3/18 to 8/3/18		Had rather hurried training to some extent, without scenery and two days work on the range, some interrupted features	
MOREUIL	8/3/18	1 pm	Rest, entrained at MOREUIL and proceeded to MOREUIL, arriving there 2 pm 9.3.18.	
LE QUESNEL	9/3/18		Proceeded by march route to LE QUESNEL	
	10/3/18 to 21/3/18		Coy training in attack and defence, stalking, FORIES and BOUCHOIR, officers went forward on a/c of FAY and ESSIGNY. Officers riding school cross held.	
BRIE	22/3/18	5pm	Entrainment to BRIE - Entrainment, train at 8pm, arrived BRIE 8 AM 22/3/18	
CHAULNES COURT	23/3/18		Marched to CHAULNES COURT arriving 10 AM, drop up in to quarters, Brch attached at HM and at night attacked by enemy shots? FAY and MORCHAIN-LA-CACHE. CAPT. MC was sent on at CHAULNES COURT and CAPT. M THOMPSON MC took command of R. Coy.	
SPGRISTO	24/3/18	9am	MARCHED to MARSES, including 6th Northumberland Fusiliers in action, eventually the Coys confused and the whole Bn. brd ordered to CROIZZE at 3-CHRIST, taking up a position commanding the Bridges. Coy were received orders to hold R. Bridgehead	
		1am	which they did unmolested by Enemy.	
MISERY	25/3/18	5am	Marched to MISERY and afterward marched to FOUCAUCOURT arriving there at 1pm	
FALHOGRE FOUCAUCOURT H.S.H.699-E-Sq	25/3/18	6.30pm 10 am	Left FOUCAUCOURT, reaching W.HOAR DEFINERY near ASKEN 2.55 filed into trenches in front of ASKEN 2.55	
FOUCAUCOURT	26/3/18	10pm	At 10 pm owing to Withdraw of Ls.40s across left as Withdrawn through "FAY and FOUCAUCOURT to HERSFELD	

WAR DIARY or INTELLIGENCE SUMMARY

Army Form C. 2118.

Place	Date	Hour	Summary of Events and Information	Remarks and references to Appendices
VAUVILLERS	24/3/18	7—	Occupied hook assembly village VAUVILLERS. Counter-attacked at FRAMERVILLE which was successful, but withdrew to VAUVILLERS later that night.	
VAUVILLERS	27/3/18		The junction of VAUVILLERS attacked until 4 pm on 27/3/18, when the Bett was driven away. Shops on left flank hampered. During the withdrawal C/O. Lt. at Thompson M.C. was wounded. The Brigade who followed command B. General RODDIE D.S.O. counter attacked during the afternoon & occupied plateau E of MAP DONVIERS.	
GUILLAUCOURT & IGNAUCOURT	28/3/18		Early on the morning 28/8/18 the Buis were ordered to take up a position at GUILLAUCOURT and during the day fought their way out at IGNAUCOURT. At night were received orders to march through MOREUIL to MERVILLE-au-BOIS. After thorough it became necessary to fall back through MOREUIL to take up position between DEMUIN and VILLERS. Capt. E.L. DOBSON in command. Although we were ordered to hold it this is the point we were pressed back & the troops took to end of hill between DEMUIN & VILLERS.	
	30/3/18		This position was held up on 30/3/18 the Bett was withdrawn to heave Honoriad through their huts to BACEUX	
	31/3/18		During the later stages of the enemy's fighting movement various detachments were attached to other commands temporarily.	

149th Brigade.
50th Division

1/4th BATTALION

NORTHUMBERLAND FUSILIERS

APRIL 1918.

CONFIDENTIAL WAR DIARY

of

4th BATTALION NORTHUMBERLAND FUSILIERS.

from

APRIL 1st 1918 to APRIL 30th 1918.

VOLUME 3

Lieut Colonel
Comdg 4th Bn. Northumberland Fusiliers

Army Form C. 2118.

WAR DIARY
or
INTELLIGENCE SUMMARY.
(Erase heading not required.)

Instructions regarding War Diaries and Intelligence Summaries are contained in F. S. Regs., Part II. and the Staff Manual respectively. Title pages will be prepared in manuscript.

Place	Date	Hour	Summary of Events and Information	Remarks and references to Appendices
VIRONCHAUX	1/4/18	12am	The 19 Infantry Brigade detained at RUE Station and received orders to march to billets in Vironchaux which were reached about 4pm. The billets were good but accommodation was very limited	
VIRONCHAUX	2/4/18		The time was spent in commencing the reorganization of the Battn. & re-equipping as far as possible. Baths were made by the Battn. & Companies were all bathed that day.	
VIRONCHAUX	3/4/18		Orders were received that the Battn. was to be prepared to move on the following day to a new area. The remainder of Bn. who had been detailed under other command's, rejoined this day. The Brigadier paid a visit to Battn. to enquire into the condition of the Officers & men who had just rejoined. Time was spent in cleaning up.	
L'ECLEME	4/4/18		The 19 Infy Brig entrained at LIGESCOURT proceeded to BUSNES, hence by march route to L'ECLEME and took over billets on the BUSNES — ROBECQ RD. The area was very scattered	
L'ECLEME	5/4/18		Company Training & refitting. Capt J.S.T. ROBSON, M.C. reported for duty with a draft of 7,250 men ?which included a large percentage of boys under 19. 1 Battn. Commanders went forward with the Brigadier to reconnoitre positions at LESTREM and VLLE CHAPELLE which the Brigade would hold in case of an attack against the Bethune Front.	
L'ECLEME	6/4/18		The Battn. proceeded by march route to billets at CENSE LA VALLEE, so bringing the Brigade closer together. In the afternoon a portion ?	JA.S

Army Form C. 2118.

WAR DIARY
or
INTELLIGENCE SUMMARY.
(Erase heading not required.)

Instructions regarding War Diaries and Intelligence Summaries are contained in F. S. Regs., Part II. and the Staff Manual respectively. Title pages will be prepared in manuscript.

Place	Date	Hour	Summary of Events and Information	Remarks and references to Appendices
L'ECLEME	6/4/18		Conf'd. The Battn. proceeded to fall in at GONNEHEM. During the day another draft arrived of 102 other ranks. The draft was of poor physique & its constituents were all under 19 years of age.	
CENSE LA VALLEE	7/4/18		The remainder of Battn. proceeded to billets at GONNEHEM. C.O. inspected billets during the morning. Orders were received to prepare to move northwards.	
	8/4/18		The Battn. proceeded by march route through ROBECQ & MERVILLE to ARREWAGE, where billets were allotted. Orders were received that the Battn. would be prepared to relieve the 5th Infce. on the right of the 91st Inft.	
ARREWAGE	9/4/18		This latter order was cancelled in the morning and orders were received that Battn. would be prepared to move at an hour's notice. At the same time further orders were received to move to assembly point on the EAST side of MERVILLE.	
do	do	9.45 am	Orders were issued and the Battn. moved off. Kipling was sent in advance to reconnoitre the route & ascertain if it were possible to get transport through MERVILLE on the townward. Very heavy shelling the whole night. During the Battn. march from ARREWAGE to MERVILLE the road was shelled & the Battn. sustained only one casualty. The Battn. had to halt at the entrance to MERVILLE to allow the 5th Battn. to pass. The sheets in places	

J.A.S.

Place	Date	Hour	Summary of Events and Information	Remarks and references to Appendices
MERVILLE	9/4/18	From 9.45 am	were found to have been badly knocked about but the Bridge were in tact. The Battn. moved to assembly point & received orders to take up position of concealment in the farms at L.30.d. The 5th & 6th Battns. went straight forward and occupied positions at TROU BAYARD & N.E. of ESTAIRES.	
do	do	2pm	The Cookers arrived with dinner which was served prior to the sending received that the enemy had occupied the 50th Bde front line & forward system of defence. We had now come under the Orders of the 151 Brigade and in accordance with their instructions, the Battn. marched in the direction of the Water Tank, ESTAIRES.	
do	do	3pm	Companies deployed from the road at the entrance to ESTAIRES, with artillery formation & moved forward to take up a position in L.23.d. Orders were received from 151 Infantry Bgde. to send one Company to flank the railway at BEAUPRÉ. "D" Company under 2nd Lt. NAPIER were immediately sent back for this purpose. Battn. Hqrs. were established at a farm in L.23.d.6.3. A.B.& C. Coys. dug in near the strong points in the vicinity of Battn Hqrs.	See line 22 below
do	do	5.30 pm	2nd Lt. Thompson & a patrol of 5 O.R. left to reconnoitre PONT LE NEUSE & get in touch with 5th D.L.I. who were holding the Bridgehead. 2nd Lt. LAWSON & a patrol of 10 O.R. left to reconnoitre PONT LEVIS & to get in touch with 5th D.L.I. there. The Battn. now came under the orders of COL. SPENCE, 5th D.L.I. The O/C 4th N.F. acknowledged his being in position to pen & one platoon to L.29.a.0.4. Sgt. Thompson who was already at that spot who now joined up by his platoon. Sgt. Wyham took a	See line 17 above

J.A.J.

WAR DIARY or INTELLIGENCE SUMMARY

Army Form C. 2118.

Place	Date	Hour	Summary of Events and Information	Remarks and references to Appendices
MERVILLE Contd	9/4/18	5.30am + on	B2 reports to 6/25 a B2. 6 reports to 5/D.L.I on the far side of the Bridge & under the command of 2Lt. LAWSON occupied a position with the guns covering the approach to the Bridge. The remainder of A Co. under Lt. NICHOLSON went forward to hold the house on the Merville canal bank between PONT DE LA NEUVE and PONT LEVIS.	
do	9/4/18	7pm	B2 remainder of the night was quiet. 2Lt NICHOLSON & his men reported to have crossed the canal further north but no definite information obtained regarding this. Rations were received in good time & distributed to Companies.	
do	10/4/18	5.40 am	The Battn. received orders to take up a position at PONT LEVIS in conjunction with the 5th D.L.I; the remainder of the Battn. to move to FME DUENNELLE & to come under the orders of the 151 Inf. Bde. The move to be completed before dawn. This order, however, did not reach Battn. until daylight.	
do	do	6.30 am	CAPT. ROBSON with 2 platoons of A Co. started for PONT LEVIS. They were held up immediately, in open ground, by heavy machine gun fire & CAPT. ROBSON was wounded. These two platoons of "A" Coy, reinforced by 2 platoons of "C" Coy, again engaged the enemy & the advance was held up by M.Gun fire. 2Lt DAVISON was wounded whilst reconnoitring a position. He was at the time accompanying the C.O. & 2nd Lt. ESSEX. The Battn. Hq. & Bn. Hq. were held up on their way to FME DUENNELLE and Batt. Hq. had to be established at L.19.c.3.4. The Position was notified to Bgde Hq & B. Coy occupied a position at PONT DE POIVRE (HARLECH STRONG POINT)

J.A.J

WAR DIARY or INTELLIGENCE SUMMARY

Army Form C. 2118.

Place	Date	Hour	Summary of Events and Information	Remarks and references to Appendices
MERVILLE	10/4/18	6:30 am	+ got in touch with a Company of 5th N.F. under Capt. Appel, who were entrenched 100x in the rear of HARLECH on the opposite side of the TROU BAYARD RD. "B" Coy immediately threw out a screen in front which reported the enemy and endeavouring to post machine guns towards our front.	
do	do	7:30 am	Information was received that the right flank of "B" Coy was in the air & were under own MG fire. Casualties to Lewis gunners of right Sgt. Major OSBORNE i/c one platoon of "B" Co. to protect the right flank of "B" Coy + eventually succeeded in establishing a line connecting A + 16 Coys. Enemy only a few casualties.	
do	do	9:30 am	The line was reported continuous.	
do	do	10/45 am	The 6th N.F. had orders to counter attack towards PONT LEWIS. The enemy out of ESTAIRES. They passed through the line of one B"Co" & drove the enemy back to the Church in ESTAIRES & PONT LEWIS but were threatened on the left flank. Two platoons of B Coy. under 2/Lt BULL were ordered to move in the direction of PONT LEWIS to report to MAJOR TEMPERLEY, O/C 6th N.F. 2/Lt BULL's party was subjected to severe machine gun fire in open ground. They were held up [mummum] & strained their objective & suffered considerable casualties. The balance [mummum] B" Co. + garrisoned HARLECH STRONG POINT. The party returned to HARLECH STRONG POINT, having reported to MAJOR TEMPERLEY + being informed they were no longer required.	

J.A.G.

WAR DIARY
or
INTELLIGENCE SUMMARY
(Erase heading not required.)

Army Form C. 2118.

Place	Date	Hour	Summary of Events and Information	Remarks and references to Appendices
MERVILLE	10/4/18	10/55 am	Bty Hd Qrs Batt. Hd Qrs. had dug in rear of the 5th N.F. Co's position. During the morning D. Co. retired from BEAUPRE, reported to Battn. Hd Qrs. & dug in rear of Batt. Hd Qrs position. The enemy now commenced to attack in front of the 5th Batt who were forced to retire on the left & left flank "in air". "D" Coy was sent with drawn. This left our left flank uncovered and reported to dig in between TROU BAYARD × ROPAS + the COL DE SAC FARM. "A" Company of the 5th N.F. at Harlech themselves held up in doing this, few casualties and reported came under MG fire of the 4th Batt N.F. & two platoons were placed to back up the Left Batt. + D.G. O/C B Co. reported that the Enemy was moving forward machine gun along & becoming able to bring enfilade fire on all the shop points at HARLECH. The enemy was unable to do much before nightfall remained in the position he had arrived at as soon as it was dark "A" Company of the 5th N.F. took over the part of the line occupied by D. Co. + D. Co. took over this Co's late position & my side started. They Battns were Much thought together reorganization ammunition	
do	do	4.90 pm		

J.S.

WAR DIARY or INTELLIGENCE SUMMARY

Army Form C. 2118.

Place	Date	Hour	Summary of Events and Information	Remarks and references to Appendices
MERVILLE	11/4/18	12.30 pm	At midnight, orders were received that A Coy of the 5th N.F. would be relieved by a Coy of the 4th E. Yorks & they were to take up a position at J.23.d.6.3. "D" Coy formed up on HQrs left & the remainder of C Coy withdrew to position lately occupied by D Coy in rear of HARLECH. Bttn HQrs moved back to Neuf Berquin.	
do	do	10 a.m.	Position was taken up & consolidated before dawn. "D" Coy on the left, "B" & "C" & RFC held men post against repeated attacks and under heavy trench mortar & Machine gun fire. HARLECH STRONG POINT was very heavily shelled at point blank range from the canal at ESTAIRES & was subjected to considerable amount of gas.	
do	do	5 pm	It became both that necessitated the removal of Bttn HQrs to Farm at J.10.6.9.6. The afternoon and evening were spent in the collection of stragglers, the reconstructing of the line for defence. The withdrawal was made through 2 g. E. Dns who were dug in, in our rear, & became necessary owing to the withdrawal of the right & left flanks. No information conveyed to our flank Companies who became aware of the withdrawal by when they found the enemy settling in behind them.	

J.A.S.
Lt.

WAR DIARY
INTELLIGENCE SUMMARY

Army Form C. 2118.

Place	Date	Hour	Summary of Events and Information	Remarks and references to Appendices
	11/4/18	2 pm	The Battn. was given instructions to bivouac in a large field 29½ D.1 rather 6½ Battn. with two companies moved forward to counterattack. The 4th Battn. moved forward at the same time. Battn. HQrs. moved to farm at L.1 & 9.6.	
	12/4/18	Dawn onwards	The Brigade received instructions to withdraw from its position at L10.6 (Sheet 36.A N.E.) and march under Col. Irvine 8th N.F. at L10.6 (Sheet 36.A N.E.) and march from K.11.d. 7.8 to Z.13.6.16. Information was received that NEUF BERQUIN was held by the enemy's machine guns which were firing down the road towards LA COURONNE. Up advance party was sent out to engage the machine guns, & were then unable to get forward until nearly daylight and were then made to obtain a position of vantage before Nieppe dawn. They did not obtain a position of vantage. The Brigade took up a position astride the NEUF BERQUIN RD at Z.13.9. The 6th Battn. got over to the right & occupied ground at K.12.c. The 4th N.F. and in support at S.K.R.d. The Guard's Brigade were found lying in mass at K.12.b. & Z.7.a. Owing to the 29th Divt. failure to come up on the left, the 149 Brig. and forces to both were & took up a position in conjunction with the Guards Brigade. The Guards Brigade counterattacked against NEUF BERQUIN	

J.A.J.

WAR DIARY
or
INTELLIGENCE SUMMARY

Army Form C. 2118.

Place	Date	Hour	Summary of Events and Information	Remarks and references to Appendices
K.12 d.6	12/4/18		6 a.m. After getting forward we were forced back down. Throughout the 4th & 5th 5/7 1st Battn marched into VIEUX BERQUIN & received orders to attack to LA TIR	All day reference
L.7.a. (Continued)			ANGLAIS. At this time the 1st Australian Divn were reported 5 miles in rear.	relieved
			Took up position between K.76 (Map 36th N.E.) and LA COURONNE in front of the BOIS DE VAL.	36th N.E.
	13/4/18		Orders were issued for the Battn to march to J.14 to occupy billets there. The men were given as much sleep as possible. Stragglers were collected from the transport lines at STEENBECQ.	
J.4.a.	14/4/18		The Brigade became attached to the 5th Divn under orders of the 97th Bgde. 15th Divn through the BOIS DE VACHES. This had been ordered to occupy in case of an enemy attack against the BOIS NIEPPE.	
	15/4/18		They retired to billets each day on the conclusion of work.	
	16/4/18		The 150751 Bgr Jas Watkins to a rest area on 15th inst. Duke to 4 inst Lieut Col B.A. GIBSON, D.S.O. arrived from England & took over Command of Battn. MAJOR J.R. ROBB, accompanied him taking the position of 2 i/c Command. Capt. G.C. GASSON, M.C. also schooled for kit on this date.	

J.R.

WAR DIARY
or
INTELLIGENCE SUMMARY.

Army Form C. 2118.

Place	Date	Hour	Summary of Events and Information	Remarks and references to Appendices
QB	17/4/18		The Battn. joined the transport at STEENBECQ and at 1 p.m. proceeded to march through AYRE to MAMETZ, where the arrived billeted.	
MAMETZ	18/4/18		2/Lts W.L. McLEAN & A. MARSHALL, also 5 O.R. joined for duty on this date. A.E. MORRIS Time was spent in reorganizing, reequipping & refitting. Inspections were carried out although the work needed knowledge by the fact that outside the Headquarters Companies the Battn. at this date, has only 7 Officers.	
do	19/4		Lieut. J.M. GOODBODY + 2nd Lt. J.A. GREANEY + 219 O.R. reported for duty on this date. Plans & reorganizing were proceeded energetically carried out.	
do	20/4		The Battalion was a constituent of the 149 Brigade was inspected by the MAJOR GENERAL commanding 50th Divn MAJOR-GENERAL H.C. JACKSON, D.S.O. The Brigade was afterwards @address by the General. the battle it was chosen in the fighting on the SOMME + then in the MERVILLE – ESTAIRES Sector.	

J.A.J.

Army Form C. 2118.

WAR DIARY
or
INTELLIGENCE SUMMARY.
(Erase heading not required.)

Place	Date	Hour	Summary of Events and Information	Remarks and references to Appendices
MAMETZ	21/4/18		The usual Church Parades of all denominations took place. The weather remained fine. The effect of the rest on the troops who had experienced the fighting was appreciable. This effect combined with the brightness & alacrity of the young new drafts from England, has increased noticeably day by day.	
do	22/4/18		Training under Battalion & Company arrangements in the morning. In the afternoon inspections, preparatory the	
do	22/4/18	9am to 4pm	Lectures by C.O. to all newly joined officers Lts. R. Walsh, T.H. Chewright, F.C. R.H. Smithwick, 2/Lts H.R.Toll, J. W. Hodges, H.Fogg & Smith. Company & Platoon arrangements for field training in the morning. Battalion inspection in the fullest tactical scheme in the afternoon, there will be special attention to the duties of the Scouts of the Company, also the institution of Junior NCOs & Tricks into the cavalry of today Field exercises. Medal Ribbons were presented by Brig Gen RUSSELL 51st Bt. to men who had	
			This being St. GEORGES DAY, the Regimental day of the N.F. Permitted festivities were arranged insofar as local conditions permitted.	
do	do	2am to	C. entertained by the S.O.S. Mess. Concert party extra food	

WAR DIARY
or
INTELLIGENCE SUMMARY.
(Erase heading not required.)

Army Form C. 2118.

Place	Date	Hour	Summary of Events and Information	Remarks and references to Appendices
Marets	23/4/18	6am	1 NCO + 41 Other ranks were provided. The Brigadier + Staff Officers were present at the funeral of the Officers. The cortege of the day spent. Issued in the evening of activity + operation on the Batts. The Commander in Chief ordered in advance announce during the day.	
do.	24/4/18	9am 9/11:30 pm	Training under the Batts. + Company arrangements, with particular attention to steadiness + smartness on parade.	
do	do	2pm to 4pm	Inspection of arms, boots, clothes + general equipment. Lectures by Platoon + Co. Commanders. 2nd Lt D. Forte + 1000R. [?] to duty.	
do	25/4/18	7am to 12:30 pm	Training under Company + Battalion arrangements. Specific training by all Cos. in section + platoon advance. Encouragement of initiative in operations, use of cover and contact, tactical handling, fire + manoeuvre. Lecture to all Officers + N.C.Os on methods of Training. Final inspections etc under Company arrangements. Col. Membery adds a postscript. H.E. Findley, M. Hawksley + S. OR Jones joined for duty.	
	26/4/18	4am	The 149 Bde entrained and proceeded to Savio from hence the main body of the Batts. proceeded by train to Brisien + thence by road. Tadmelois	

S.D.J.

WAR DIARY or INTELLIGENCE SUMMARY.

Army Form C. 2118.

Place	Date	Hour	Summary of Events and Information	Remarks and references to Appendices
Nom Marck	26/4/18		Route to Cologues and where the Batt. was expected. Whilere settled into huts.	
	27/4/18		D. Co. of the 4th N.Z. being billeted by an earlier train on 26th, having been divided in train unloading party to the Brigade did not join the 4th NZ at Cologues until 2am 28/4/18. The 4th N.Z. arrived at Cologues at 5am 28/4/18. In the afternoon preliminary inspection of arms, equipment, also huts took place.	
Cologues	29/4/18		Training out of doors was interrupted by wet weather. Lectures & close inspection of huts etc. were carried out. Lecture was given in the afternoon to all officers of the 49 Infantry Bge. by Brig. Genl. Riddell, D.S.O.	
do	30/4/18		Effective training under Batt. & Co. arrangements in open warfare tactics, sectional advances with particular attention to Lewis Gun tactics, from 9am until 3 p.m. The usual inspections were carried out. The attention of Company Platoon & Section Commanders was again called to the Scarcity of	

J.R.J

WAR DIARY
or
INTELLIGENCE SUMMARY.
(Erase heading not required.)

Army Form C. 2118.

Place	Date	Hour	Summary of Events and Information	Remarks and references to Appendices
COLOGNES	30/4/18		Smartness in saluting & the necessity of strict discipline & that the men must go around & up & down line cleanliness among the troops.	
			Casualties during April.	
			Officers Ranks Officers Name	
			Killed 16 1 2nd Lt A.N. Lawson	
			Wounded 185 5 " W.A. Kipling, C.M. Dawson	
			Missing 122 Capt J.G. Colson, M.C. 2/Lt J Crosher	
			W.Y.D.N.Con 12 Now 2/Lt T.H. Clarke	
			2/Lt H.E. Buck	

JNS

149/50

CONFIDENTIAL
WAR DIARY
of
4th BATTALION NORTHUMBERLAND FUSILIERS
from
1st May 1918 ———————————— 31st May 1918.

VOLUME 4

_____

M Goodbody Lieut. & /Adjt.
for
Lieut Colonel
Comdg 4th Bn. Northld Fusrs.

WAR DIARY or INTELLIGENCE SUMMARY

Army Form C. 2118.

Place	Date	Hour	Summary of Events and Information	Remarks and references to Appendices
COLOGNES AISNE	1/5/18		The Battn. participated in a Divisional tactical scheme of open warfare. That whole of the 149, 150 & 151 Brigades being engaged. The training in the handling of sections & platoons attached previously received special attention in the Battn. seemed to have transferred itself. The rug sup. by Brig. was of great assistance to the Coys. Commander. The wound inspection inspected by the boys Commander.	
do	2/5/18	5am 7am to 12.30pm	were carried out by Companies & lectures on the morning's scheme at 3—7pm. Training by Companies on the handling of sections in the advance & competences of attack were practised.	
		2pm to 4pm	with after special instruction in leapfrog movements. The whole inspectors were employed in the afternoon with increased attention to field of guards & county	
do	3/5/18	7am to 12.30pm	Company training in open warfare. First practice instruction in Lewis fire to all teams.	
		2pm to 4pm	Inspections etc. by all Coys. & Adjns. A well attended concert, arranged by the Medical Officer, was given in the evening.	

J.D.

WAR DIARY
or
INTELLIGENCE SUMMARY.
(Erase heading not required.)

Army Form C. 2118.

Place	Date	Hour	Summary of Events and Information	Remarks and references to Appendices
COLOUGNES	4/9/18	7.30	A Tactical scheme in open warfare was carried out by the Batt.	
		10.45	The practice of this scheme would appear to be of great instructional value to N.C.Os, Platoon & Company Comdrs.	
		2 p.m.	Inspections & Equipping of Transport etc.	
		5 p.m.	Lecture by O/C Battn. to 2 i/c Coys.	
COLOUGNES	5.6.18	6 a.m.	The Battalion proceeded by march route to CONCEVREUX a distance of 15 miles arriving at 2.30 p.m. The marching was well maintained & the march discipline throughout was good. The O/C Battn. accompanied by an Advance party from Coy Comdrs & four other ranks preceded the Battn. & made a preliminary reconnaissance of the sector to be taken over from the 1st Battn. of the 33rd French Regiment. The Battn. Coy Commdrs. proceeded to the Hdqrs. of their respective French Companies whom they were to take over. The Coy Commdrs. & their orderlies remained in the line & one Officer of the 4th N.Z. remained at the Hdqrs. of the 1st Battn. 33rd French Regt.	

J.A.J.

WAR DIARY or INTELLIGENCE SUMMARY

Army Form C. 2118.

Place	Date	Hour	Summary of Events and Information	Remarks and references to Appendices
CONCEVREUX	6/5/18	10am	Inspectors were carried out, otherwise as much rest as possible was allowed to the troops. Arrangements for taking over the line were carried forward. The O/C Battn. visited the Hdqrs. of the 1st Battn. 33rd Regt. & discussed the general dispositions with the French Command & viewed the necessary instructions to the Off. of the 4th N.F. who remained at the French Battn. Hdqrs. The Off. of the 4th N.F. returned to Brigade Hdqrs. in the Hdqrs. of the 33rd French Regt., & later in the day afnn. visited 1st Battn. 33rd French Regt. Hdqs. accompanied by the Brigadier Genl. cmdg. Infantry Brigade. It is hoped the Battn. Runners were on this day all to exploit the line & C.Ts.	
CONCEVREUX	7/5/18		Platoon Guides from each Company were met at an arranged rendezvous by French guides. The guides of the 4th N.F. were taken to the posts of their various platoons to be shown the time of the concerning French sections — so that they would be able to take up occupation of the line & were fully instructed to the line they would be able	

Army Form C. 2118.

WAR DIARY
or
INTELLIGENCE SUMMARY.
(Erase heading not required.)

Instructions regarding War Diaries and Intelligence Summaries are contained in F. S. Regs., Part II. and the Staff Manual respectively. Title pages will be prepared in manuscript.

Place	Date	Hour	Summary of Events and Information	Remarks and references to Appendices
CONCEVREUX	7/5/18		Continued to carry out their duties with efficiency by night	
	7/5/18	8.30 p.m.	The Battalion was relieved at PONTAVERT by the 6eme 1/4 Bn of the French Infantry and despite the extreme darkness of the night and the difficulties of an initial relief between troops having no language in common, the relief was quietly & successfully completed by all Companies	
FRONT LINE	8/5/18	3.45 a.m.	The relief was reported complete by all Companies. The work of CAPT. RICOTTE 1st Bn 33 French Regt, was pleasing, praiseworthy & his painstaking work to clear up points of defence etc etc were extremely helpful in a difficult tricky relief. The French Interpreter attached to 19 Infantry Brigade - Lt BEREST rendered most useful assistance. The line was very thoroughly explored & schemes for improvement of trenches & existing schemes of support & defence were discussed & amended. A Runners relay post was established near the Hdqrs of the CENTRE Company this being very necessary owing to the	

WAR DIARY or INTELLIGENCE SUMMARY

Army Form C. 2118.

Place	Date	Hour	Summary of Events and Information	Remarks and references to Appendices
FRONT LINE	8/9/18		Scattered shelling the line. The balances to be covered. Telephone communication to the Front Line was not available.	
do	9/9/18 to 10/9/18		Inspection carried out and Coy arrangements were established by the Adjt. Work of deepening the trenches was commenced by RIGHT & SUPPORT Companies. The Brig Genl of 149 Infantry Brigade visited the line. The observation posts were established at the ROYAL DE LA PLAINE. Patrols from the 3 Companies holding the line went out on 9th to ascertain for the purposes of warning our own & Enemy wires & for evidence of any enemy movement.	
do	10/9/18	9 pm	The artillery S.O.S signals were tested by pre-arrangement with artillery. These promptly responded by the guns.	
do	11/9/18	10-11 pm	An attempt to spread to the enemy wire would appear to have been made on the right of Batt front. Our artillery was very active.	
do	12/9/18		took in the line was captured. There was no rally of incident during the day.	

J.A.J.

Army Form C. 2118.

WAR DIARY
or
INTELLIGENCE SUMMARY.
(Erase heading not required.)

Instructions regarding War Diaries and Intelligence Summaries are contained in F. S. Regs., Part II. and the Staff Manual respectively. Title pages will be prepared in manuscript.

Place	Date	Hour	Summary of Events and Information	Remarks and references to Appendices
Front Line	13/5/18		Battalion employed on shovel work in trenches.	
"	14/5/18		Relieved by 2 N.F. & Battalion moved into Reserve area at CENTRE DEVREUX. Relief completed 4.30 AM 15/5/18	
	15/5/18		Day spent in cleaning up.	
	16/5/18		On Divisional Orders the Battalion moved into Corps Reserve at CONCEVREUX village. One Coy & Bn HQ in Pillets in the village & 3 remaining Coys in camp in the vicinity. The C.O., 2nd in command, 2 officers per Coy reconnoitred RIGHT & LEFT BDE SECTORS	
	17/5/18		Companies at the disposal of Of. Coys in the morning & afternoon due to to improving & taking in AISNE Canal.	
	18/5/18		Same as on the 17/5/18	
	19/5/18		Battalion moved into Support at VILLE-AU-BOIS relieving 5th N.F. Relief completed at 1.30 AM 20/5/18	
	20/5/18 21/5/18		Repairing trenches, relaying duckboards, forming Reserve dumps behind Battle line positions.	
	22/5/18		Two Cooks of French trenches went up in Support line during the afternoon shoot of MM	

WAR DIARY or INTELLIGENCE SUMMARY

Army Form C. 2118.

Place	Date	Hour	Summary of Events and Information	Remarks and references to Appendices
Front line trenches	24/4/15		8th East Kent Battalion took over the line during the afternoon & relieved 20th on outpost commencing at 3 P.M. The line along Road 44, 1809, a TRENCH DE LA PLAINE - Batt 49 on left, Supp-batt on BOYAU - TRENCH DE LA REDOUTE - TRENCH DARDENELLES, 100y TRENCH EPINAL + H.Q. at Batt. H.Q. at P.C. KLEBER. There was a disposition of supports carried out successfully & complete by 3 A.M.	
			Head Cover continued throughout morning on new higher men-out trench adjustments employed. Attitude was certainly showing of hostile guns & rifle fire.	
		7.30am	Wire received from Brigade saying that an enemy attack on a large scale was to be expected at 3.30 A.M. Bombardment on our line to commence at 1 A.M. Full defensive measures to be taken.	
		6.30pm	Comdg Off. to meet Brigadier, Major attached staff at Batt HQ to discuss details 2 P.M. with reference to the Brigade left flank, liaison & possible reinforcements for the new position of attack had been arranged. Orders were to Coy Comdrs. information as to Enemies lines of attack. All Coys were warned. No attack commenced at 12 midnight & morning passed without incident.	

(A9475) Wt W2335/P360 60,000 12/17 D. D. & L. Sch 5702 Forms/C2118/15

WAR DIARY or INTELLIGENCE SUMMARY

Army Form C. 2118.

Place	Date	Hour	Summary of Events and Information	Remarks and references to Appendices
Front Line	21/4/17	11 PM	2nd in Command made personal reconnaissance to COMBEREIX with Chauser. Correspondence Points preparatory to Barrage to Commence in Enemy's lines	
	28/4/17	4 AM	Enemy put down a most extraordinarily intense barrage on the whole of the forward area (Every sort of H.E. gas, much Shrapnel, attempting to mass their Battle positions) every indication was caused that of the shelling	
		5 AM	Enemy attacked along the whole line, on the Bn. front they appear to have crossed behind the OUVRAGE de LA CARRIÈRE in a S. Easterly direction and handled the Route 44. The numbers of the enemy opposed by a Company during this attack was two hundred. B. Coy. fire broke up the attack, some fresh of the enemy	
		4.4 PM	Attack occurred in fact to our front behind Tanks which L/Col Beloni were occupied by our own troops, however the lines of posts about B de WARABAIE on our right. The enemy however the lines of the line of posts about B de WARABAIE on our right. The enemy however succeeded so quickly that notwithstanding the Lieut. put forward were immediately forced to the copy by a heavy behind them in B de SIEGFRIED further moves of the Coy. that more between. L Battle line commences action. Our Artillery by this time were	

WAR DIARY or INTELLIGENCE SUMMARY

Army Form C. 2118.

Place	Date	Hour	Summary of Events and Information	Remarks and references to Appendices
	27/9/18	6:15 AM	practically the pel. was no longer effective in supporting the attack. It was	
		6:45 AM	The Battalion was thrown in an the direction of VIS-AU-BOIS. Started Bn. M noo passed in the 2 legs of the M Plat Bn (11 HLI) being in rect of the Battle line. The remainder of B Coy under Capt ALLEN with	
		8 AM	Bn H.Q. under Lt.Col GIBSON (about 70 men in all) went about to CENTRE MARCEAU, where telephone communication was established with Bde H.Q. and Col Gibson spoke to the Brigadier & said he was holding out with his H.Q. & about 70 men. This was the last message received from the Battalion.	
		5-30	Line of Redoubts not attacked from the right. CENTRE MARCEAU attacked in force from the right front & rear. held out for some time, however finally withdrawing to the BUTTE de L'EDMOND where they fought out to the last round. Machine Gun Battalion made a further stand at the Col Gibson was killed & Capt J.V.GREGORY morally wounded, also R.S.M. FEWSTER. One or two men eventually got back to LONGEVREUX noted. From this time the 17th M.K. Bn ceased to exist as a fighting unit	

Army Form C. 2118.

WAR DIARY
or
INTELLIGENCE SUMMARY.
(Erase heading not required.)

Instructions regarding War Diaries and Intelligence Summaries are contained in F.S. Regs., Part II. and the Staff Manual respectively. Title pages will be prepared in manuscript.

Place	Date	Hour	Summary of Events and Information	Remarks and references to Appendices
CONCEVREUX	27/9/14	8.30AM	All details were organised at CONCEVREUX under Major R R ROBB to carry a Bridge Head at the Canal bridge S of CHAUDARDES. This bridge was later blown up by the Royal Engineers.	
		1PM	Withdrew to eastern edge of CONCEVREUX to conform to position of the 3rd WORCESTERSHIRE REGT, who were unable to advance though the large trees of ROUCY. Several attempts of the enemy to work down the Right bank were beaten off with loss. The enemy escaped from a position with loss.	
		3.15PM	Order received from the Brigade Major to withdraw if hard pressed by the enemy. We re-crossed the woods SE of CONCEVREUX also on the CONCEVREUX-MEURIVAL RD. Withdrew to the High ground South of CONCEVREUX & reorganized all details by battalions under their own officers.	
		4PM	Took up a position in prepared line across CONCEVREUX-VENTELAY RD (front N of point 200 where track crosses the road) Ref. Soissons 22. 1/100.000) in touch with 3RD WORCESTERSHIRE REGT on the right & LANCASHIRE FUS. on the left.	

WAR DIARY or INTELLIGENCE SUMMARY

Army Form C. 2118.

Place	Date	Hour	Summary of Events and Information	Remarks and references to Appendices
	27/5/18	4 PM	This position was held till 9.30 PM. Operation of what attack enemy casualties were inflicted on the enemy.	
		9.30 PM	The 3rd Worcestershire Regt. withdrew having outflanked on both right.	
		10 PM.	Withdrew & occupied a new line south of LE FAITE FARM. The enemy was then observed in the northern outskirts of VENTELAY as a further advance was	
		11 PM.	made & a new position established south of VENTELAY across the ROMAIN – VEMELAY	
			MONTIGNY Rd. – VENTELAY Rd. do.	
	28/5/18	5.30 AM	This position was held till enemy had worked round both flanks & new	
		6 AM.	Line were taken up on high ground N.E. of MONTIGNY from the line was then occupied by troops of 19th Brigade Co. H.Q. and B. and C. companies moved to BASIEUX & small	
	29/5/18	1 AM	available fighting troops were detailed to form into a divisional Composite Battalion.	
		12 noon	Bn. H.Q. Transport moved via CRUCHY, & N/Wy & away the MARNE towards	
			front to JONY. Bivouacs	
	2/5/18	10 AM	Moved to on ORBAIS – SURGY Rd.	
	3/5/18		Moved via CHAMPAUBERT to LILLETTE in CONGY.	

WAR DIARY
or
INTELLIGENCE SUMMARY.

Army Form C. 2118.

Casualties + Reinforcements during the Month of May 1915.

CASUALTIES

OFFICERS				O.R.			
K	W	M	NYD	K	W	M	NYD
2	5	16	—	3	40	485	53

REINFORCEMENTS

OFFICERS	O.R.
11	116

M Rodhoty Lt
O/a of W Mort Hrs

CONFIDENTIAL
WAR DIARY
of
4th BATTALION NORTHUMBERLAND FUSILIERS

FROM

1st JUNE 1918 — 30th JUNE 1918

VOLUME IV.

30/8

V. M. FitzHugh
Lieut-Colonel
Comdg 4th Bn NORTH⁰ FUS

Army Form C. 2118.

WAR DIARY
or
INTELLIGENCE SUMMARY.
(Erase heading not required.)

Instructions regarding War Diaries and Intelligence Summaries are contained in F. S. Regs., Part II. and the Staff Manual respectively. Title pages will be prepared in manuscript.

Place	Date	Hour	Summary of Events and Information	Remarks and references to Appendices
CONGY	1-6-18		The morning was spent in reorganising equipment as far as stores would allow. Ammunition was given as much rest as possible.	
	2-6-18	10 AM	Our officers & 50 other ranks were sent to the 2nd Machine Gun Bn for Instruction.	
		11·15 AM	Orders were received that all available officers & men to move to VERT-LA-GRAVELLE where they found a company of the 149 Brigade Composite Battalion.	
			C.O. & Staff & Transport received orders to move to AULNEUX	
Aulneux	4-6-18		Details of the battalion in billets & fields	
	5-6-18		The 149 Bde Composite Battalion moved up to the Trenches & unsuccoured MajorG.R.Ratt	
	6-6-18		If [?] NSM Trench up 1st Royal Berkshire Regt arrived to take over command of the 14th & 15th North[?] Tire.	
	7-6-18		On the departure of the 149 Brigade Composite Batt, the details were attached to at AULNEUX	
			detail ordered to move to BROYES	
BROYES	8-6-18 to 19-6-18		at BROYES	
	19-6-18	8·45 PM	Officers & men with the 149 Bde Composite Batt returned to details from the line	

WAR DIARY
or
INTELLIGENCE SUMMARY.

Army Form C. 2118.

Place	Date	Hour	Summary of Events and Information	Remarks and references to Appendices
BROYES	20.6.16		Battalion resting, but 4th day being out over 3 per non. at.	
	25.6.16	6-7AM	On company moved from the neighbourhood formed bath and 147 Brigade Contact Battalion which was commanded by Lt. Col W. M. Kilby (4th M. Bde Fus)	
LES ESSARTS		8-30AM	A. Cola (A.M. Brownhill Edalgesou-Miff + Transport Junior commands of Maj. F. Bell arrived at LES ESSARTS where Stigarmi under the orders of Brigadier General Marshall (150 Inf Bde)	
	25.6.16	3-30pm	Transport forward under orders to hand up to succeed to the Base	
	26.6.16		Supplies for Brigade found by P.M.L. Receiver, Q.M.S.	
	27.6.16		Q.M.S.A. Pickering and horses the Transport all remaining much of LES ESSARTS to arrange for wagons for the Base.	
	28.6.16		Received near E. Bages special with the General high the actions who had gone for menury cording of the of the Scorpion Battalion the 148th Brigade & omitted Battalion handed to the 4 M.d.s.were his.	
BROYES	30.6.16		with the batt as organised from LES ESSARTS	

Army Form C. 2118.

WAR DIARY
or
INTELLIGENCE SUMMARY.
(Erase heading not required.)

Instructions regarding War Diaries and Intelligence Summaries are contained in F. S. Regs., Part II. and the Staff Manual respectively. Title pages will be prepared in manuscript.

Place	Date	Hour	Summary of Events and Information	Remarks and references to Appendices
			CASUALTIES REINFORCEMENTS	
			K W M	
			Officers — — — 2	
			O.R. 2 3 — 29	

Army Form C. 2118.

WAR DIARY
or
INTELLIGENCE SUMMARY.
(Erase heading not required.)

WO 36

CONFIDENTIAL

WAR DIARY

of

4th BATTALION NORTHUMBERLAND FUSILIERS

from

1st July 1918 — 31st July 1918

VOLUME IV

[signature] Lt. COLONEL
COMDG. 4th Bn. NORTHD. FUSILIERS

WAR DIARY or INTELLIGENCE SUMMARY.

Army Form C. 2118.

(Erase heading not required.)

Place	Date	Hour	Summary of Events and Information	Remarks and references to Appendices
Breyes	1-7-18		147 Inf Brigade left BROYES, 4 Northumberland Fus moved with the rest of the Brigade to labours of Morlancy & St SOPHIE FARM.	
St Sophie Farm	2-7-18	9.30 AM	Capt Arkwright took the battalion for an hours arms drill & company drill. Remainder of the day given up to cleaning & resting etc. The Brigade organised a Concert in the evening.	
Châlons tourn	3-7-18	8.0 AM	The battalion left to entrain at FÈRE CHAMPENOISE at 11-30 AM. In the Battalion Zone.	
Fère Champenoise	10.40 AM	FÈRE CHAMPENOISE was reached at 10-45 AM & entraining was completed by 11-15. The train left at 11-33 AM.	
Pont-Remy	4-7-18	11-15 AM	Train arrived at 10-15 AM, but the battalion did not entrain till 11-15 AM.	
		1.0 PM	Detraining complete by 1-0 PM, at 1-15 PM the battalion left PONT-REMY & marched for HOOGINCOURT where it arrived to be billeted	
Hoogincourt	4-7-18	2.30 PM	Battalion in billets by 2.30 PM.	
"	5-7-18		Orders received to reduce all battalions to the establishment of a Service battalion. All surplus personnel to be despatched to the Base. This meant reducing us by 64 officers & other ranks which were to be known as the Cadre battalion	
	6-7-18		Most of the Cadre Battalion personnel going to the Base completely but no orders to move.	

Army Form C. 2118.

WAR DIARY
or
INTELLIGENCE SUMMARY.
(Erase heading not required.)

Place	Date	Hour	Summary of Events and Information	Remarks and references to Appendices
Hucqueneaux	1-7-16		Coy Musketry training still carried out by the whole battalion	
"	2-7-16 to 10-7-16		Company training in the morning, afternoons free	
			Disposal of left as through	
"	11-7-15		All personnel proceeding to have inspected at YONVILLE by Major General H.C.	Major General J. Otbaun
			For room G.S.O. to take the run fully equipped heavy marching order, all ranks	
			good polish. Afterwards paraded and congratulations to such men of the	
			Brigade that had not presented them selves unwell at Montmorency	
			We received much allowance	
"	12-7-16		Usual training carried out	
Happy	14-7-16		149 Inf Brigade concentrated at HAPPY	
	15-7-16		Personal proceeded to the Base dispatched from Pont-REMY	
			We started the morning Course B.	
	16-7-16			
Rouxmesnil	17-7-16		Cadre Bn moved by bus to H.Q.15 Coro near DIEPPE same camp	
			ROUXMESNIL	
			Cadre B. a training & awaiting orders as to disposal of	
	31-7-16